THE FINE
PRINT

Also by David Cay Johnston

Free Lunch: How the Wealthiest Americans Enrich Themselves at Government Expense (and Stick You with the Bill)

Perfectly Legal: The Covert Campaign to Rig Our Tax System to Benefit the Super Rich—and Cheat Everybody Else

[the fine print]

THE FINE
PRINT

THE FINE PRINT

HOW BIG COMPANIES USE "PLAIN ENGLISH" TO ROB YOU BLIND

DAVID CAY JOHNSTON

PORTFOLIO / PENGUIN

PORTFOLIO / PENGUIN
Published by the Penguin Group
Penguin Group (USA) Inc., 375 Hudson Street, New York, New York 10014, U.S.A. •
Penguin Group (Canada), 90 Eglinton Avenue East, Suite 700, Toronto, Ontario, Canada
M4P 2Y3 (a division of Pearson Penguin Canada Inc.) • Penguin Books Ltd, 80 Strand,
London WC2R 0RL, England • Penguin Ireland, 25 St. Stephen's Green, Dublin 2, Ireland
(a division of Penguin Books Ltd) • Penguin Books Australia Ltd, 250 Camberwell Road,
Camberwell, Victoria 3124, Australia (a division of Pearson Australia Group Pty Ltd) •
Penguin Books India Pvt Ltd, 11 Community Centre, Panchsheel Park, New Delhi – 110 017,
India • Penguin Group (NZ), 67 Apollo Drive, Rosedale, Auckland 0632, New Zealand
(a division of Pearson New Zealand Ltd) • Penguin Books (South Africa) (Pty) Ltd,
24 Sturdee Avenue, Rosebank, Johannesburg 2196, South Africa

Penguin Books Ltd, Registered Offices: 80 Strand, London WC2R 0RL, England

First published in 2012 by Portfolio / Penguin, a member of Penguin Group (USA) Inc.

10 9 8 7 6 5 4 3 2 1

LIBRARY OF CONGRESS CATALOGING IN PUBLICATION DATA
Johnston, David.
   The fine print : how big companies use "plain English" to rob you blind / David Cay
Johnston.
     p. cm.
   Includes bibliographical references and index.
   ISBN 978-1-59184-358-0
 1. Invoices.   2. Corporations—Corrupt practices.   I. Title.
   HF5681.I7J64 2012
   364.16'8—dc23   2012019318

Printed in the United States of America
Set in Janson Text LT Std
Designed by Elyse Strongin, Neuwirth & Associates, Inc.

While the author has made every effort to provide accurate telephone numbers, Internet
addresses, and other contact information at the time of publication, neither the publisher
nor the author assumes any responsibility for errors, or for changes that occur after publication. Further, the publisher does not have any control over and does not assume any repon-
sibility for author or third-party Web sites or their content.

For David Crook

[CONTENTS]

[AUTHOR'S NOTE]

When Major League Baseball came to San Francisco in 1958, someone gave my father two Giants tickets. Dad had no interest in what he called commercial sports, but Mom was a baseball fanatic, so one chilly May evening she took her third-grader to his first ball game.

Peppered with my questions, my gray-haired mother found a way to keep my mind occupied. "Imagine if you could figure out how to make everyone in Seals Stadium give you a nickel!" she said. I took the implied arithmetic problem and ran with it.

By picking a nickel, my mother had complicated the math. I diligently counted blocks of seats and multiplied by five, remembering numbers as I moved on to the next section, starting over when I made a mistake. After the seventh inning I declared my answer: $1,100, about $8,800 in today's money. My mother folded back a page on the program that listed the number of seats and showed me her penciled-in calculation.

"Very good," she said of my estimate, "but *how much* is only half the answer. Now, tell me *how* could you get a nickel from everyone here?"

That second question is the one that stayed with me—and that inspired this book. Half a century later, I'm still pondering, but in a bigger way, how it applies to your life and mine. As in: *How have all of us consumers ended up paying so many extra charges on electric, phone and other bills?*

This book is about the many ways that corporations extract from you those extra nickels—which add up to thousands of dollars. Many of the mechanisms require the government's cooperation; some of them are the result of seemingly unconnected sources; others are hidden in plain sight.

I promise you, however, the explanation is right there before you, whether you've done the reading or not. It's in the fine print.

Jacking Up Prices

The distribution of wealth is not determined by nature. It is determined by public policy.
—**Eric Schneiderman, New York State attorney general**

1. **Friends and colleagues** have always known that Adam Leipzig husbands his own money and reliably earns profits on funds others entrust to him. As a young executive at Disney, Leipzig oversaw *Dead Poets Society; Good Morning, Vietnam;* and *Honey, I Shrunk the Kids.* Later, as president of National Geographic Films, he was behind *March of the Penguins.* His films have brought in $2.1 billion, seven times what it cost to produce them. That makes him a Hollywood rarity—a reliable steward for investors in the risky business of moviemaking.

Because it was so small, the one thing Leipzig never gave much thought to was his monthly phone bill. When it came, Leipzig checked to see how many long-distance calls, if any, had been made and wrote a check. But his casual view changed one day near the turn of the century during a meeting at the AT&T offices in Los Angeles.

Leipzig had wrangled a meeting with AT&T marketing executives to propose a strategic alliance to help him start his own film production company. Leipzig left with everything he wanted, but a decade later the terms of his successful deal were mostly forgotten. What remained vivid in his memory was what the phone guys had said about the future of his and everyone else's telephone bills. Their private comments differed dramatically from what everyone in America had been hearing for a quarter century about the costs of telephone calls and, for the previous five or so years, about this wondrous new thing called the Internet. The promise of cheap and abundant telecommunications service, to be available almost anywhere, was becoming a major theme in telecommunications industry marketing.

But that was not at all what the telephone guys said in private while meeting with Leipzig.

"They said their corporate strategy was that, within a few years, AT&T wanted to draw at least $100 a month from each client household," Leipzig recalled. "They would do this with phone service, and also things they were not offering at the time, or had not expanded as much— mobile, Internet and cable."

As your monthly phone bill probably tells you, this is exactly what has happened. At the time, Adam Leipzig's home phone bill ran $35 a month. A decade later, the total amount due AT&T every month was more than $200, even though he buys his cable television service from another company.

What the marketing executives had forecast had indeed come to pass.

THE RISE OF FALLING PRICES

Since 1974, politicians, pundits and professional economists all have said that, thanks to competition, the cost of telephone service would fall. The Justice Department sued that year to break up the American Telephone and Telegraph Company, saying Ma Bell's monopoly hindered new technologies and shouldered aside competitors who wanted in on the lucrative business of long-distance calls. (Back then calls were so expensive that many people kept little sand dials by their telephones when calling loved ones long distance so as not to go a second too long saying good-bye and be charged for another full minute.) Eventually the antitrust case was settled by negotiation and, in 1984, Ma Bell spun off seven regional telephone monopolies known as the Baby Bells.

AT&T kept the lucrative long-distance business, but even before the breakup, another monopoly business, a railroad, found a way to compete in long-distance calling. Southern Pacific Railroad began offering limited long-distance service in 1972. SP microwave towers, which kept the trains running on time, sent signals along the narrow rights-of-way that the federal government had given the railroad in the nineteenth century. These towers had the capacity to handle calls, too, and by 1978 SP was providing a cheap long-distance system connecting business customers in Los Angeles, San Diego and Anaheim, California, with those in three East Coast cities, Boston, New York and Philadelphia.

Southern Pacific Communications would eventually evolve into to-day's Sprint Nextel, but by the 1990s, a number of competing systems were being served by a growing network of glass fibers buried alongside the tracks. These braided glass strands, each thinner than a human hair, held vastly more capacity than the microwave system, which in turn was far more powerful than the old copper wires used to make the first commercial telephone call in 1878 and still in use today in most homes and small businesses. In the last decade of the twentieth century, the whole country buzzed with talk of a new Information Superhighway that would connect everyone in America; the oft-expressed expectation was that, thanks to competition, prices would fall lower and lower. Some published studies even showed that the cost of long-distance calling would fall more than 99 percent, which was not exactly good news for AT&T as a dedicated long-distance company, nor for its nascent competitors. In Washington, awestruck lawmakers marveled at the idea that every word and image in all 22 million books in the Library of Congress could be sent in the blink of an eye to any place connected by the new fiber-optic cables.

Across the country from our friend Adam Leipzig, Bruce Kushnick in Brooklyn, New York, had his own epiphany. Visiting an aging aunt, Kushnick discovered twenty years' worth of monthly telephone bills. Kushnick worked as a telephone industry consultant, paid to extol the virtues of the coming new era of digital communications.

Kushnick knew a research gold mine when he saw one, and he set to work. When he cross-checked his aunt's telephone bills over the years, he could hardly believe the numbers. His aunt paid $9.51 for her local phone service in 1984. By 2003 her bill had swollen fourfold to $38.90. In the two decades since the breakup of the AT&T monopoly, even after adjusting for inflation, his aunt's telephone cost $2.30 for each dollar paid in 1984. And that was without any charges for long-distance calls.

His little history lesson prompted Kushnick to think about the telephone bill itself. Old telephone bills—from the era of the Great Depression of the 1930s, for example—often consisted of three lines. One was the monthly charge. The second was the cost of long-distance calls. The third was the total.

With the passing years, Kushnick noted, the bills had gotten more and more complicated. When AT&T started offering phones in colors, colored phones came with an extra charge. So did the immensely popular Princess telephone for the bedroom in 1959. In 1963 the first push-button phones were introduced (called Touch-Tone), and people paid extra to escape rotary dialing. Two years later came sleek Trimline phones with lighted dials—along with another extra charge.

The publicly switched telephone network, as it was known in the industry, was upgraded for emergency calls to 911. Then it was upgraded again with ANI (automatic number indicator) so that emergency dispatch centers would know the numbers of callers, and later with ALI, or automatic location indicator. The cost of ALI was justified, as it saved the lives of many people in the midst of medical emergencies or assaults, even if they were unable to say where they were. But the public paid both for its installation and for some other things, too, as some of the money collected was diverted to other uses, including new equipment the phone companies said was necessary to make ALI work.

Soon after the railroad rights-of-way microwave towers made possible the first sliver of long-distance calling competition, telephone bills became even more complicated. In the late 1970s, while the breakup of Ma Bell was under negotiation with the Justice Department, AT&T began seeking limits on free directory-assistance calls. It seemed a curious move—Ma Bell executives and spokesmen at the time told anyone who would listen that free directory-assistance calls encouraged more calling—but the AT&T shift away from free directory assistance was brilliant in the way that it quietly raised prices.

State utility regulators were told that telemarketing companies were taking advantage of free directory assistance, placing many thousands of calls to 411. That, in turn, was described as a hidden cost borne by residential and small-business customers. Thus, AT&T was able to argue that the consumer would pay a little bit less if fewer operators were employed looking up numbers for "junk calls."

The state utility regulators might have just slapped a charge on any business that made large numbers of directory assistance calls. Or a rule could have been adopted that applied only to telemarketing firms and commercial customers. Instead, as the telephone company had requested, the state regulators limited how many free calls to directory assistance *any* customer could make.

At first, the limit was ten calls. Over time, the limit was trimmed in stages to zero; by 2008, "free" had become a fee, with many customers paying $1.99 each time they called directory assistance, adding more lines of fine print to telephone bills. Verizon Wireless and some other companies did not list charges for calling directory assistance separately, but hid them in plain sight among the monthly list of calls made, a portion of the bill many people typically find tiresome to examine line by line.

Today it's typical to be charged for *not* being listed in the telephone directory, and, by the way, it's not a one-time fee to defray the cost of flipping an internal computer signal, but a monthly fee. Think of it as a charge for no service. Over the years the white pages, which used to be dropped free on every doorstep, became less common and less thorough; they no longer appear in some communities. That translates to an increased number of calls to directory assistance—for which a fee is collected. While various white-pages listings appeared on the Internet, the telephone companies spent little to keep them up to date, which of course drove more business to paid 411 services. When new services such as call waiting and three-party calling were introduced, they bore stiff additional charges, too.

With AT&T's breakup into Ma and the seven Baby Bells, new charges were introduced for regional calls, those that were neither local nor long distance. Known as Local Access and Transport Area or LATA, the implementation of this system also meant that, in some metropolitan markets, the circle shrank within which unlimited calls could be made at no extra charge. In some cases a call to a neighbor went from free to dear because of illogical LATA boundaries.

New costs came at the consumer from all angles. Until the 1984 breakup, regulations required customers to use the telephone set installed by Ma Bell. After the breakup, customers were told they could either buy or rent their phone. At first, the rental seemed cheap, but gradually people learned how little a telephone costs to make and also realized how much an open-ended rental could cost.

And then there was the expense associated with making sure the phone line in your house actually worked. Ma Bell got state public utility commissions to transfer ownership of the telephone line at the point where it entered your home or office. Once that happened, customers had to pay to fix any wires inside their homes or businesses that, say, got wet or gnawed by a rodent. But there was an option, namely a monthly "wire maintenance" fee, which added yet another extra charge for what once had been included in the basic price.

Bit by bit, the line items grew, and others were added. It was easy to miss the escalating prices because they came separately over time—a nickel on one line of the bill, a quarter or two on another. With many small line items, people tended not to notice how the total was creeping upward much faster than the rate of inflation or the size of their income.

Kushnick found his aunt's bills printed on multiple slips of paper, making it hard to spot everything at once. He noticed some charges were for services his aunt did not use; a few were for services she couldn't possibly use because her telephone was too antiquated. And the monthly rental for the phone itself? Kushnick calculated that his aunt had paid more than twenty times the price of the instrument with that small monthly rental fee.

One of the fastest-growing items Kushnick found on his aunt's bill was labeled "FCC Subscriber Line Charge." Other phone companies call this "FCC Charge for Network Access" or "Federal Line Cost Charge" or "Interstate Access Charge." Variations include "Federal Access Charge," "Interstate Single Line Charge," "Customer Line Charge," "FCC-Approved Customer Line Charge" and even "End User Fee."

These may sound like government fees, or perhaps a disguised tax on telephone users that goes into federal coffers. Not so. Each of those labels identifies the charge for connection to the long-distance network. The government does not collect a penny from that charge. All the money goes to the phone companies.

According to Federal Communications Commission rules, phone bills are supposed to be easy to understand. The FCC truth-in-billing policy supposedly "improve[s] consumers' understanding of their telephone bills." According to the FCC:

> Section 64.2401 of the rules requires that a telephone company's bill must: (1) be accompanied by a brief, clear, non-misleading, plain language description of the service or services rendered; (2) identify the service provider associated with each charge; (3) clearly and conspicuously identify any change in service provider; (4) contain full and non-misleading descriptions of charges; (5) identify those charges. . . .

Despite the misleading labeling of the network "line charge," the FCC has approved it for years, officially helping confuse consumers. Among the honest descriptions the FCC might have required would be "long-distance system access" and "telephone company network charge."

Inspired by his study of the evolution of the phone bill, Bruce Kushnick decided to find out how many people were misled by terms like "FCC Subscriber Line Charge." In a survey of one thousand Americans, he found three people who understood their phone bill, which means 99.7 percent did not. Round to the nearest whole number, and Kushnick's finding was that 100 percent of those surveyed did not understand their phone bill. In effect, *no one* understands his or her telephone bill, which amounts to a powerful rebuke to FCC policies that clearly harm consumers and benefit the telephone companies. In the years since that survey, however, the FCC has made no meaningful changes to rules that allow phone companies to confuse people. Don't blame the FCC staff for that. As with all government agencies, the bureaucrats do what the politicians tell them to do.

PROMISES, PROMISES

What Leipzig and Kushnick encountered were early signs that the lower prices made possible by competition and digital technology were just empty promises. This involved more than money, since the telephone industry, together with the cable television industry, quietly saw to it that written into the fine print were laws and regulations that made it easier for them to minimize their investments in new technology and to serve only the customers the companies wanted.

Since 1913 Americans had enjoyed a legal right to a landline telephone at any address, but by 2012 that right had been legislated away so quietly that my Reuters columns were the first to report this trend. The right to a landline was taken away without any news coverage in Alabama, Florida, North Carolina, Texas and Wisconsin. In Kentucky and New Jersey enough attention was aroused that consumer groups fought the changes, but they faced powerful obstacles. AT&T hired thirty-six lobbyists to work the Kentucky state legislature. In California the consumer group The Utility Rate Network (TURN) counted 120 AT&T lobbyists, one for each member of the Golden State legislature.

The telecommunications companies wanted to build the most profitable electronic toll road possible. Their aim was, first, to spend as little as possible on technology, which ultimately meant slow Internet service for many customers. Second, they wanted to serve areas where lots of customers could and would buy a monthly pass to get on this electronic highway; potential customers in sparsely populated areas were at best incidental to such plans. Third, they wanted to set prices as high as the market would bear, even if it meant many people could never afford to access this electronic roadway.

Lost in the rush to profitability was the crucial fact that the federal government had established an underlying policy to make telecommunications services available to all at reasonable prices. Compared to the rest

of the modern world, American phone companies, along with cable television companies, have done a spectacular job of building only what and
where they wanted while shoving the cost on to their captive customers.

Instead of increased competition between the telephone and cable
companies, a new cartel emerged in the first decade of the twenty-first
century. While telephone and cable companies posed in public as rivals,
Verizon made a deal to sell its branded services over cable company
Comcast's lines, and vice versa. The only risk of real competition arose
when some local governments favored the idea of building a municipal
telephone, cable television and Internet access system that would be
faster and cheaper. The industry responded like sharks, determined to do
in the opposition and protect their predatory position. Later in the book,
we'll see how those and other efforts to kill competition fared (see chapter 5, "In Twenty-ninth Place and Fading Fast," page 50).

READING BETWEEN THE LINES

How the promise of cheap, competitive and unlimited telecommunications service has been turned into a reality of expensive, monopolistic
and limited service is just one part of the larger transformation in the
American economy since the late 1970s. A host of large industries, including banks, credit card lenders, electric utilities, health care, oil pipelines,
Hollywood studios, property insurance, railroads and water companies,
all have worked quietly to rewrite America's economic playbook in their
favor.

In the chapters that follow, we'll look at how legislatures have rewrit-
ten basic business laws, some whose principles date back thousands of
years. Too often the goal has been to thwart competition, artificially inflate prices, hold down wages by decimating unions, reduce worker benefits and then restrict or bar access to the courts by those aggrieved.
Businesses have gotten policies adopted that have allowed some managers to run corporations as, effectively, criminal enterprises, something
modern management and economic theory regard as outside their fields
of expertise (and at best implausible) but that criminologists have a name
for: control fraud. That means, in short, that those in control run the
fraud, as we shall see.

While schoolchildren are taught about heroic figures who raised the
capital to build new factories and fill offices, these days large companies

rely on taxpayers for that money. Almost every brand-name company is in on these deals; state and local governments alone spend at least $70 billion a year of taxpayers' money to subsidize factories, office buildings and the like, according to Professor Kenneth Thomas, a University of Missouri–St. Louis political scientist. That burden comes to $900 per year for a family of four. My only criticism of Thomas's work is that I believe he understates the cost by an unknown but considerable sum.

The worst of these are laws in nineteen states that let companies pocket the state income taxes withheld from their workers' paychecks for up to twenty-five years. Hard as it is to believe such laws exist, they do, and they are spreading fast. General Electric, Goldman Sachs, Procter & Gamble and more than 2,700 other big companies have these deals. It is not just American companies, either. Siemens, the big German computer maker, the Swedish appliance maker Electrolux and a host of Japanese, Canadian and European banks have similar arrangements with states from New Jersey to Oregon. In many of these subsidy programs, no jobs are created. Instead the state income taxes are given to companies that agree to move jobs from one state across the border to another, as AMC Theatres agreed to do in moving its headquarters from Kansas City, Missouri, to Leawood, Kansas, just ten miles away. AMC will get to pocket $47 million withheld from its workers, a boon to its major owners: J. P. Morgan, Apollo Management, the Carlyle Group and the firm Mitt Romney cofounded in 1984, Bain Capital Management.

From the corporations' point of view, the best part is that the workers are left in the dark. None of these states requires that workers be told that their state income taxes go to their employers—that they are in effect being taxed by their bosses. GE says that it did tell its Ohio workers about how it updated its operations there, investing $126 million and pocketing $115.3 million of tax monies. GE shareholders paid just eight cents on the dollar for the investment.

Legislatures passed these laws, presidents and governors signed them and the courts have endorsed them. In many cases they effectively gut state constitutional provisions and laws banning gifts to business.

In New York, lawyer James Ostrowski filed a lawsuit on behalf of more than fifty citizens, ranging from serious libertarians to liberal Democrats, challenging a gift of at least $1.4 billion of state taxpayer funds to a company controlled by Abu Dhabi's hereditary ruler, Sheikh Khalifa bin Zayed Al Nahyan, one of the wealthiest people in the world. The sheikh's company, GlobalFoundries, is building a microchip factory in the Hudson

River Valley near Albany. Back in 1846, the New York State constitution banned gifts to corporations or other business entities, a provision that the voters reaffirmed in 1874, 1938 and again in 1967. In each case the vote was by a margin of two to one, which would seem to make the desires of voters clear.

In deciding Ostrowski's suit, two justices said such gifts were plainly illegal. But the court majority found a way around this. They reasoned that while the state government could not make such gifts, the legislature could create an economic development agency, give it the money and, in turn, the agency could give it away to the sheikh and any other business owner. If parallel reasoning were applied to drug deals, the kingpins who finance the drug trade could never be convicted of a crime as long as they do not touch the drugs.

The court also showed its contempt for those who challenge giveaways in its final order in the case, which ordered Ostrowski to pay $100 because he asked for a rehearing to show the factual errors in the court ruling.

You'll learn in this book how other courts, including the United States Supreme Court, have diminished the rights of consumers, voters and workers while enhancing corporate power. One instance was the Lilly Ledbetter case, which demonstrated the willingness of the court majority to favor corporations over people. Ledbetter retired in 1998 after almost two decades at a Goodyear Tire & Rubber plant in Gadsden, Alabama. Only when she was leaving did she learn that the men holding the same job she had held all earned significantly more—as much as $18,000 a year more. Paying men 40 percent more than women for the same work looks like an easy case of discrimination. But the Supreme Court said that Ledbetter's legal right to sue ended 180 days after the discrimination first took place, which was so many years earlier that the court ruled she had lost her right to sue. But how would Ledbetter have known she was being discriminated against? Only by a tortured reading of the statute could the majority rule against Ledbetter.

Bits and pieces of the complex story of business gaming government and gaining unfair advantage over consumers have been reported in the press, most often on the business pages. That coverage, however, tends to be narrow, typically portraying what are fundamental issues as disputes between competing industries, say, telephone companies versus cable companies or truckers versus railroads. Looked at from a larger perspective, these disputes were really about how to raise prices, limit

Corporate Power Unlimited

[A] corporation is a legal person created by state statute
that can be used as a fall guy, a servant, a good friend or
a decoy . . . a person you control . . . yet cannot be held
accountable for its actions. Imagine the possibilities!

—**Wyoming Corporate Services, Inc.**

2. **Just a few** blocks from the Wyoming state capitol sits a modest
brick house with a neatly manicured lawn at 2710 Thomas Avenue. As my
Reuters colleague Brian Grow revealed in 2011, this unimposing building
in Cheyenne is the headquarters of more than two thousand companies.

This is the home of Wyoming Corporate Services, which, for a fee,
will create a company, set up a bank account, appoint officers and directors (including a chief executive officer) and even provide a lawyer as a
corporate director so the company can invoke attorney–client privilege.
Wyoming Corporate Services will also make any required regulatory
filings. It can do all of this without anyone being able to ascertain, without a court order, who is behind any corporation it creates. As the Wyoming Corporate Services Web site notes, "Imagine the possibilities!"

Inflated ad copy? Perhaps. But let's try imagining exactly what it could
mean.

Let's say you're driving to work when a radio station reports that as-
tronomers have discovered a comet with an unusual tail that the earth
will pass through in a few days. When night comes, you enjoy the cosmic
light show in the sky, then you go to bed and the event is soon forgotten.

As the years pass, however, you and others begin to notice that a few
of us—say one in every thousand—has stopped aging. These people
never get sick. In an accident they can be crushed and bleed to death, but
otherwise they are immortal. That is not the only change. Whatever

and tested (and therefore profoundly conservative) principles of business developed over thousands of years. Allowing corporate values to overwhelm us is not necessary—I will close with some suggestions and solutions—but, in the meantime, our wealth, our well-being and our freedom are being diminished daily.

their interests before the comet, they now have a single desire. All they care about is money. They will do anything to get it as long as their actions are not illegal. They are neither moral nor immoral, but calmly amoral. As their wealth grows, they hire very smart people to help them make even more money.

If such immortal, amoral and greed-driven people walked the earth, we would have to rewrite our laws governing property. Property law assumes a finite human lifespan, and thus whatever property and power one builds up will be passed on when that person's time runs out. But our new class of immortals could just keep accumulating wealth and power forever. In time they would probably own every single asset on earth worth having.

Here's the kicker. The immortal being I've just described exists: it is the modern corporation. Unless it bleeds so much cash that it goes bankrupt, the corporation can exist forever. Even if it does go bankrupt, modern American laws allow a fresh infusion of cash from banks and investors to revive it. Because a corporation is not a natural person but an artificial entity, it has no conscience and is therefore amoral. The corporation can do anything legal in order to make money. The values of its officers and directors will shape the company, but by and large, legality alone rules. To be sure, some corporations are scrupulous because the managers of the moment have high ethical standards. But some other corporations will act illegally because their managers believe they will not get caught, that the law is unfair or because illegal conduct by competitors forces them to do likewise or go out of business.

In any case, they're in business to serve the interests of their shareholders, not John Q. Public.

A BLESSING AND A CURSE

Of course corporations can and often do make our lives better. Without corporations we would see far less enterprise. Corporations create wealth, which benefits those who possess it. Without the corporation, innovation might stagnate, and some of the comforts, services, pleasures, and much else that we value in our lives might not come to pass.

But certain corporate attributes can also be a curse.

To maximize gain, companies lobby for less government. Many seek reductions in the ranks of the white-collar police. These are auditors from the Internal Revenue Service, or tax police; examiners from the comptroller of the currency, or bank police; Securities and Exchange Commission investigators, or Wall Street police; and others whose job is to investigate and enforce the laws of commerce.

People who work for corporations seek these budget cuts and rule changes, but corporations are not people. And, in the eyes of the law, that has traditionally been an important distinction. Unlike individuals, who must take responsibility for their conduct, corporations' legal responsibility for their conduct (and misconduct) has benefited from limits to that responsibility established by law. The rationale for this is that people who want to build a business would not take the same risks if failure meant they would lose not just the time and money they put into their business, but their houses, cars, stamp collections, and everything else they have; limits on liability mean that they do not face such risks and they can go about their corporate business, creating enterprises and generating wealth.

While limiting liability has eased the path to profitability, it has also obscured a corporation's responsibility to function for the benefit of society. The greater good is an idea that's thousands of years old, but in the recent past corporations have been permitted to lose sight of that important notion.

I can date the moment it began to fade.

In a 1970 article in the *New York Times Magazine*, Milton Friedman argued that the sole duty of a company is to its shareholders, not to the interests of workers and surrounding communities. Friedman closed his piece with these words:

> There is one and only one social responsibility of business—to use its resources and engage in activities designed to increase its profits so long as it stays within the rules of the game, which is to say, engages in open and free competition without deception or fraud.

This is a bottom line with lots of implications. Workers may toil their entire lives, communities may tax themselves to create infrastructure a corporation needs, and vendors may invest their entire fortune to supply the corporation—but none of these parties, Friedman said, has significant legal rights or moral claims.

The idea was radical. It was not supported by the development of the law, the regulation of business and the advancement of civilization over thousands of years. But in a surprisingly short time, Friedman's ahistorical thinking has come to dominate our society. The corporate elite, the majority of billionaire investors and the officeholders in the legislative,

Back on earth, the jobs and pay situation for the vast majority of Americans can be summed up in a single word: dismal. Wages, adjusted for inflation, have stagnated for more than a decade. The median wage—half make more, half less—hovered at just over $500 a week for twelve years. In 2010 the median wage fell back to the level of 1999, according to the Social Security Administration's income data. In 2010, like the dozen years before it, one in three workers made less than $15,000 a year, while just one in four earned $50,000 or more; and less than 1 percent made $200,000 or more.

It gets worse when you look beyond wages to all income measured in inflation-adjusted dollars. The 2010 data on Americans' adjusted gross income (the last line on the front page of your tax return) showed that the top 1 percent of the top 1 percent had a great year. Compared to 2009, the top of the top saw their incomes soar 21.5 percent. These 15,600 households captured 37 percent of all the increase in income in a country of more than 300 million people.

At the same time, the bottom 90 percent saw their average incomes decline, down a fraction of a percent. The highest income household among the bottom 90 percent made $108,024. The average for the bottom 90 percent was much lower, just $29,840. That was down $4,842 from 2000.

More shocking still, the average income of the vast majority of taxpayers in 2010 was just a smidgen more than the $29,448 average way back in 1966. The difference after forty-four years was just $392, not enough for anyone to notice. In comparison, the average incomes of the top 1 percent of the top 1 percent increased in that same period by $18.7 million. That means while the vast majority went nowhere, the top of the top enjoyed nearly quadruple their 1966 income. Since tax rates on the top fell steeply, with the top rate cut in half and capital gains taxed at just 15 percent, much of this group enjoyed eight times more after taxes.

Another revealing piece of history: the-rich-get-richer pattern in the present is the opposite of what happened in 1934, the year after the Great Depression officially ended. Back then the income of the vast majority soared almost 9 percent, anticipating four decades of real income increases. But those at the top of the top saw their incomes dip, down 3.4 percent in 1934 compared to 1933. (For the record, 1933 had been the best year ever for the stock market, which fuels incomes at the very top but has little effect on the vast majority.)

More recently, when the economy collapsed in 2008—a collapse worse by some measures than the Great Depression—many among the vast majority experienced at first hand a new era of massive numbers of pink

FALLING INCOMES

George W. Bush said in 2000 that his tax cuts would spur prosperity and make us better off than in 2000. Instead, average incomes, adjusted for population and shown in 2012 dollars, fell sharply. Total incomes would have been almost $5 trillion higher had we stayed at 2000 levels.

YEAR	AVERAGE INCOME	CHANGE PER TAXPAYER	CHANGE FOR ALL TAXPAYERS
2000	$65,543		
2001	$61,361	($4,182)	($544,708,123,359)
2002	$59,146	($6,397)	($832,086,227,161)
2003	$59,332	($6,210)	($809,989,376,790)
2004	$62,348	($3,194)	($422,354,984,737)
2005	$64,881	($662)	($88,906,102,176)
2006	$66,029	$486	$67,237,795,856
2007	$67,225	$1,682	$240,537,500,383
2008	$61,801	($3,742)	($533,025,140,235)
2009	$58,041	($7,502)	($1,053,940,926,118)
2010	$59,243	($6,300)	($899,947,788,311)
2000-10	($6,300)	($36,020)	($4,877,183,372,647)
PERCENTAGE	(10%)		

Source: Author calculations from IRS Statistics of Income tables.

slips. My analysis of the Medicare tax database reveals that every thirty-fourth person who had worked in 2008 went through all of 2009 without earning one dollar. Most of those long-term unemployed failed to find any work in the next two years, in part because, since the turn of the new century, the national population has grown six times faster than jobs.

Among the world's thirty-four modern economies, America ranks second in the share of workers earning low wages. One in four employed Americans in 2010 was classified as a low-wage earner, just a smidgen below the share of low-paid workers in South Korea and far above the share of the same groups in Germany, Norway and other countries that remain broadly prosperous.

Adding to the distress of this growing chasm between the top and bottom is the decreasing number of jobs that come with benefits. More than one in four Americans goes without health insurance for part of each year. America's largest employer, Walmart, cut the hours of tens of thousands of its workers so that they would no longer be eligible to buy into a company-sponsored health-care plan. Other employers have withheld wage increases, saying they had to divert more money to health-care insurance.

It's not news that health-care costs devour an ever-larger share of the national economy. America will soon spend half of all the money in the world that is spent on health care or, more accurately, sick care. In 2011 health care consumed every sixth dollar of U.S. economic output, and medical finance experts warn that health costs could rise to one in four dollars. Devoting so large a portion of our economic output to health care means less money for everything else, from educating young people to maintaining roads and from inspecting food for dangerous pathogens to just having a little extra money to go out to dinner.

A look at the retirement system finds more bad news. Some corporate pensions are turning out to be more air than assets, and years of underfunding by many state governments reveal promises made but not funded. Worsening the problem is the legalized looting of pension plans when companies are sold and resold. And what of those do-it-yourself retirement schemes that promised to make the thrifty millionaires by the time they hit their golden years? As 2012 began, the total stock market, including reinvested dividends, was worth a third less than in 2000. Your 401(k) probably became what I call a 201(k).

THE RISE OF CORPORATE POWER IN AMERICA

American schoolchildren are taught that the American Revolution was a protest against taxation without representation. But what launched the colonists toward independence was more nuanced than that. The concern wasn't so much high taxes as a tax break for a monopoly.

Contrary to what many Americans believe, including members of today's Tea Party, the original Boston Tea Party and the smaller ones that followed in other colonial cities were never protests against high taxes. They could not have been, as an examination of official documents at the British Library in London reveals. In that era, taxpayers in the mother country paid twenty-five to fifty times as much in taxes per person as the American colonists. What the colonists who filled Old South Church in Boston on December 16, 1773, were protesting was a tax exemption intended to bail out investors in the British East India Company. With tons of tea that it couldn't sell, the threat of bankruptcy loomed. That would have meant ruin for friends of King George III in an era when debtors went to prison.

According to historian Benjamin Woods Labaree in his definitive *The Boston Tea Party* (1964), most Bostonians were drinking Dutch tea that fall, not because it was better but because it was cheaper. But the British Parliament had granted the East India Company a tax exemption, meaning the British tea would sell for less than Dutch tea. That might have seemed attractive to customers, but only in the short run, as a royal monopoly was to be strictly enforced. In time, tea prices would rise.

The Founding Fathers, who were sensitive to the potentially unbridled power of the East India Company, would be shocked by the rise of corporate power in our time. Early in the years following American independence, corporations were regarded with deep suspicion. Back then a corporation was allowed to exist for only a single purpose and for a limited period of time, usually twenty years. To retain the privilege of a corporate charter, the owners had to show that the corporation served a public purpose. Hiring people was not enough; that was understood to be necessary to do business. The idea that the government would give a corporation money to create jobs was, in the late eighteenth century, beyond imagining. In short, corporations were narrowly defined entities.

Not until well into the nineteenth century did the evolution of corporations into "people" begin. That story begins with a property tax dispute, one that hinged on the issue of whether the Fourteenth Amendment, adopted to make sure freed blacks were treated equally under the law following the Civil War, could be applied to companies.

The Southern Pacific Railroad was fighting a property tax imposed by California counties in what is now called Silicon Valley. The decision rendered in the case, *Santa Clara County v. Southern Pacific Railroad*, came not from the justices, but amazingly from the pen of the official court clerk, J. C. Bancroft Davis, who just happened to be a former president of Newburgh and New York Rail. Davis's one-paragraph statement asserted that the court did not need to hear the case to conclude that corporations were persons under the Fourteenth Amendment and thus were entitled to dispute the tax with the county authorities. Even though the Supreme Court never heard the case, corporations as of that moment were granted personhood in matters of property.

Very much later Associate Justice William Rehnquist, who would subsequently be elevated to chief justice of the United States, noted that the personhood grant applied only to property. Rehnquist warned in a 1978 case that it was one thing to treat corporations as persons when it came to property rights, but altogether different, and dangerous, to give corporations political rights. Rehnquist wrote that Congress, thirty state legislatures and the highest court in Massachusetts were among the many bodies that had

> concluded that restrictions upon the political activity of business corporations are both politically desirable and constitutionally permissible. The judgment of such a broad consensus of governmental bodies expressed over a period of many decades is entitled to considerable deference from this Court . . . A State grants to a business corporation the blessings of potentially perpetual life and limited liability to enhance its efficiency as an economic entity. It might reasonably be concluded that those properties, so beneficial in the economic sphere, pose special dangers in the political sphere.
>
> Furthermore, it might be argued that liberties of political expression are not at all necessary to effectuate the purposes for which States permit commercial corporations to exist. . . . Any particular form of organization upon which the State confers special privileges or immunities different from those of natural persons would be subject to like regulation, whether the organization is a labor union, a partnership, a trade association, or a corporation.

A bit more than a quarter century later, however, Rehnquist's warning was summarily rejected when, in 2010, under his successor Chief Justice John Glover Roberts, the Supreme Court proclaimed corporations the equal of people in politics. In the case *Citizens United v. Federal Election Commission*, the court went far beyond the narrow issues before it, holding that no law may constrain the spending by corporations, unions, nonprofits or others to influence elections and, further, that the names of those spending money can be kept secret. The notion is one that the framers of our Constitution would never have embraced, yet Roberts and his confreres insist that their guiding principle is strict adherence to the original intent of the framers. The so-called conservatives who so often rail against what they call judicial activism scarcely acknowledged this act of extreme judicial activism.

Such judicial activism will play a major role in many of the stories that follow about corporate power and how customers, investors, workers and others are abused, often with no way to seek redress for their grievances or losses. Keep in mind that justices Antonin Scalia and Clarence Thomas insist that they are "originalists," meaning that they apply the intent of the framers, as best they can discern it, to interpreting our Constitution as a document fixed in time. No honest originalist could possibly have signed on to *Citizens United*, but intellectually corrupt justices who worship corporatism, disdain the poor and enjoy the perks of power did so.

It is difficult to overstate the significance of the ideas that Milton Friedman launched in 1970, now compounded by the *Citizens United* decision and the power granted to make corporate values, already dominant, pervasive in every aspect of American life.

Citizens United is to the expansion of corporate power what the big bang was to the beginning of existence—it is the whole universe.

Buffett Buys a Railroad

Monopoly of one kind or another, indeed, seems to be the
sole engine of the mercantile system.

—Adam Smith, 1776

3. **In Wyoming's Powder** River Basin, where the high plains merge
into the high desert, the countryside takes on a pale green hue in spring
as melting snow reveals fresh shoots reaching toward the sun. Soon,
though, the summer wind robs the plants of their moisture, tanning the
countryside. Just beneath this shifting palette, spread across a million-
plus acre expanse larger than Delaware, lies a reddish-brown rock called
clinker. Here and there pieces of this natural ceramic litter the surface,
like giant shards of pottery smashed eons ago by rampaging Gargantuans.

Looking at the landscape today, one would hardly imagine that the
Powder River Basin was once a lush tropical swamp. Crocodiles basked
beneath palm trees covered with thick vines watered by more than a hundred inches of warm rain each year. Life flourished in this languid atmosphere sixty million years ago, each plant and animal competing and
cooperating until its time ran out and its remains sank into the continually renewed waters. Over five million years, their gooey black residue
formed a deposit hundreds of feet deep.

About 55 million years ago, when magma from deep inside the earth
raised the land, the fresh water drained away. Between the Black Hills
of South Dakota, with their rich veins of gold, and the majestic Big
Horn Mountains to the west, dirt and debris slowly covered the former
swamp. Heat from the molten rock far below began to dry the goo, cooking it into the black rock we call coal. From the skies, lightning strikes

ignited fires that over eons burned off perhaps 90 percent of the coal, creating natural furnaces that fused rock and dirt above the coal into ceramic clinker.

Cut to the present: this little-known ancient swamp now plays a role in the American economy as a whole and in your wallet in particular. Once again, the trick is to look beneath the surface, to see more than the headlines and to understand the fine print.

Just as geologists can read the layers of rock to understand what the Powder River Basin was like in earlier eons and how a tropical swamp was transformed, so can the record of human choices be peeled back to reveal how America has been transformed from a land of growing economic plenty into a hollow shell. In just a third of a century, the widespread liquidity that nourished the economy—reliable streams of cash going to workers and owners alike—has, like the rainfall that sustained the ancient swamp, dried up. Once so many greenbacks rained down every week or month that the share of people who had too little was shrinking. Today, instead of receding, poverty spreads while the middle class shrinks.

What caused this economic disaster in a few decades is no more a mystery than what happened in Wyoming over a span of 60 million years. Grasping the explanation requires knowledge, but the principles are not complicated. That said, those who have profited from the transformation do their best to describe their actions in language as alien as the Latin Mass was to Catholics before Vatican II brought in the vernacular.

CLINKERS, CARBON AND COAL

Four decades ago the Powder River Basin was insignificant; today every fifth lightbulb, computer screen and factory stamping tool is powered with the residue of the plants and animals that thrived in the lush valley in northeastern Wyoming. Starting our journey in the Powder River Basin provides a clear vector to follow in order to see how our economy got off track.

At its core, this is a story of well-established principles being replaced with radical and untested theories that, more than three decades of experience now reveal, are destructive. We built lofty economic superstructures not on foundations of granite but of sand. And when economic storms came, as they always do, giant waves of red ink eroded those foundations, leading to the subsidence of all that was built upon them. The problems with the theories and the practices that grew from them are reflected in the bills you get in the mail every month, and help explain how the prices you pay are subtly, and artificially, inflated while the quality of goods and, especially, the quality of services are cut.

What the record shows is the creation, by our elected leaders and their appointees, of a multitude of privatized systems designed to redistribute wealth and income upward. These systems destroy the benefits of capitalism by replacing the rigors of market competition with what I call *corporate socialism*. But let's start with one of the basic drivers of modern life, carbon energy in the form of coal, precisely that black stone found in the Powder River Basin.

A century ago, coal bins were common features of residential and commercial basements. Although hardly anyone has coal delivered to their home or store anymore, Americans today consume a per capita average of nineteen pounds of coal a day. That's three and a half tons of coal per person every year, consumed in ways as distant from our direct experience as Wyoming is from crocodiles.

Just four decades ago the Wyoming coal industry hardly existed. Coal had been mined there since the 1800s, but for local use. American power plants mostly burned coal from other ancient swamps more than a thousand miles to the east because these were closer to big cities and industrial centers. Appalachian coal also contained more energy—two tons of West Virginia or Pennsylvania coal generated the same heat as three tons of coal from the remote Powder River Basin. The much older Appalachian coal was bone dry and more compressed while Wyoming coal, though dry to the touch, still held trapped molecules of water from its fetid past.

Then in 1970 Congress changed the market for coal in a decision that touches your pocketbook every day. We use Wyoming coal now because the ancient western swamp contained freshwater while the eastern swamps were salty. As the eastern coal dried, as much as 5 percent of the anthracite became sulfur. When burned, the sulfur mixed with sunlight and other molecules, then fell back to earth as acid rain. This rendered the soil and water in the Adirondack and Catskill mountains toxic, poisoning maple, hemlock and spruce seedlings and trout eggs. Acid rain was even said to have discolored or "etched" paint on some cars.

When President Richard Nixon signed the Clean Air Act in 1970, he took a step toward making northeast forests and waterways healthier. But by igniting demand for sulfur-free Wyoming coal, Nixon also set in motion major changes that are central to how big business is using government to remake the American economy.

Today, every seven seconds a railroad car is filled with more than a hundred tons of Powder River Basin coal. Every twelve minutes a train linking at least a hundred cars heads west or east or south. After the cargo is dumped at power plants, it is crushed and ground until it is finer than face powder. Pressurized air blows this explosive dust into huge furnaces, and the heat from the furnaces boils water, which turns huge turbines that spin giant copper ropes looped around powerful magnets, creating every fifth watt of electricity in America. Coal stands at the center of this transformation because electricity is the defining technology of the modern world. From the radio that awakens us to the automatic door opener that lets our car into the garage at night, electricity makes modern life possible.

Visit the ruins at Pompeii and Herculaneum and you will see that these ancient Roman resorts bear a resemblance to the modern world. Their streets were lined with barbershops, restaurants, bars and laundries laid out much as those shops are today. What's different is the scale. Ancient towns were built to suit humans, with streets about as wide as the promenades in today's shopping malls because everyone walked.

Without this electricity, there would be no internal combustion gasoline engines, which rely on an electric spark to ignite the fuel. There would be none of the elevators that make high-rise buildings feasible, no automated traffic lights, no pumps to move water uphill. Without electricity, bauxite could not be melted to make aluminum, so jetliners, unimaginable to the ancients, would still be impossible.

Today coal is crucial to the generation of electricity. With such a huge demand for coal you might expect that there would be heavy competition to mine, move and burn the black rocks. After all, competition is what America is known for; it's the fuel that powered the nation's economic engine, raising living standards further and faster than anyone dreamed possible before we broke free from British rule more than 230 years ago.

Millions of people have come to the United States believing that anyone with a dream, a commitment to hard work and a bit of luck can reap the economic rewards of their endeavors. Yet today the potential to compete and achieve is leeching out of the American economy; in place of strivers, America is witnessing the rapid rise of monopolists and their close cousins, oligopolists.

The rigor of competition, which forces businesses to be efficient or fail, is being weakened bit by bit: a law here, a regulation there, a court ruling over there. These events tend to be reported as discrete events or even to go unnoticed. Because these changes take place over time, sometimes over a span of more than a decade, only rarely are the dots connected in political debate or in the news, revealing the larger outline.

The markets are supposed to be policed, but, posing as friends of the taxpayer, politicians from both parties have increasingly handcuffed the white-collar detectives at the federal agencies. Price fixing, price gouging, price manipulating and other anticompetitive practices have become more common, becoming the norm—and sometimes the standard—of conduct. Meanwhile, leaders chosen from the industries they are supposed to regulate are named to the regulatory boards. Compromising relationships are formed—but seldom observed—as journalists, aware that the public's attention is more easily drawn to the sensational than the substantive, focus more frequently on cheap news, like whom the Kardashians are dating this week.

Complicating all of this are corporate teams armed with spreadsheets and databases that make instant calculations. When one airline changes its prices, every other airline adjusts the prices for countless seats on thousands of flights in a matter of minutes. This ability to match almost instantly any competitor's price poses fundamental challenges to the idea of price competition.

In order to penetrate the strata of obfuscating language and seemingly disconnected laws and regulations of the marketplace, with its fluidity and its boundless opportunities, let's mine one story to see why prosperity is eluding more and more people.

In 2009, financier Warren Buffett decided to buy out shareholders in the BNSF Railroad. BNSF had been formed by the mergers of many railroads, the last two giants supplying the name: the Burlington Northern and Santa Fe. The BNSF was a consequence of a massive consolidation of railroads that began after a major change in federal law in 1980 that its sponsor, Representative Harley Staggers, a West Virginia Democrat, said would ensure robust railroad competition. Remember that name.

Buffett paid a stiff premium for the BNSF railroad shares he did not own, but told the world he did so gladly. "It's an all-in wager on the economic future of the United States," Buffett announced—a line that appealed to the patriotic instincts of broadcasters, print reporters and politicians. He got ample press coverage, but few questions were asked about the deal. Buffett sealed his message with a promise that he would make the economy better. "Our country's future prosperity depends on its having an efficient and well-maintained rail system," Buffett said.

The facts of the deal were clear enough: Buffett's Berkshire Hathaway holding company paid $100 per share for the 77 percent of the company it did not own, offered in cash or in shares of Berkshire. Add in the piece of the company Berkshire already owned and $10 billion of debt the railroad owed, and the deal established a value for BNSF of $44 billion.

One question nobody asked at the time was just what attracted Buffett to the railroad in the first place. Nor was there much analysis by financial journalists of how the railroad and its competitors were performing as investments. Business writers, like those they cover, tend to look forward rather than back. And they have a soft spot for positive news—a subtle but powerful bias.

Had you put a dollar into an index mutual fund comprised of the entire American stock market at its peak on March 23, 2000, just before the Internet bubble collapsed, you would soon have lost more than a third of your money, including reinvested dividends, after taking inflation into account. Your investment would be down to less than sixty-seven cents by the day Buffett announced his deal in 2009. Had you put a dollar into BNSF, however, your dollar would have grown to $3.75.

How did BNSF stock do so much better than the market?

You probably have guessed that hauling coal from the Powder River Basin is big business for BNSF; certainly it's profitable. But look a little deeper and you'll find that Buffett's railroad also ships grain. For many farmers, especially in the Dakotas and Montana, BNSF is often the only rail line farmers can use to send their wheat to buyers. So the railroad provides a necessary service, right?

A look at government data shows that BNSF routinely gouged farmers who had no alternative shipper, charging much more than what is known as its variable cost to ship their grain (variable cost acknowledges that a corporation's expenses will vary with production volume). The Surface Transportation Board (STB), which regulates some railroad prices, allows the rails leeway, permitting charges up to 1.8 times its variable cost before asserting that the costs have become price gouging. But BNSF routinely charged farmers 2.5 to 4 times its variable cost in the decade before and after the turn of the millennium. According to government documents, BNSF jacked up some prices 40 percent faster than the economic data showed was warranted based on costs.

BNSF got away with this because, buried in the fine print, there are rules about who can file price-gouging complaints. Even though farmers bear the cost of shipping their wheat to market, grain companies who buy from farmers contract for most shipping. Two of the biggest grain shippers are Cargill, the privately owned business that is the world's largest grain dealer, and Archer Daniels Midland or ADM (a major beneficiary, by the way, of a long-running subsidy for ethanol that was also involved in the global price-fixing scandal for another product, lysine). Under rules of the Surface Transportation Board, Cargill, ADM and their like can file complaints, but typically farmers don't have standing. They can't sue.

Customers who have access to only one railroad are known as captive shippers. As in any business, captives are likely to be mistreated and, in one two-month period at fall harvest time, official data show, BNSF failed to provide more than twenty-two thousand grain-hauling cars when they were scheduled to be filled with wheat and other crops. More than 70 percent of these railcars that arrived late were in the Northern Plains—Montana, the Dakotas and Minnesota—where farmers were BNSF captives. Missed shipments can cost farmers a great deal (grain prices change from one day to the next) and that's exactly what happened repeatedly: prices slipped during the time grain went unshipped.

Congress periodically holds hearings into how railroads are operating. A steady stream of complaints about railroad price gouging are heard, but few real changes are made. Congress was given clear evidence of price gouging in 2008 when a study by Escalation Consultants showed that, depending on the commodity being shipped, BNSF was the worst or second-worst offender. But nothing happened.

Wayne Hurst, past president of the Idaho Grain Producers Association, complained in 2007 that since that 1980 change in railroad law, "the degree of captivity in many wheat-growing regions has increased dramatically." Farmers were getting hit with a double whammy of "unreliable service and higher" rates. Hurst traced the problem to a wave of consolidations in the railroad industry. Less competition meant railroads could lower the reliability of service, cutting where and how often they would pick up grain and other crops. Increasingly, they refused to pick up partially filled railcars, forcing farmers to truck wheat to central pickup points. The railroads "view efficiency as hauling larger and larger movements of a single crop from a single origin to a single destination," Hurst said, rather than supporting a diversity of farmers and grain users, which would facilitate a competitive market.

All that means farmers have to spend more to haul grain by truck to a central pickup point, which also shrinks the number of buyers they have bidding for their crop. That means less competition not just in rail services, but in the grain business too.

Ironically, railroading was the first industry subject to price regulation by Congress when it created the Interstate Commerce Commission (ICC) in 1887. While complaints by western farmers about price gouging and lousy service prompted the law, the railroads played a major role in shaping the legislation as it moved through Congress. Subsequently the STB replaced the ICC, but things haven't changed a great deal.

In recent public talks, board members focused largely on the concerns of the railroads rather than their customers. In 2009, for example, the acting chairman of the STB, Francis P. Mulvey, told a conference that railroad profits were up, the numbers of rail workers slashed and the share of shipping on barges and trucks down. Still, he said, most railroads "are not revenue adequate on a system basis."

"Revenue adequate" is bureaucratese for "not charging high enough prices." What could be sweeter to the ear of anyone in a regulated industry than to be told they should charge higher prices? Warren Buffett was presumably listening: within a year of hearing that the official line was that railroads were not charging high enough prices, he made his move to own all of BNSF.

WARREN WORKS THE RAILROAD

Mulvey's remarks on revenue adequacy are consistent with how government agencies created to control rapacious conduct now regularly facilitate it. Looking over the backgrounds of appointees to a host of federal and state regulatory boards, strikingly few have any background as advocates for consumers, whether that consumer is Joe Sixpack or a mighty corporation that depends on a regulated industry for services. While industry-friendly regulators have always been around, when I started covering these issues in the late 1960s and on into the early 1980s, these boards typically included one or more people *not* beholden to the industry they were supposed to monitor. And more than a few of these boards had well-informed critics, some of them successful business owners and executives with no ties to the industry they swore to regulate in the public interest.

Congress knows all about this, but does nothing. Hurst, the Idaho grain farmers' leader, pointed to studies by the Government Accountability Office, the investigative arm of Congress, from 1999, 2002 and 2006. He said they "all point to the same conclusion—that the [Surface

Transportation Board] is not adequately protecting large parts of the country from market abuse where no competition exists."

This was not supposed to happen after Congress adopted the Staggers Rail Act in 1980. A related law, known as the Long-Cannon Amendment (named after senators Russell B. Long and Howard Cannon), required that railroads take steps to maximize competitive pricing. Together the Staggers Act and Long-Cannon were sold as ways to ensure competition and give shippers better deals. In some cases it has, but overall the Staggers Act has been a powerful weapon wielded against any hint of real competition, not least because it permits railroads to sign secret contracts with customers.

The Staggers Rail Act is to transparency in railroad freight rates as Wyoming clinker is to that ancient swamp. It acts as a rock-hard shield to hide the information that could lower prices and foster actual competition. Information, not secrecy, promotes competition. Secrecy enhances the power of monopolists. And monopoly power is money. As Toby Kolstad, president of Rail Theory Forecasts, put it: "In recent years, freight rate increases for coal shipments have provided much of the increased earning power of the railroad industry."

Thanks to the Staggers Act, from the moment that coal is loaded onto the railcar until you pay your electric bill, every step of the journey is crafted to take as much money as possible out of your pocket by avoiding the rigors of market competition; inflating costs; avoiding taxes; shifting the costs of safety and environmental protections on to you; and making the billing as complex and incomprehensible as possible.

The demand for more coal to generate more electricity underlies a calculus that is, once again, complicated and yet not so hard to discern if you know how and where to look. At each step along the way, our government now helps rail and other companies pick your pocket by erecting barriers to complaints, as with the wheat farmers who are technically not customers even though they pay the freight. This makes it virtually impossible for consumers to bring rate cases. Then there is the growing practice of granting automatic rate increases under the guise of adjusting for inflation or imagined higher costs, while simultaneously stopping the collection of data needed to evaluate business practices.

Railroad price gouging is so out in the open that the industry's own commentators write and talk about it freely. Few citizens, however, are aware of it because industry's specialized journals attract few readers. Much commentary is also couched in dense bureaucratese, a language as alien to most people as ancient Greek.

Protecting railroads from competition has an obvious implication: every time you turn on a light in your home or buy a product made with the help of electricity, you're paying more than you would in a competitive market. When a business has a monopoly, as railroads do in many parts of the country, regulation is supposed to act as a substitute for competition, a proxy for market forces. But that assumption breaks down when regulators identify with the industry more than with customers; then the captains of industry get both undeserved riches and the wherewithal to further the tilt of the system in their favor. Easy profits enable them to make more political donations and offer more jobs to former regulators and their spouses, some of whom know how to get politicians on the oversight committees to make sure that no matter what is said, nothing happens to harm the protected industries.

In a competitive market, when companies raise prices, they lose business as customers switch to other suppliers or cut back on spending. But a railroad with an iron grip on its customers will likely keep every one of them, even when prices go up. When an industry can raise prices in the absence of increased demand, it is said to have "market power," and the result is usually twofold. First, it means more money for the railroad owners; second, it comes at a price to society that economists call a "deadweight loss."

Government policy enables this subtle transfer of wealth from you and others to railroad investors. Here is what the Justice Department's Antitrust Division told Congress about market power in the railroad industry and the shortcomings of regulation by the Surface Transportation Board:

> One reason for the current market power enjoyed by the U.S. Class I railroads is the past mergers that have already been allowed by the STB—some of which . . . were either opposed by the Antitrust Division or recommended only with more stringent conditions than were imposed by the STB. The result of these mergers has been two mammoth regional duopolies in which neither duopolist aggressively seeks to poach business from the other. Thus, had antitrust jurisdiction rested with the Antitrust Division at the time these mergers were proposed, the industry likely would be more competitive today.

This means the cozy duopolies—one in the West, one in the East—can escape the rigors of competition and enjoy what are in effect monopoly profits so long as each cooperates in keeping prices high and does

not compete for more business by cutting prices. Keep in mind that 44 percent of the tonnage hauled by railroads is coal. But the coal buyers are not a competitive group, either. The corporate-owned electricity business is also highly concentrated, if not to the degree of the railroads. Just fifty companies collected 95 percent of electric revenues in 2010, the year Buffett bought total control of the BNSF railroad. One of the biggest of those fifty electric companies was MidAmerican Energy Holdings. Its subsidiaries serve customers from Oregon and California east to Illinois. MidAmerican is owned, in turn, by Buffett's Berkshire Hathaway.

Like most electric utilities, MidAmerican is not all that sensitive to the price it pays for shipping coal, whether it comes from its corporate sister BNSF or another railroad. That's because state regulatory commissions let companies add to customer bills whatever they pay for coal and other fuels, as long as the price is deemed reasonable. Because "reasonable" means what other monopolies are charging, once again there is no downward pressure on rates paid to haul coal.

Owning complementary monopolies dovetails with Buffett's announced policies to buy businesses with both minimal competition and the power to raise prices. Owning a monopoly is nice. Being able to leverage one monopoly, a railroad, say, with another, such as a coal-buying electric utility, is like winning the lottery every day. But what's terrific for the winners is costly for those of us who pay the price every day.

Wall Street even measures companies by their success in creating barriers to competition. The investment research firm Morningstar rates companies using a "moat index" to measure success at avoiding the rigors of market competition. Pay close attention, especially to the last line, of what Morningstar candidly says:

> The concept of economic moats is a cornerstone of our stock-investment philosophy. Successful long-term investing involves more than just identifying solid businesses, or finding businesses that are growing rapidly, or buying cheap stocks. We believe that successful investing also involves evaluating whether a business will stand the test of time.
>
> The concept of an economic moat can be traced back to legendary investor Warren Buffett, whose annual Berkshire shareholder letters over the years contain many references to him looking to invest in businesses with "economic castles protected by unbreachable 'moats.'"
>
> Moats are important to investors because any time a company develops a useful product or service, it isn't long before other firms try to

capitalize on that opportunity by producing a similar—if not better—
product.

Basic economic theory says that in a perfectly competitive market,
rivals will eventually eat up any excess profits earned by a successful
business. In other words, competition makes it difficult for most firms to
generate strong growth and margins over an extended period of time.

There you have it—competition "eats up any excess profits." And so
what the serious investors want is to avoid competition, which in turn
destroys the benefits of market capitalism that Adam Smith figured out
back in 1776.

Another Buffett strategy is to earn profits today but pay taxes in the
future. MidAmerican is a major beneficiary of Congress's profit-now,
pay-later corporate tax laws. In 2009 MidAmerican's income tax bills,
Buffett wrote in his annual letter to his shareholders, came to just $313
million on a pretax profit of $1,846 million. That is less than 17 percent—
and less than half the posted corporate income tax rate of 35 percent,
which MidAmerican gets to include in full in the price it charges every
customer every month. That means customers of MidAmerican pay electric bills calculated on the assumption that the utility is paying 35 percent income tax, although in fact the government collects only half the
money.

As a result of my work a few years back, Oregon passed a law requiring
that electricity and natural-gas utilities taxes must be paid over to government or given back to customers. As soon as it was enacted, Buffett's
lobbyists began working to restore the system that let Berskshire Hathaway's PacifiCorp electric utility in the Beaver State pocket taxes, divert-
ing them from public coffers to Berkshire Hathaway's accounts. In 2011
they had spread around enough money that the law was repealed. Once
again, Buffett is profiting off taxes paid by his captive Oregon customers.

Despite owning a monopoly railroad in an industry that ships more
than 40 percent of its freight to a small number of monopoly buyers, one
of which is another Buffett company, Buffett argues that railroads are not
monopolies. Indeed, he told Berkshire Hathaway shareholders in 2010
that his Burlington Northern Santa Fe Railroad faces intense competition:

The business environment in which BNSF operates is highly competitive. Depending on the specific market, deregulated motor carriers
and other railroads, as well as river barges, ships and pipelines in

certain markets, may exert pressure on price and service levels. The presence of advanced, high service truck lines with expedited delivery, subsidized infrastructure and minimal empty mileage continues to affect the market for non-bulk, time-sensitive freight. The potential expansion of longer combination vehicles could further encroach upon markets traditionally served by railroads. In order to remain competitive, BNSF and other railroads continue to develop and implement operating efficiencies to improve productivity.

As railroads streamline, rationalize and otherwise enhance their franchises, competition among rail carriers intensifies.

BNSF's primary rail competitor in the Western region of the United States is the Union Pacific Railroad Company. Other Class I railroads and numerous regional railroads and motor carriers also operate in parts of the same territories served by BNSF. Based on weekly reporting by the Association of American Railroads, BNSF's share of the western United States rail traffic in 2009 was approximately 49 percent.

By controlling, in effect, half of the rail traffic in the West, BNSF is by definition half of a duopoly, and BNSF's circumstances a far cry indeed from intensely competitive. Although Buffett says he is worried about so-called monster trucks that could carry two-thirds more freight than the eighteen-wheelers on the road today, they would still be able to haul only about half what a railcar can carry. Plus it only takes a two-man crew to move a hundred or more railcars, meaning that moving the same weight by truck would requires two hundred drivers. That clearly doesn't sound like a challenge in the making for BNSF.

That trucks work best for shorter hauls or goods that have to be moved faster than rail is a long-accepted fact (think fresh fruit and vegetables that need to get from Arizona or California to stores in Massachusetts or Mississippi before they rot). Likewise, it is a maxim of transportation that the freight put on a ship crossing the ocean gets moved for less than the cost of rail transit across the continent and that, in turn, is often less than the cost of trucking it to its final destination. But neither trucks nor ships pose a threat to the coal, grains and other freight that make BNSF so profitable.

Yet the American Association of Railroads also tries to sell this claim of intense competition to the public, noting that since 1980, when "deregulation" began:

Railroads' earnings have typically been insufficient to cover the total costs of their operations and provide a reasonable return on investment.

In fact, freight railroads have consistently been in the bottom quartile of all U.S. industries in terms of profitability. Even in 2006 and 2007, when railroads had record traffic . . . , [the] industry's profitability was still below average compared to other industries.

This assertion is belied by Justice Department analyses, and my own, which show that railroad profits rose at an accelerating pace in the 2000s. Rail profits became so robust in the Great Recession of 2009 that the *Journal of Commerce*, the daily newspaper of the freight industry, headlined an article "US Railroads Are Holding Up as the Healthiest Segment of the North American Freight Carrying Industry."

Buried deep in a Surface Transportation Board report is profit data that could prompt Buffett to dance a jig. In 2008 the industry's revenue for each mile each ton of coal was shipped shot up 22.1 percent over 2007. This was the year when the Gross Domestic Product, our key measure of economic activity, was virtually flat in real terms and the Bush administration asked Congress for $700 billion to rescue Wall Street. This was the year when the worst economic meltdown since 1932 ravaged the country. But the price of shipping a ton of coal rose 22.1 percent. (That $700 billion figure, by the way, was the equivalent of all of the federal income taxes you and everyone else in America paid from New Year's Day through Labor Day that year.)

So here we are, talking again about that black residue in the Powder River Basin. How could railroad shipping rates explode when the economy was falling apart? Economic theory says that railroads and others should have been cutting prices to keep from losing business in a recession, especially since the volume of freight being shipped fell. That they did not shows why it's nice to own legal monopolies, especially when faux "free market" ideology spouted by politicians empowers you to extract more and more from customers instead of coping with the rigors of market competition. When it comes to hauling coal, railroads enjoy monopoly routes, which in turn means monopoly pricing.

Another example? Monopoly power has meant railroads can shortchange maintenance of the rail beds. When derailments shut down coal shipments from the Powder River Basin in 2007, the railroad blamed coal dust, saying it weakened the rail beds. Burlington Northern Santa Fe increased prices to coal shippers, charging them for measures to reduce how much coal dust flew off its trains as they moved down its tracks. What Buffett and other railroad owners really did was simply raise prices—prices that they knew would be passed on to electricity consumers, making them pay more each month.

A little-known STB policy helps further inflate railroad prices and profits. In judging how much railroads should charge for hauling freight, the Surface Transportation Board uses a standard measure called "cost of capital." But the cost the STB applies is a fifth higher than what Wall Street analysts use. Inflating the cost of capital distorts economic decisions. Ultimately, artificially inflated costs destroy jobs in industries that depend on goods shipped by rail, including chemicals, coal and grains.

For much of the twentieth century railroad executives complained about union work rules, which they said forced them to retain people whose jobs were no longer necessary. The railroad companies called it worker "featherbedding." Now we have, by government policy, what might be called "capital featherbedding." But you won't hear the railroad executives gripe about that.

Railroaded

Federal government policies force us to pay monopoly prices.

—Terry Huval, 2012

4. **In the heart** of Cajun country, Lafayette Utilities System should be able to negotiate a competitive price with the rail companies. From Kansas City on south, two railroads, the Kansas City Southern and the Union Pacific, rumble across Arkansas, delivering Wyoming coal to Louisiana. The presence of rolling stock competing for business would seem to suggest that negotiating with the two railroads would produce a good price. Unfortunately, the game of monopoly has advanced too far for that to happen.

Although both railroads trace the eastern shore of the Red River to Lafayette, the utility's power plant is twenty miles back upstream on the west side of the river. As it happens, the west bank is Union Pacific's exclusive province. Well, you might say, why can't Lafayette negotiate competitive rates from Wyoming to the Lafayette rail yards, then pay Union Pacific a monopoly rate to haul its coal the last twenty miles to the parish's Rodemacher power plant? Sadly, it doesn't work that way, and Lafayette pays a monopoly rate for the entire 1,520-mile trip.

"We are a classic captive customer," said Terry Huval, who runs the Lafayette Utilities System. "On ninety-nine percent of the route we have competitive rail service, so we would like to negotiate for competitive rates on that portion, but we cannot." The reason is the "bottleneck" decision of the Surface Transportation Board.

In 1996, the STB ruled, in essence, that if any portion of a trip is on a monopoly rail line, the monopoly rail can charge monopoly prices not just to the nearest junction with another railroad, but all the way. One implication is that bottlenecks become a good thing for railroads. In the case of coal, two-thirds of which moves under this monopoly-pricing rule, bottlenecks have become a very good, very profitable policy for the carrier, but not the customer.

As usual, the implications are broad. Across America nonprofit electric utilities like Lafayette's, as well as corporate-owned utilities, pay higher freight charges because the government rule favors monopolies (Warren Buffett surely understood this when he willingly paid a premium price to own all of the Burlington Northern Santa Fe). And what of the customers of the utilities that burn coal? The costs get passed on to them because, under rules that apply to corporate-owned utilities, the rates customers pay may include any reasonable amount paid for fuel, making these utilities largely indifferent to how much the railroads charge to deliver coal.

You're probably wondering what this means to your monthly electric bill. Thanks to Congress, you're not really allowed to know that.

Recall the Staggers Rail Act, the 1980 law that was going to bring competition to the railroad industry. Under the terms of the legislation, railroads do not have to publish the prices they charge to haul freight the way that, say, Amtrak and passenger airlines do. Instead, the Staggers Act encourages railroads to negotiate individually with their customers on the theory that this will promote competition. The Staggers Act also lets the railroads *require* that the contract terms be kept confidential, even when the customer is a public entity such as the Lafayette Utilities System.

"I'd tell you the terms of our contract if I could," Huval said. Even though he couldn't tell me the particulars, he did describe the big picture. According to Huval, Union Pacific's monopoly pricing costs his community about $6.5 million per year. And the figure keeps rising.

Union Pacific's picking of Lafayette's pockets works out to more than a dollar per week for every man, woman and child in Lafayette, more than $200 annually for a family of four. That's more than enough to finance a 10 percent cut in Lafayette property taxes. Or it could cover free electricity to Lafayette schools and colleges, relieving taxpayers of that burden, with enough left over for a small property-tax reduction.

Looked at another way, that $6.5 million per year could be spent on local goods and services for the benefit of Lafayette's businesses and workers. Instead, it is extracted from the wallets of local residents and businesses and sent to Omaha, home to both Union Pacific and BNSF owner Warren Buffett.

Lafayette is far from alone in being railroaded into paying higher prices. Charging monopoly rates for an entire route, not just the small portion served by one railroad, is common. Few rail customers have direct access to two or more lines, and railroads work hard to make sure they can protect their monopoly pricing power. Since half the electricity in America comes from burning coal, we can multiply the numbers from Lafayette by all the communities whose electric power comes from burning coal and reach the unsurprising but still shocking conclusion that billions of dollars are being extracted through monopoly pricing. The total cost of monopoly pricing nationwide is easily $6 billion per year; if Lafayette's experience is in the middle range of price gouging, the cost may exceed $8 billion per year nationwide.

In a quirky turnabout, the "bottleneck" decision from 1996 was challenged by another utility, none other than Warren Buffett's MidAmerican Electric Holdings. In early 1999, the decision of the Eighth Circuit Court of Appeals made clear the judges did not agree with the policy; still, they upheld the bottleneck decision. The decision found that, since the rationale given for "bottleneck" pricing was neither arbitrary nor capricious, it would stand.

COUNTING CARS AND CALCULATING COMPETITION

Monopoly rates allowed by government rules are just part of the story of how monopoly railroads pollute the economy. The official data on how many freight cars the railroads own suggest a decline in the American rail system, but the actual number of railcars in use has gone up, not down. The explanation for this apparent contradiction is that railroads now demand that more customers supply their own railcars.

Let's go back to Lafayette, a city of a little more than 120,000 people. As a railroad customer, it had to pay half the $16.5 million cost of buying 246 aluminum railcars. The railroad paid nothing, since customers of neighboring electric-utility systems paid the balance. For residents of Lafayette, the cost came to about $200 for every household for the new cars.

Big railroads also erect "paper barriers" to block competitive pricing. The big railroads go to the myriad little mom-and-pop railroads, making offers they cannot refuse: agree to an exclusive relationship—or get cut off. As Mark Cooper, director of research at the Consumer Federation of America puts it, paper barrier contracts memorialize, in essence, the edict "Thou shalt not compete or do anything that promotes competition."

What does the railroad industry have to say for itself? In speeches, in testimony to Congress and in disclosures to shareholders, rail industry leaders describe a tremendously competitive market, one in which the railroads are under siege by truckers, barge operators and pipelines trying to take away their business. As you would expect, each railroad has reliable expert witnesses who testify in trials and present politicians with studies that show how tough it is to make a profit running a railroad. Even more powerful than expert witnesses are the government insiders with whom the railroads have established relationships that serve their interests—often at the expense of the consumer. Two quick examples: When Linda Morgan left the Surface Transportation Board in 2002 she was its chair; she joined Union Pacific as one of its top lawyers. Less than four years later, her successor, Roger Nober, left the government board only to resurface, exactly one year and one day later, as executive vice president and chief lawyer at Buffett's BNSF. They are just two of the many who reaped the rewards of having been reliable industry allies while in government.

The rail industry is quick to challenge anyone who questions its power, its misleading use of statistics or its stranglehold on the economy, asserting that critics really want to destroy a crucial mode of transportation. This is poppycock, of course, but given how little most journalists know about business—and especially business law—outraged railroad voices with one simple message often succeed in drowning out those that describe the complexities of a modern octopus that has businesses and communities in a stranglehold.

Lafayette's Huval offers a fair-minded view from the middle of the fray. He reports that his nonprofit electric utility "supports a strong national coal delivery network by rail," before adding a crucial qualification: "It is in the national interest to have a railroad system built on reasonable, not predatory, pricing and service."

That brings us back to another common complaint concerning monopoly railroads: quality of service. In a competitive environment, there's pressure not only to match or better a competitor's prices but to provide reliable service so the customer will not shift allegiances. But just as the wheat farmers in Montana and Idaho sat powerless, their harvests sitting trackside while prices fell, so electric utilities suffer from sporadic coal deliveries. In 2005 and 2006 the Union Pacific provided such atrocious service that the Lafayette Utilities System had to import coal from Venezuela (which, by the way, was shipped by barge). At times the system had to truck low-quality lignite coal from northern Louisiana to keep the lights on. Competitive businesses would pay dearly for providing such unreliable service, but government-protected monopolies can disregard customer need yet keep on making huge profits.

The so-called unit train is a transport practice that has worsened customer service in recent years. The most efficient way to run a railroad is nonstop between two points, with two or three locomotives pulling a hundred or more fully loaded railcars at slow speeds. Such unit trains are extremely efficient because once a train is moving, fuel consumption drops dramatically (as we're reminded often by the CSX Transportation commercials boasting of moving a ton of freight more than two hundred miles on one gallon of diesel). The same principle applies to airplanes, which gulp fuel on takeoff but sip at cruising altitudes; thus, a direct flight from New York to San Francisco consumes much less fuel than connecting flights that carry the LaGuardia passenger to the same final destination but connect at St. Louis and Salt Lake City.

That said, neither passengers nor every piece of freight shares the same cost-effective destination and point of departure. When in-between and tangential destinations are factored in, a network develops. Though that's part of the fabric of modern economic life, it runs counter to the ideal model for reducing rail operation costs by scheduling fewer trains that pull more cars with fewer stops. Increasingly, manufacturers and farmers have been pressured to alter their business to suit the railroads.

In the past, manufacturers constructed their factories near mainline railroad lines, often with a siding so they could load boxcars with their products for pickup every day or two. But in the new world in which railroads dictate to customers, the manufacturer must face added costs, cash-flow impacts, and slowed delivery times when the train stops only once a week. Such erratic rail service forces some businesses to switch to trucking, which can cost four times as much. It's also one of the myriad reasons why 56,000 American factories have closed and jobs moved to China in recent decades. Today trains run an average of 900 miles between stops, half again as many as the 600 or so in the 1970s. More long-haul unit trains, fewer stops and inflexible rules have meant, in short, many fewer freight cars stuffed with American-made goods.

If you're a farmer or small manufacturer whose heavy product requires rail for efficient transport, you face three choices in order to stay in business. The first is to ship by truck to a central point for rail pickup, with added costs that eat up profits. Second, you can keep more supplies and finished goods at the factory while trying to persuade customers to keep more product on hand, a practice that means more capital will be tied up in inventory, reducing profit margins (yours and/or your customers'). Third, you can move your factory to China, where labor is extremely cheap and shipping goods across thousands of miles of ocean may actually be more cost-efficient, given the increased costs and uncertainty imposed by the remaining few railroads.

"The focus of U.S. transportation policy in the nineteenth and twentieth centuries was on extending the benefits of transportation to more locales and to more citizens," said Gerald McCullough, a University of Minnesota economist who studies railroads. But the Staggers Rail Act has shifted that priority. Its stated purpose is to promote "a safe and efficient rail transportation system" and the Intermodal Surface Transportation Efficiency Act, which created the Surface Transportation Board, has as its goal a system that is "economically efficient." But in practice a switch has been effected as the board focuses more on the welfare of railroads than the customers or the larger economy they serve.

The evidence of a lack of competition in the rail marketplace is more than anecdotal; the numbers tell the same story. In 1978, two years before Congress adopted the Staggers Rail Act, the railroads actually were highly competitive, with thirty-six big lines known as Class I railroads. The industry and Staggers said this robust competition did not produce enough profits, an argument that ran counter to the traditional thinking that the economy thrives on competitive enterprise. Once the Staggers Rail Act took effect, the number of Class I railroads quickly shrank and, by 2004, there were just seven Class I railroads.

Economists have a simple technique for measuring whether an industry is competitive or tending toward monopoly. It is called the Herfindahl-Hirschman Index, or HHI. The formula squares the market share of each company, then adds up the squares. It's easier than it sounds. In an industry with one firm that has 100 percent market share, the HHI score will be 100 x 100 or 10,000. Or, if fifty firms each have 2 percent of the market, then the score would be 200 (2 x 2 = 4; 4 x 50 = 200). On the Justice Department scale, scores up to 1,000 indicate competitive markets, while scores higher than 1,800 are seen as solid evidence that competition is weak to nonexistent.

In 1978, when America had thirty-six Class I railroads, the HHI score was 589, indicating robust competition. By 2004, however, just seven remaining Class I railroads meant the HHI score had soared to 2,263, reinforcing what was already obvious: little competition survived in the marketplace. Although the text of the 1980 Staggers Rail Act cites competition four times as the goal of the law, the effect has been the opposite.

(To say that there are seven Class I railroads is also misleading. Twin duopolies, one west of the Mississippi River, the other east, dominate rail freight hauling. In the West there are the Union Pacific and Warren Buffett's Burlington Northern Santa Fe. In the East there are CSX and Norfolk-Southern. As long as each of the big players elects not to cut prices to take major customers away from its rival, these duopolies function as price-inflating, profit-making machines to the detriment of the overall economy.)

Another look over our shoulder at the not-so-distant past is informative. In the nineteenth century, the Grange movement of yeoman farmers arose mostly in response to railroads charging such high prices for poor service that family farms could not survive. Grain traders, millers and others have been treated no better by the railroads today, but protest is muted in our time in large part because politicians are insulated from popular dissent by the nature of our campaign finance and voting systems, which require huge infusions of cash that come from a small but very rich segment of the public. Therefore the voices politicians hear are those of the rich and of lobbyists whose concerns are underwritten by larger interests.

There is another thing that the railroads became much more adept at after the Staggers Act and its false promise of competition. From 1978, just before passage of the Staggers Act, to 2004 the amount of freight moved per worker grew sixfold, a reflection of the fact that many workers were being laid off. No doubt increased labor productivity is good for railroad profitability; very likely it would be good for the economy as a whole if it added overall to economic efficiency. But in cutting their workforces, the railroads pushed goods onto the highways, which today means less efficient burning of fuel and more trucks around you when you go to work or drive your family on a vacation down an interstate highway.

Let's take one more look back. So ruthless were the nineteenth-century railroads that, as the reformer Henry George wrote in his 1879 book *Progress and Poverty*, railroad monopolists approached the burghers of small towns "as a robber approaches his victim." The railroads demanded whatever would make them richer, threatening to move their line a few miles this way or that to compel submission. You can still visit the ruins of once-thriving little towns in the Great Plains that became ghost towns because the town fathers dared to resist the demands of railroad barons.

Jumping to our time, railroad ownership is more concentrated than in 1887 and the abuse of power as great or greater. The subtitle of Henry George's book is as apt now as then: *An Inquiry into the Cause of Industrial Depressions and of Increase of Want with Increase of Wealth.*

In Twenty-ninth Place
and Fading Fast

It sounds like you don't want any competition down there
in Glasgow.

—Judge Ronald Meredith

5.　**A 1999 television** commercial encapsulated the telephone industry's promise of the future along the Information Superhighway. A
grizzled salesman drops his bag in the sparse lobby of Roy's Motel and
Café, then asks the unaccommodating young woman at the front desk
about amenities.

"What kind of rooms you got?"

"King size."

"You got room service?"

"Donuts and coffee," replies the young woman, not bothering to look
up from her book.

"Got entertainment?"

As the camera closes in on her lips, she says, "All rooms have every
movie ever made in every language, anytime, day or night."

Astonished, the aging man asks "How is that possible?" As his words
die away, the camera shifts outside to the windswept Mojave Desert,
where an old Route 66 highway sign morphs into the logo of one of the
Baby Bell telephone companies. In voice-over, the actor Willem Dafoe
answers the question. "Could your business use the bandwidth to change
everything? Ride the light. *Qwest.*"

Qwest was just one of the telephone companies that shaped the promise
of connecting us to the World Wide Web, even from fleabag motels in the

Without basic data, state and federal legislation will be shaped by the information the companies choose to make available, information that will focus on company needs rather than the needs of customers. The result must be—and is—laws and regulations written to the detriment of millions of people, especially captive customers.

Regulation of prices acts as a proxy for customers where no market exists because of monopolized industries or where market competition is minimal, as with our national telephone duopoly of AT&T and Verizon. Prices are not the only concern, either. Access to service, quality of service and resolution of disputes are also important issues, as more Americans are discovering under the new rules—and many more will once AT&T and Verizon achieve one of their basic goals: to enhance profits by shedding unwanted customers, a goal they were in sight of in 2012.

Even in a market where more than one telephone service is available, competition is not robust. Many people can chose Internet calling via unregulated services such as Skype and Vonage if they buy broadband Internet access, which may well come from AT&T or Verizon. People can also switch to cell phones, where AT&T and Verizon also dominate. AT&T and Verizon also own traditional landline systems that are legal monopolies. Through one technology or another, the AT&T–Verizon duopoly controls more than 60 percent of the telephone business in America.

Any competition between telephone companies and cable companies is illusory. Verizon announced in 2008 that it would stop building out its FiOS (fiber-optic system) once it reaches about 16 million of America's more than 100 million households. In New Jersey, for example, a state law that Verizon drafted says it must run FiOS past homes and businesses in seventy cities, but it is not required to actually wire every property for service. Verizon has no plans to wire the rest of the state. Instead, it has made deals with Comcast to sell its services using Comcast cables. Verizon said it anticipates similar deals with other cable providers to sell over their systems.

The cross-marketing deal Verizon and Comcast made is not competition, but the start of a cartel. It is much closer to the intertwined corporate ties that dominate the economies of Japan and South Korea than the American ideal of competitive markets. It reinforces the economic interests of telephone and cable companies by not extending lines to rural areas or poor neighborhoods and not wiring apartment buildings where few people could afford the new services.

Cable companies jacked up prices, too. Since 1995, average cable prices have been rising 2.6 times faster than the cost of living, reaching an average of almost $53 a month for basic, no-frills service in 2009, FCC reports show. Some cable companies are not content with annual price hikes. Comcast raised prices twice in ten months in 2011 and 2012 on its 1.8 million Boston-area customers. Service that cost $58 in 2009 came to almost $67 in early 2012, increasing at more than twice the rate of inflation.

The strongest evidence that the cable companies exert monopoly power to raise prices comes from a survey of prices for basic service plus the most commonly purchased extra features such as handheld remotes and premium channels like HBO. In 2008, the worst economic year since the Great Depression, when the national economy shrank and millions lost their jobs, cable prices rose. What is more astounding is that, for the first time in decades, there was no inflation that year. A dollar was actually worth 3.6 percent more in 2009 than in 2008. But the cable companies raised prices 5.9 percent that year, according to a survey that the FCC relies on. That's a real price hike of 9.5 percent.

Of course, the FCC figure may be wrong, too, as it might understate actual increases. According to SNL Kagan, a market research firm, the average cable television bill in 2011 was $78, almost double the $40 price in 2001 and significantly higher than the FCC figure. Had the price just increased at the rate of inflation it would have gone up only $11, not $38.

What do these prices mean? In 2010 half of all workers made less than $507 a week, according to Social Security Administration wage data. After taxes, then, a single person at the median wage had to work for two full weeks, plus most of the following Monday, just to make enough, after taxes, to pay the annual cost of cable service.

While cable prices rose sharply from 1999 to 2010, the median wage, adjusted for inflation, was essentially flat during those twelve years. That means cable television consumed a growing share of people's incomes, leaving them less money to buy other goods and services. Because they are monopolies or part of a duopoly in most localities, the cable companies leave the consumer with a simple choice: submit to cable-company pricing or go without the service.

LET'S GO TO GLASGOW, KENTUCKY

One community unwilling to submit to monopoly pricing was a small Kentucky city whose name recalls the Scottish heritage of its early settlers. Cable service wasn't merely a convenience for the 15,000 people in

Glasgow, as the nearest broadcast stations are across the Tennessee border in Nashville, ninety-five miles away, too far for TV signals to carry over the air. But Glasgow residents complained of poor service and high prices from their monopoly cable provider, Telescripps (later acquired by Comcast).

The Scots have a proverbial reputation for being thrifty. After all, Scotsman Adam Smith first identified and explained market competition in his 1776 book *An Inquiry into the Nature and Causes of the Wealth of Nations.* So perhaps it is not surprising that there was popular support in Glasgow for creating competition by building a city-owned cable system. In 1987 the Kentucky town built its own broadband system, spending $10 million (in 2012 dollars), about $667 per resident. Once municipal cable became available, prices plummeted. The cost of basic service dropped by half; the cost of a handheld remote fell from $4.95 a month to under a buck.

The handheld-remote charge illustrates how modern price gouging works. Cable companies typically just provide one when signing up a customer. Many people assume the company-owned remote is required to change channels to avoid getting up to push the tiny buttons on the cable box, but in fact you can buy your own remote at an electronics store for under $10 retail. Remotes are so inexpensive that most companies don't require their return with the cable box when service is cancelled. However, the remote the cable company rents you comes preprogrammed, while a remote you buy retail involves some setup.

Telescripps charged nearly $5 a month for the remote, generating an annual profit on devices in the range of 2,000 percent. Telescripps' charge was high, but even at the seventy-five cents a month some cable companies charge today for a remote channel changer, the annual profit remains several hundred percent annually.

Under historic notions of fair commerce, either price would be considered unconscionable. But cable companies are free to charge such high prices, having persuaded Congress to enact a law in 1992 that bars cities and towns from granting exclusive franchises to provide cable service. Congress also forbade localities to regulate prices. All of that might seem like a guarantee of competition, but in the cable marketplace, the opposite often proves true.

Cable systems are capital intensive, meaning their biggest cost is wiring homes and running the necessary equipment. The most efficient way to operate a cable system is to sign up as many homes as possible; the greater the density of customers, the lower the initial capital costs per customer and the higher the eventual profits. That's obvious enough.

A company that wants to enter the market and compete must bear the cost of stringing cable, wiring homes and then convincing existing cable customers that it will be in their interests to switch to the company's services. The argument is easy enough to make when a product is obviously different—a one-piece swimsuit instead of a bikini or an SUV instead of a sedan. But while the lineup of channels may differ slightly, one cable system is pretty much like another. As a result, price is likely to be determinative. Let the competition begin, right?

In practice, the technically nonexclusive franchises in most localities and the ban on price regulation hasn't resulted in widespread competition of the sort the industry's expert witnesses said would happen. Look around: Where do you see Comcast going into a territory served by Cox? Or Cox taking on Time Warner? Each stuck to its existing territory and raised prices. As with the twin railroad duopolies in the West and East, there's an unspoken understanding that, so long as none of the monopolists tries to poach customers from another by cutting prices, everyone gets to earn fat profits, all thanks to Congress.

Now, let's go back to Glasgow, Kentucky, and the city-owned cable system. Telescripps looked askance at its upstart competition, which charged much less, threatening Telescripps' profits. Telescripps took the Glasgow Electric Plant Board to court. Telescripps spread campaign money around and lobbied state and local politicians. A study by the Progress & Freedom Foundation said the Glasgow municipal system was a money-losing disaster propped up by taxes. The study's conclusions were unsurprising to those who knew that the foundation was not an independent research organization, but a front for the big telecommunications companies. Newt Gingrich founded it when he was Speaker of the House to raise money from telecommunications companies lobbying the terms of the 1996 Telecommunications Act.

Billy Ray, the Glasgow municipal system superintendent, admits that the study findings were true—sort of. The system was indeed in the hole when the study came out, but the reason had nothing to do with inefficiency or mismanagement. "The Progress & Freedom Foundation study neglected to mention that the only reason was all the money we had to spend on lawsuits fighting Telescripps," Ray said, as well as "all of the dirty, underhanded, dishonest tactics they used to stop us so they could keep their monopoly."

For a pretrial hearing in its federal lawsuit against the city, Telescripps brought in Burt Braverman, a high-powered Washington media lawyer. Braverman laid out the company's grievances before federal district court judge Ronald Meredith in Bowling Green, a jurist well known for his rock-hard conservatism. The judge listened to Braverman and then, looking down from the bench, told the lawyer that "it sounds like you don't want any competition down there in Glasgow."

Braverman later wrote an article denouncing "curious and disturbing" municipal cable television systems, claiming they lose money and are "fundamentally unwise and unfair, and amount to bad public policy." It was like most such attacks by the telecommunications industry: long on rhetoric but short on hard facts. Braverman is one of the most influential figures shaping cable industry policy, working hard to make sure it favors the industry rather than its customers, so his words deserve attention. He wrote that the "justification for municipal forays into cable—the need to subject private cable providers to competitive discipline—rings hollow" because of growing competition from commercial providers. He also claimed that municipal systems "divert scarce public funds to the provision of nonessential services that can be more than adequately provided by private enterprise."

Experience shows otherwise. Municipal systems cover their costs from subscriber payments, not taxes. They make money for the public, unlike tax-free debt financing, which Congress has now made available to many private enterprises. Municipal systems are run as a public service rather than a profit-making venture—with the emphasis on service. Municipal systems generally use newer and faster technology than commercial cable companies offer, in some cases allowing cities to attract large digital businesses with big payrolls. Chattanooga, Tennessee, became in 2011 the only American city with a one-gigabyte Internet, providing municipal service that is two hundred times faster than the commercial system average. Many other municipal systems offered speeds five to twenty times faster than the commercial purveyors.

Glasgow upgraded its system twice since 1987 but continued to charge significantly less than Comcast in surrounding communities. By 2010 Glasgow residents had saved a total of $30 million compared to what Telescripps and, later, Comcast charged. That amounts to more than $2,000 per Glasgow resident over twenty-three years. These savings alone come to triple the original $10 million cost of building the system.

So Glasgow residents saved substantial money and got a superfast and efficient Information Superhighway; elsewhere Americans spent, on average, more than $3,000 each. Many do not now have and under current law never will get on that digital highway. Unwilling to invest to match the Glasgow system, Comcast dropped its lawsuit and sold out in 2002, accepting $3 million from the city for its wires and equipment in and around Glasgow. Yet ten years later, Comcast still advertised that it served the city. I put in the home addresses of both Billy Ray and the mayor at Comcast's Web site, which said service was available, even though it is not. You won't be surprised to learn that the listed prices were higher than the city charges.

A handful of other cities and towns followed the Glasgow example to improve their local economies. One was the tiny Alabama town of Scottsboro, which built a municipal system in 1998 to get television signals from Chattanooga. The city offered 150 channels. That put Scottsboro in competition with Charter Communications, the cable company controlled by Paul Allen, one of the cofounders of Microsoft, a company that grew fabulously valuable by pursuing monopolist strategies in personal computer software. But Congress's rule about pricing came to Charter's rescue.

Charter, which has more than 6 million subscribers nationwide, immediately cut its price to under $20, about a quarter less than the city charged. It also forgave old bills owed it by former customers if they returned to Charter. The municipal system began bleeding customers.

"Charter was still charging much more in the surrounding area," said Jimmy Sandlin, the Scottsboro municipal system manager. "It was classic predatory pricing. Charter used its profits from all of its other customers to subsidize selling service in Scottsboro at below cost so it could run us out of business."

Sandlin fought back. He sent a letter to everyone in town showing the much higher prices charged in the suburbs. Sandlin told people that unless they stayed with the city system, a short-term bargain from Charter would soon enough become a larger expense once the city system failed. The campaign worked, and people stopped leaving the city system for the Charter offering; many others came back. Since then the city has expanded its service, adding Internet and telephone, all at prices far below what commercial providers charge in the surrounding communities.

Terry Huval, whom we met earlier at Lafayette Utilities System, believed that economic growth in his city was held back by the costly and slow information systems available in his Louisiana city from Cox Communications, the nation's third largest cable provider and a subsidiary of Cox Enterprises, which is controlled by a wealthy Atlanta newspaper family. At the special election to decide whether to build a municipal broadband system, Huval predicted that just 5 percent of voters would turn out. He was wrong: 30 percent cast their ballots to approve overwhelmingly an expanded municipal electricity network that includes telecommunications.

Places like Chattanooga, Glasgow, Lafayette and Scottsboro that have built their own municipal systems are attracting new industries and enjoying savings at the same time. Communities stuck with the emerging cartel of AT&TVerizonCenturyLinkComcastCoxTimeWarner pay higher prices for much slower connections. In large parts of the country, the unwillingness of the cartel to invest in infrastructure means that residents there face continued reliance on nineteenth-century copper-wire technology or mid-twentieth-century coaxial cable for television and Internet.

In the twenty-first century, economic growth requires the ability to move huge volumes of information instantly. The Internet is to the digital age what highways and airports were to economic growth in the twentieth century and what railroads and canals were to the nineteenth century. America prospered in its first two centuries because of massive public investments in the common modes of transportation that business needed to carry its goods. As it proceeds into its third century, the United States suffers from massive overcharging for poor-quality telecommunications services that carry its information.

The economic interests of these companies simply are not in line with those of the country. Corporate executives look first to the profit statements they issue every ninety days and then to annual figures, not to what is best for all of us a decade or two into the future.

LIVING IN THE INTERNET SLOW LANE

There's a mountain of data from numerous surveys that helps reveal how the companies that most Americans and most businesses must rely on for Internet access are damaging the economy. Let's take a short hike up that steep trail.

The United States invented the Internet, so it ranked number one when the first file was transferred between distant computers in 1969. Taxpayers financed that project through DARPA, the Defense Advanced Research Projects Agency of the Department of Defense. Browsers, which made it easy to use the Internet, also were first used here. Mosaic Netscape, the first popular browser, became available in 1994, spawning the dot-com (and, by the way, the dot-con) era(s) on Wall Street. That browser was the product of research at Indiana University.

By 2011, America's Internet leadership was strictly historical, as we lagged far behind the rest of the modern world by every standard measure except one.

South Korea has taken the lead in average Internet speeds. Its average download rate was 18 megabits per second, according to Pando Networks, which helps Internet game and video companies move their data efficiently from servers to customers. Romania came in second at 15 mbps, Bulgaria was next at 13 mbps with Lithuania and Latvia tied at 11 mbps. Next came Ukraine, Moldavia, Sweden and Norway.

America was settled well back in the pack—in twenty-ninth place. It was really twenty-ninth and falling, however, because of a continuing failure to make wider investments in universal high-speed access using glass fiber. Under current government policies, we're likely to be stuck in the slow lanes for a very long time.

The average broadband download speed in 2011 in the United States was just five mbps. That means that a large file someone in Seoul could download in one minute would require closer to four minutes in the United States.

For an extra fee, American companies like Time Warner do offer some urban and suburban customers souped-up service with speeds up to 50 mbps. However, the qualifier "up to" remains a big caveat. Customers complain at message boards about much slower downloads, sometimes only 60 percent of the advertised speed. When lots of people use the same connection point, known as a node, speeds can slow to 15 mbps.

The Central Intelligence Agency, the Organization for Economic Co-operation and Development (which counts the United States among its thirty-four member nations) and other organizations issue annual reports measuring Internet speed, quality, market penetration and other factors. All of these rankings put the United States in the middle of the pack and falling further back from year to year.

We do consistently rank at or near the top in one category: price. The average American consumer pays 60 percent more than a South Korean user. By one measure Americans pay thirty-eight times the Japanese rate to transmit data. Americans who buy a triple-play package (cable television, Internet and telephone bundled together) typically pay four times what the French pay. The French get live television from around the world, not just domestic shows. The French also get unlimited free telephone calls to seventy countries; Americans typically get free international calls only to Canada. The French Internet is ten times faster downloading and twenty times faster uploading than what most

Americans can buy. For all this the French pay a total of €29.99 (about $40) per month.

Millions of Americans, including my household, pay $160 or more, including tax, for a triple-play package. Taking into account the much more expansive and faster services the French get, and depending on how much use one makes of them, Americans pay six to ten times as much for their triple-play packages as the French.

Since most Americans don't travel abroad, they have no idea that the quality of our nation's Internet services are slowly devolving toward the third world's standards. Even for those who do know how poorly our network compares to the rest of the modern world, there is little they can do to improve their own service. Most Americans have only two Internet choices—pay the local monopoly provider or go without. In places with two broadband providers—typically a telephone company and a cable television company—pricing and speeds are likely to be interchangeable. And now even the appearance of competition is disappearing with the cartelization of the industry.

Having looked at the numbers, what are their economic implications?

We've all heard the talk about the twenty-first century's economy being digital. And about how the industrial economy that began in the mid-nineteenth century, which produced vast numbers of good-paying jobs into the late twentieth century, is giving way to a new world of services.

One practical consequence of this transition is that, because many of those services are delivered over the Internet, many white-collar jobs are at risk. As long as Internet traffic moves down two-lane country roads instead of the Information Superhighway, America's economy will lack momentum, too.

The Internet's digital economy has resulted in a new way of defining jobs, with the categories *tradable* and *nontradable*. The first kind of job can be sent offshore, the second cannot. The shift of tradable jobs offshore explains most of the wage stagnation in America, especially among blue-collar workers. Millions of factory workers lost their jobs as fifty thousand factories closed in the last three decades, many thanks to government policies that traded jobs to the benefit of Wall Street under free-trade policies.

In terms of job creation, tradable jobs accounted for only 2 percent of newly created positions between 1990 and 2008, according to Professor Michael Spence, an economist at New York University's Stern School of Business, and researcher Sandile Hlatshwayo. Their analysis of jobs data found that 98 percent of new jobs were positions that require physical presence here and that the two largest providers of nontradable positions in 2008 were in government and health care. Government at all levels accounted for 22.5 million jobs in 2008, health care some 16.3 million jobs.

Yet in the digital economy, what might appear to be comforting news may not be. Consider that any job done at a computer is also tradable. And, as the Spence report explains, "The tradable side of the economy is shifting up the value-added chain, and higher-paying jobs may therefore leave the United States, following the migration pattern of lower-paying ones."

This trend is already visible. Tax returns for clients of the Big Four accounting firms are routinely prepared in India, not the United States. Architectural, engineering, design and statistical firms send growing volumes of work offshore. *Los Angeles Times* display ads are put together in India, not Southern California, because the finished digital page can be transmitted halfway around the world in the time it takes to carry it from one office to another in Los Angeles. The labor cost savings are huge because India—like China and the rest of Asia—is filled with educated workers who work for a fraction of what Americans with the same skills cost.

The hard truth about the digital age is that future American jobs, and how well they pay, will be determined in good part by whether America climbs back from twenty-ninth place in Internet speed or continues to slip further behind countries like South Korea, with their lower wage scales and superior Internet.

The few places in America where local government leaders recognized this years ago are now prospering relative to the rest of the country because they are attracting digital businesses. But instead of emulating such successes, the monopolists seek rules that let them force their captive customers onto the slow digital lanes while charging heavy tolls. To stop more cities from building high-speed Internet systems, the monopolists get laws passed to shut down the competition where they can. In North Carolina they got a law essentially banning municipal systems. Robust profits remain the top priority for the growing cartel; world-class service that engenders economic growth goes largely unmentioned.

So what has happened to that promise so brilliantly packaged in the Qwest ad from Roy's Motel? Looking back, we see a massive scheme that took $360 billion from telephone customers, and at least $100 billion from cable customers, to build a new fiber-optic system that serves only those the telephone and cable companies wanted to serve in densely populated areas (provided they were not poverty-stricken). Instead of universal service, we are getting a retrenchment made possible by companies selling the public on one idea and then getting laws written that let them serve only those customers who can afford high prices. Curious, isn't it, how politicians who denounce Social Security, Medicare and even public education as wealth redistribution schemes never mention these privatized systems that take from the many to benefit the few?

Worse yet, the system as constructed is so behind the times that, while highly profitable for the telecommunications monopolists, it retards the growth of the American economy. It operates outside the reach of market forces that could discipline the market and punish companies that abuse customers.

In short, our Internet-telephone-cable cartel has left us with the worst possible outcome. As Susan P. Crawford, a former White House special assistant for technology and innovation, concluded in late 2011: "We now have neither a functioning competitive market for high-speed wired Internet access nor government oversight." The promise captured in that Qwest commercial of universal, high-speed Internet access has proved to be nothing more than a mirage.

Profits Upkeep Commissions

We don't maintain anything, we just wait until it breaks
and then fix it.

—Anonymous NV Energy lineman

6. **One spring evening** in 2010, Ben and Rita Weisshaar pulled into the driveway of their home in the Nevada high desert north of Reno. As they did, a neighbor came over to alert them to danger.

"You've got quite a light show going on out back," the neighbor reported. They soon saw that, sure enough, at the far end of their lot an eerie green light was emanating from a canister of electrical equipment high on a power pole. As they watched, it sparked, settled down and dimmed, only to light up and spark again. Ben called NV Energy, Nevada's largest electric utility, and was told that someone would call back.

"Did you tell them it is arcing real bad?" asked Rita, who had retired from an office job at the utility. "You better tell them it's really bad."

When his call was not returned, Ben rang again. Finally, around ten that night, a woman at NV Energy called to say that the "trouble man" on duty advised that there was no emergency and that the couple should not be alarmed. The Weisshaars went to bed.

When the couple awoke at six o'clock the next morning, their bedside alarm clock had stopped a half hour earlier, along with every other electric appliance in the house. Rita remembered thinking to herself that it was a good thing she had kept her battery-powered telephone. She rang NV Energy to report the service outage.

When the troubleshooter arrived, the canister was so hot he could not touch it. He told the Weisshaars they were lucky a fire had not started.

Only then did it dawn on the couple that they had taken a big risk in accepting NV Energy's assurances the night before.

"It was the middle of May, so the wooden fence was all dried out and, if it caught, it would have just gone up in flames, and then fire would have leaped into the sagebrush," Rita recalled. "We live in a development on the edge of acres and acres of dry brush with only one way out. If the sage had caught fire, we could have all been trapped, everyone in the area."

As the repairs were being made, Rita asked why the arcing had occurred. The service man told her the company had cut spending on maintaining electric boxes and other gear. "We don't maintain anything, we just wait until it breaks and then fix it," she remembers him telling her. "That stuck with me," she said, "because when I worked for Sierra Pacific Power, before the merger that created NV Energy, it was a very responsible company that took good care of the lines, did all the maintenance work needed and took good care of its workers. Not anymore. All they care about now is cutting costs and increasing profits."

AGING INFRASTRUCTURE

The problem the Weisshaars encountered with poorly maintained equipment is widespread. America is using up its infrastructure instead of rebuilding it. We grow slowly poorer as roads crumble, dams weaken on their way to deadly collapses and the electric utilities siphon off funds customers pay for reliable power.

One indicator of this? From 1983 to 2010, the number of Americans rose 36 percent, but the number of utility workers fell 15 percent. As the electric grid and the pipes carrying water and natural gas under high pressure age, more workers are needed for maintenance, repair and replacement, not fewer.

Traveling a few miles west of the Weisshaars to Northern California, we find ourselves in Pacific Gas & Electric territory. PG&E owns 2.3 million power poles that, according to PG&E experts then seeking to charge higher rates, need to be replaced, on average, every fifty years. That means replacing about forty-six thousand poles annually. The case made, regulators approved higher rates, including money to replace that many poles.

PG&E diverted much of that money. It replaced just 15,000 poles in 2002 and 2003, less than a third of the number its own experts testified should be replaced. Then it cut the number of replacement poles drastically in 2004, explaining that it had "shifted resources to higher priority work, thus decreasing the number of pole replacements." Replacement fell to about 3,300 poles a year. At that rate, seven hundred years would be required to replace PG&E's poles.

For an industry with no future—say, buggy whip makers after Henry Ford started making horseless carriages—a strategy of testing the life expectancy of existing equipment might make sense; the end of business is in sight. However, if a competitive business fails to replace aging equipment or to set aside money to do so, the company might one day confront unmanageable repair costs that could put it out of business. But a monopoly utility is different: it can actually *gain* by letting the electric grid fall apart.

When PG&E makes customers pay for new poles, but then does not install them, costs are subtly pushed into the future and company profits are inflated. That makes executives and investors happy. When the inevitable day comes and aging poles start crashing? No worries then, either, as a profitable solution is probably in the offing. Another rate hike will address the emergency by undertaking a massive pole replacement program.

A typical scenario might unfold like this: Although the state utility commission staffs across the country should know how maintenance money is spent, continuing staff cuts and lower salaries lead to a decline in time and talent; the disclosures in the fine print that should be highlighted can be, and regularly are, missed. Politicians signal the utilities commission staffs not to make a ruckus. The electric grid slowly degrades. By the time a crisis hits, the commissioners who looked the other way and the utility execs have all moved on, leaving a mess for someone else to clean up.

Best case for the utility? If no one pays attention, an emergency rate increase to pay for work customers already paid for may become a permanent rate increase. This scenario isn't fiction. It's happened again and again.

THE STRANDED CONSUMER

In the 1990s, when half the states decided to break up electric-utility companies, failure to pay attention proved costly. Customers lost tens of billions of dollars in the first step of the process; then customers had to pay a second time, with interest, for costs they had already paid for in advance, inflating even more the transfer of wealth from customers to utility company coffers.

All this was done under the guise of "deregulation," but the harsh truth is that there's really no such thing. Everything has rules. Deregulation is just a disingenuous name for new regulation, too often under rules that favor corporations over their customers.

This story is as old as commercial electricity. Not long after the first lights were strung on Wall Street and in the *New York Times* newsroom in 1882, utilities came to be viewed as natural monopolies whose prices could not be set by the market. These utilities generated power, they transmitted it, and they distributed it to customers. That amounts to a vertically integrated system in which all the steps were controlled by one business.

Often these utilities operated under still another corporate structure—an unregulated utility holding company. A holding company structure allows "pyramiding," which permits investors with only a small amount of capital at risk to control vast enterprises, which can then be loaded with debt that can be put into the controlling owners' pockets.

This technique works fine as long as there is enough income to pay interest on the debt. Sam Insull, the creator of the modern electric utility, made a fortune doing this until he ran out of cash to pay the interest on the bonds sold by his utilities, which extended from Chicago to Oregon. By 1932, just eight utility holding companies controlled almost three-fourths of the nation's electricity production, an extremely risky concentration of ownership. The danger became a painful reality that year when the heavily mortgaged Insull Trusts collapsed, plunging the nation into the deepest part of the Great Depression. The investments of 500,000 shareholders and 600,000 bondholders were wiped out.

In 1935 Congress enacted the Public Utility Holding Company Act to rein in such abuses. The law served the nation well, but was repealed in 2005 at the urging of the industry and the energy-friendly Bush administration. The repeal came on the heels of laws passed by half the states in the 1990s requiring utility holding companies to sell off their generating plants. This seemed, on the surface, to convert the utilities into companies that only distributed electricity. The distribution-only utilities were supposed to buy their energy in the new market for power, which, in theory, would also encourage investors to build competing power plants.

On paper it looked like a smart move; in the real world it was a costly disaster for customers and a huge new opportunity to rob customers without their knowing it.

While generating electricity was supposed to become a competitive business—and produce lower costs—regulators in many states gave the existing utilities an advantage on upstart competitors. The states let the power plants be transferred within the same corporate family to a new sister company. One sibling made electricity, the other bought it. Since there was a parent company on top of both—a utility holding company— there was cooperation rather than competition within the corporate family to maximize prices and profits. It was a system both easy to game for profits and a trap for unwary investors, who ventured into what they thought was a competitive market only to lose everything.

The robbery began when utility holding companies said that transferring their power plants to their newly formed generating subsidiary would cost them money, lots of money. They called it "stranded costs." They asserted that a power plant in a monopoly was worth a lot more than one in a competitive environment, where profits should be smaller. Thus, they argued, these plants would lose value and should sell, or be transferred, for less than they were worth under the old vertically integrated monopoly utility system. Whether stranded costs were real or fabricated would have been established had they actually sold the plants to the bidders, but that didn't happen.

The concept of stranded costs, lifted from economic texts, was fed to politicians, journalists and customers, who swallowed it whole. But this first step in a process that was supposed to result in smaller electric bills actually increased prices because of the need to recover the theoretical stranded costs. Many utilities agreed to temporary caps on electric rates, but that was little more than a distraction.

The talk of caps and stranded costs also diverted attention from another issue: taxes. When it came to tapping customers for tax dollars, the utilities took a vacuum cleaner to customers' pockets and wallets, sucking up pennies and hundred-dollar bills alike.

Although the value of power plants was supposedly less in a competitive market, the utilities said that they would have to report to the IRS that they made a profit when they transferred ownership to the new sister companies that would generate electricity. Of course, a profit would mean that corporate income taxes were due.

The argument is convoluted (one might ask, for example, Where's the profit in offloading a plant with a value diminished by the shift from a monopoly system to a supposedly competitive market, where profit margins would be thinner and the risks greater?). But even as it gets more complicated, the workings are worth examining.

Congress requires companies to keep two sets of books, one for share-holders and one for the tax man. An annual deduction is permitted on both for the declining value of the power plants as they age. These de-ductions differ, however, as the rate of write-off is slower on the share-holders' books and much faster on the IRS ledgers. That means an electric-power plant might be worth five times as much for shareholder reporting as for tax reporting. A power plant sold for more than its listed value on tax returns would create a gain for tax purposes, even if, on the reports made to shareholders, it appears to have been sold at loss. The difference between the two is roughly the "stranded cost."

What are the implications? Let's look at the case of PSEG, a New Jersey utility that used to be known as Public Service Electric & Gas. Colin Loxley, the company executive who testified on these matters, said the company had $3.9 billion of stranded costs at the end of 1999. The report he prepared for state utility regulators noted that in addition to getting a rate increase for the supposedly stranded costs (because the sale was for more than the value on the books kept for the IRS), the utilities commission would "need to provide for income taxes" on money paid to offset the stranded costs. So a seeming loss for shareholders—the stranded costs—meant a rate increase to cover the cost and an even big-ger rate increase to cover the taxes on what the company said the IRS would view as a profit.

The New Jersey Board of Public Utilities promptly gave the company higher rates to cover the stranded costs plus the taxes on the gain from the stranded costs. This, in turn, required even *more* money because the extra money to cover taxes increased profits, so the award to cover taxes had to be increased or, in utilities jargon, *grossed up*. The utilities board also let the company sell bonds to recover these costs immediately, add-ing interest costs that, over two decades, would nearly double the total cost to customers.

In sum, these items amounted to more than $5 billion in costs, taxes and interest, a total that was imposed on customers just to transfer own-ership of power plants from PSEG's right pocket to its left pocket. Had the law been written differently, that transfer could have been accom-plished at no more expense than the salaries and hourly fees paid to law-yers needed to write transfer contracts.

After the deal was done, customers were still getting the same power from the same company generated at the same electric-power plants. They were just paying PSEG more.

But we're not quite done. The regulators skipped over another little detail: the utilities had already collected taxes in the monthly bills paid by customers. Loxley testified that in 1999 PSEG had more than a billion dollars in its ADIT, or Accumulated Deferred Income Tax account. Measured in 2012 dollars, that was nearly $800 for each of PSEG's 1.8 million residential customers. ADIT accounts should have been tapped to pay any taxes due, but in transactions like PSEG's, they generally were not.

Most of the consumer watchdogs around the country missed this, too, but Dan Sponseller didn't. He's a Pittsburgh utility lawyer and he saw a good case for getting the money back for customers. Sponseller also suspected that little or no taxes were actually paid, creating a windfall for any company that was awarded higher rates for stranded costs, taxes and interest. Sponseller found an aggrieved PSEG customer, Richard G. Murphy II, and filed both a lawsuit and a complaint with the New Jersey Board of Public Utilities on Murphy's behalf.

PSEG sought dismissal of the cases. Significantly, PSEG never denied what Sponseller said happened. When I spoke to company spokesmen, they declined to make executives available. But there was never any denial of the statements Sponseller and his client made in official papers. Instead PSEG argued that this was a settled matter beyond review by anyone, anywhere. It was an argument that struck me as akin to a bank robber who spends his money openly after the statute of limitations for prosecution has passed.

There was also a big problem with PSEG's assertion that the billions it got were not subject to review. The law specified that the actual costs were to be compared with the estimates of stranded costs so they could be adjusted as needed as many times as necessary in the future. The industry term is to "true up" costs and revenues. But PSEG made a clever argument against such a review.

The company said that when the deal was closed with the Board of Public Utilities approval, that constituted the only allowable review. And since the utilities board had not acted on that day to change the terms, PSEG argued that it never could. Sponseller worked hard for several years to keep his case alive, but it died before a New Jersey state judge who agreed with PSEG, and thus avoided the admittedly arduous task of learning all the subtle tax rules. Not surprisingly, the utility board was also hostile.

I sent some of Sponseller's expert accounting reports to Jeff Gramlich, who teaches accounting at the University of Southern Maine and once, with a colleague, figured out an incredibly complex tax dodge involving

Chevron, Texaco and the Indonesian government. Gramlich and other utility accounting experts who agreed to look over the Sponseller materials (some did not want to be quoted because they work for utilities) all came to the same conclusion: customers had their pockets picked.

PSEG has about 2 percent of the electricity revenues for all of the jurisdictions across the country in which vertically integrated utilities were broken into pieces. If the costs imposed on its customers were typical, then around $200 billion was taken from customers. That would be around $2,500 per household.

IT'S GOOD TO BE A UTILITY

There is another way that monopoly utilities use the tax system to rob you. While your payroll and income taxes are taken out of your paycheck before you get paid, Congress lets companies earn profits today and pay taxes years later. For example, Pacific Gas & Electric had about $450 million of deferred taxes in 2011. The company, on page 282 of a 334-page report it filed with the California Public Utilities Commission in its 2011 rate-hike case, explained how long it holds on to this money before paying the government. In some cases the delay is thirty-seven years.

The $450 million is a huge sum, and hard to grasp. But imagine that you could get just $45,000 today from your job and not have to pay your taxes for thirty-seven years. At 3 percent, inflation would reduce the value of the taxes you would owe by two-thirds. Meanwhile, if you earned a real return of 5 percent annually on the money in your deferral account, after thirty-seven years each dollar would have grown to close to six dollars. To paraphrase Mel Brooks in *History of the World Part I*, it's good to be a utility.

These and other tax benefits flowing to corporate-owned utilities are enormous. From 1954 to 2006, corporate-owned electric utilities got tax benefits worth $450 billion, according to a study for the American Public Power Association by MSB Energy Associates of Madison, Wisconsin. In 2006 alone another $11.6 billion in tax benefits was added to the total. That is almost a dime a day from every man, woman and child in America who get their electricity from a corporate-owned utility, about $150 per year from each affected family of four.

From the utility's point of view, things are likely to get even better because of the clamor in Washington to reduce corporate income taxes. Since 1993 the corporate tax rate has been 35 percent. But during the

Bush administration special rules were added that lowered the real corporate tax rate for utilities. The Obama administration got Congress to
do more to cut actual rates. In 2012 Congress was moving to lower the
rate to 25 percent. If the rate is cut, as seems likely to happen, the utilities
will get a windfall, unless state utilities boards make adjustments. Almost a third of the money in the utility deferral accounts—those ADIT
funds—would no longer be owed, but instead would be pocketed by the
utilities. That is a huge boost to their finances and a further drain on yours.

Utilities are understandably eager to make sure government looks
upon them with the soft gaze of a lover and not the flinty stare of a skep-
tic, especially when it comes to their finances. More than a century of
experience has taught corporate-owned utilities how to keep politicians
focused on corporate interests rather than what is good for country or
customers. One way is to raise money from regulated industries to spend
on travel for those who regulate the companies. That is just what Mike
Peevey did after his term ended as president of the California Public
Utilities Commission. Peevey helped create the California Public Utilities Commission Foundation, which held a fund-raising dinner where
tables sold for $20,000 each. Among the buyers were Pacific Gas & Elec-
tric, San Diego Gas & Electric and Southern California Edison, the utility that Peevey was president of before he became its chief regulator.

Bill Bagley, another former commissioner, told the *San Francisco
Chronicle* that he saw no reason for anyone to look askance at the utilities
giving money to pay for travel by PUC commissioners and staffers. "Basically, every utility will be contributing—so if it's a conspiracy, it's a
massive conspiracy," Bagley said in 2011.

Indeed, it was a massive conspiracy, in this case to undermine the public interest. That the idea was embraced by the utilities and various politicians shows how thoroughly corporate values permeate California's
utilities commission, which up until the end of the century was regarded
as the best utility regulatory body in the country because it actually balanced utility interests with those of customers. Under Peevey it became
the utilities' best friend.

The California Public Utilities Commission Foundation soon met a
well-deserved early death, but the idea of free travel for politicians and
officials paid for by utilities didn't die with it. Each year more than a
dozen California state lawmakers enjoy a free trip to Hawaii. In 2011
they checked in to the luxurious Fairmont Kea Lani hotel in Maui, part
of a chain owned by a billionaire Saudi prince. Among those headed to
the land of the lei was the speaker of the state assembly, Los Angeles

Democrat John Perez, who said he could not imagine anyone thinking the trip was questionable. Another traveler was Tom Berryhill, a Republican state senator from Modesto who opposed efforts by the South San Joaquin Irrigation District to buy out PG&E. The district said it could cut prices 15 percent and improve service.

California law prohibits state lawmakers from taking more than about $400 in gifts. The Maui trip was quite a lavish working vacation, costing $13,000 per lawmaker. The lawmakers could go because of a loophole. While gifts from corporations and others were limited, no restriction was placed on travel paid for by nonprofit organizations. The nonprofit sponsor in this instance was no charity in the traditional meaning of that word. It was the misleadingly named Independent Voter Project, a front for PG&E, Southern California Edison and other special interests eager to get five days with lawmakers to educate them on what they want state government to do for them.

On the other side of the country, another kind of influence jacks up electricity costs for consumers and small business owners in New York.

Niagara Falls generates massive amounts of cheap electric power. Buffalo journalist Jim Heaney likens Niagara Falls to an eternal Saudi Arabia, a place where, long after the last drop of oil has been extracted from the Middle East, the waters of the Great Lakes will keep spinning turbines to generate electricity. All that cheap power could foster an economic boom in western New York, historically a center of innovation and manufacturing. Cheap power is doing just that on the Canadian side of the border as automakers and others flock there. Out west, Grand Coulee and nine other dams on the Columbia River have made the Pacific Northwest economy flourish for more than seven decades.

But in New York the cheap power benefits only a few. Just ten corporations get two-thirds of the cheap power not dedicated to the handful of publicly owned electric utilities in New York. Among those with long-term contracts to buy power at well below the rates anyone else pays are Intel, Occidental Petroleum and Olin, a chemical company. The biggest share—a fourth of Niagara Falls' power—goes to Alcoa for its aluminum smelters at the eastern end of Lake Ontario. This power is so cheap compared to what other industrial customers pay that, over thirty years, Alcoa will save the mind-boggling sum of $5.6 billion. That is ten times the entire profit Alcoa earned worldwide in 2010. So what does all this cheap power subsidize?

About a thousand jobs, filled by workers who earned an average of less than $60,000 each per year. Divide up the subsidy, and it amounts to about $150,000 per job annually. Paying the workers in full to stay home would thus save $90,000 per job each year. That makes the Alcoa subsidy the equivalent of throwing your money over Niagara Falls. The subsidy also means that while Alcoa reports profits to investors, those profits come not from the competitive markets, but this subtle gift of a public resource.

What makes these sweetheart electricity deals even more astonishing is that the state studied them years ago and recognized that the power was being wasted. The knowledge, however, did nothing to alter the behavior of the politicians or the companies. Alcoa insisted on, and got, a thirty-year contract for Niagara Falls electric power at giveaway rates.

In one California city the leaders grew tired of being robbed by PG&E. The town is Manteca, home to about sixty-five thousand people. Located in California's Central Valley, Manteca's environs look more like the drier parts of Texas than the forested coast eighty miles away. The farmers who settled there in the late nineteenth century realized that water was key. They spent their own money to build and maintain the South San Joaquin Irrigation District waterworks, which captures the runoff from melting Sierra Nevada snows. The early farmers' foresight means that today Manteca's prosperous almond growers pay about $8 an acre foot for reliable, clean sweet water, while other California farmers pay up to a hundred times that much for salty, less reliable flows. The dams that the irrigation district built—without federal subsidies—also produce electricity, generating sales that ease tax burdens.

The irrigation district wants to buy out PG&E in the area. The farmers understand that if they can get rid of PG&E, their electric power costs will fall by at least 15 percent. They hired as their general manager Jeff Shields, who has taken on corporate utilities four times in the past. In one case he forced the sale of corporate-owned utility assets and, when a judge ruled that the proper value for these was their cost less depreciation, known as book value, the utility decided to let it go. Had the utility appealed and lost, the decision by a California court of appeals would have established book value for future takeovers by public agencies.

One September morning in 2009, under a cloudless sky, the district held a public hearing. Men in blue jeans with big belt buckles, starched plaid shirts and cowboy boots and women in flowery dresses took seats in what is normally the parking pad for irrigation district trucks. The well-maintained metal roof overhead looked neat and clean in contrast to the dusty mess visible through a chain-link fence surrounding the local yard for PG&E crews. The ranchers voiced strong support for buying out PG&E, their every word captured by a video crew sent by the utility to record the proceedings.

Three speakers stood out that crisp morning. Two were young men in dress shirts who railed about government abusing its power of eminent domain to condemn PG&E property. Neither acknowledged that PG&E, like all utilities, also has the power of eminent domain and can force you to live with a power pole in your garden. You will be compensated, but the utility's idea of fair compensation may seem to you like a token fee for their destruction of the value of your property.

The third speaker was a PG&E executive who stood out because she wore a sleek tight dress and red-soled Louboutin high heels more appropriate to a San Francisco office than a country town. PG&E, she said, would sue the district like it had never been sued. She tossed out figures for the value it would get a court to award for its property, figures that if applied to the whole company would make it one of the most asset-rich companies in America, worth many times what it told its shareholders it was worth.

When the session ended, the woman raced off before I could interview her. The farmers who stayed to sip coffee said they were not worried about the threats, though they considered them bad manners. "That's the PG&E way," one rancher said. "They are bullies, pure and simple, with no regard for anyone or anything except their profits."

"Pure greed," the farmer's wife said. Others nodded in agreement.

Among the many things that upset these ranchers and other Mantecans besides high rates and bad service was how anyone who built a new home or business had to gift the electric wires and natural gas lines to PG&E—and then pay taxes on the value of those gifts and taxes on the value of the taxes.

Dennis Wyatt, the no-nonsense editor of the daily *Manteca Bulletin*, figured out how much these gifts cost: $7,000 for the wires and pipes for the average new home valued at $250,000. Of that amount, Wyatt calculated that $2,380 was for the taxes and the taxes on the taxes. "This isn't chump change," Wyatt told his readers, since the grossed-up taxes alone inflated the value of the typical new home in Manteca in 2009 by 1 percent.

For years Wyatt explained to readers how the Public Utilities Commission fixed this rule to benefit PG&E at the expense of customers, news that no other major news organization in California reported. Jeff

Shields, as wily an opponent as PG&E has ever encountered, put all the obscure and damaging evidence he could find in the public record in front of the irrigation district customers, many of whom learned of these matters by reading Wyatt.

One evening in his tiny office at the *Bulletin*, Dennis Wyatt stared at his computer. He was trying to come up with a shorthand way to communicate to his readers how the Public Utilities Commission was serving the interests of PG&E to the detriment of its customers, who had no alternative for electricity and natural gas.

After midnight, Wyatt started focusing on the word "public," with its implication that the Public Utilities Commission existed to serve the commonweal. He had a little epiphany when he looked at the acronym PUC in a new way.

In reality, Wyatt wrote, what PUC really stood for was *Profits Upkeep Commissions*.

"We Lead the Industry with Integrity"

When you are the captain of the ship, you are responsible
for everything that happens to the ship.

—Judge Kern A. Reese

7. **Walking along the** 1500 block of Tulane Avenue in downtown
New Orleans in 2007, I saw a curious sight. On the sidewalk was a thin
pad of crumbling cement; bolted to its top was a piece of sheet steel about
a foot square. The steel seemed to have a great puncture in its middle; in
fact, the round, jagged-edged hole was the result of a violent storm that
had shorn off the light pole once mounted there.

I visited this site on a September day when New Orleans seemed so
steamy you could almost sip the moisture from the air. My guide was a
man named Joe Seeber, and he directed my eye to the dark pit at the
hole's center and a tangle of black and white cables inside. The ends of
the wires were wrapped in black electrical tape, creating bulges that, in
the stylized manner of modern art, might be said to resemble Medusa's
deadly tresses, as if she lay in wait beneath the pavement, her headdress
of vipers waiting to strike anyone who dared to gaze upon her.

Spotting a telephone repair crew up the street, I asked the two work-
men to take a look.

"Live wires!" exclaimed one of them, showing us a meter holding
steady at 227 volts. "Dangerous! Stay back!" he warned as I drew closer to
see the meter's needle.

The four of us were standing in front of Charity Hospital, where the
poor and those without insurance sought care for illness and injury until

flood damage caused by Hurricane Katrina forced it to close in 2005. But there in front of Charity's white towers, in the heart of the city's hospital district, people were ambling by as they do every day. All that stood between a pedestrian and a potentially fatal shock were the black tape turbans wound around Medusa's electrified split ends.

"Been that way for more than eleven years," Joe Seeber said.

The two telephone guys shook their heads in disbelief. "Someone needs to fix this," one said as they walked back to their truck.

Joe Seeber knows more about this than anyone. That snarl of live wires nearly got him jailed, even though he had nothing to do with the storm that snapped off the light pole in March 1996. The pole fell on a street vendor, leaving him permanently disabled.

How a falling light pole almost got Joe Seeber imprisoned is a story that reveals how corporate America abuses its power, aided by government, to punish those who dare to challenge its privileges.

JOE SEEBER'S CRUSADE

Entergy, the electric-utility holding company that is the most powerful corporation in New Orleans, decided to silence Seeber. His offense? Seeber had exposed how Entergy cheated the people of New Orleans out of millions of dollars.

Joe Seeber owns TriStem Consulting in Hewitt, Texas. TriStem examines electric bills that utilities send to cities and state agencies, colleges, charities, factories and shopping malls. From his base in Hewitt, halfway between Austin and Fort Worth, Seeber dispatches teams across the country to count the streetlights for which utilities charge taxpayers, just to be sure they exist. Many do not. His teams compare the wattage shown on power bills to the actual bulbs in streetlights (often utilities charge for high-wattage bulbs, even though they install smaller lamps that consume less juice). TriStem finds streets that have been dark for months or even years, with lights that residents and business owners have complained need to be replaced, but for which the billing has never ceased.

New Orleans is not alone in being overcharged by Entergy on its electric bills. Seeber has caught the company cheating taxpayers in states throughout the South. Entergy owns four other utilities—one each in Louisiana, along the gulf coast of Mississippi, in East Texas and Arkansas.

All of these Entergy utilities have billed taxpayers large sums for power that was never used.

Late in 2009, the small East Texas town of Beaumont got a report from TriStem detailing how Entergy billed for nonexistent streetlights and overstated wattage on other lamps. Seeber included photographs with addresses so that anyone could check his work. Three decades earlier, one of Seeber's first audits had uncovered $100,000 of bogus Entergy charges to Beaumont taxpayers, but in 2009 the City of Beaumont sued Entergy for fraud. "After an inspection and audit," the Beaumont lawsuit charged, "shocking trends were discovered" about "Entergy's unethical and fraudulent billing practices." Within days four other East Texas towns—Conroe, Huntsville, Nederland and Port Neches—filed similar lawsuits based on TriStem audits of Entergy bills.

Although it serves many poor areas, Entergy is an enormously profitable company. From 2006 through 2008, Entergy reported profits of more than $5 billion. Customers of its utilities paid the company more than $800 million to cover its corporate income taxes for those three years. Yet Entergy did not pay a dollar of corporate income tax to the government. Instead, Entergy got back almost $58 million from the government. That gave Entergy a real federal tax rate of *minus* 2.4 percent.

In 2009, Entergy paid just $43 million in income taxes on a pretax profit of nearly $1.9 billion for an effective income tax rate of just 2.3 percent, according to its own annual disclosure statement.

Although many of its customers are impoverished, Entergy's chief executive officer, J. Wayne Leonard, is paid exceptionally well for his performance as head of a holding company with five monopolies, among other investments. According to Equilar, a company that tracks executive compensation, Leonard's 2009 pay came to $27.3 million. Entergy's board had been so generous that, as 2009 ended, Leonard's stock equity and pension were worth more than $92 million. These figures are based on the way the government requires companies to calculate executive wealth, though history shows that official figures often understate the real wealth of executives.

Despite this fortune, Entergy directors awarded Leonard $15,871 to pay part of his 2008 income taxes. They also gave him life insurance and financial-planning assistance. He got free personal use of Entergy jets. The captive customers of this monopoly, together with customers of other electric utilities that buy power from Entergy's electric-power plants, were the source of the money that ended up benefitting Leonard.

Sustaining this kind of pay would be difficult in a market economy, where competition would drive down prices as people shopped for the best bargains. That kind of shopping means thinner profit margins. Or, as Adam Smith observed in 1776, a business in a truly competitive market will make just enough profit to justify remaining in business. In a competitive market the bargaining power of shoppers drives down the price of executive labor to a level that correlates with the value the executives add to the company.

Disproportionate compensation wouldn't exist if regulators set prices close to what a competitive market would produce. The various state utility commissions are supposed to set prices as a proxy for the market, achieving through investigation, hearings and policies a list of prices close to what a market would produce. But the utilities often convince regulators that they must earn very high profit margins. For utilities, rates of return are based on invested capital. The average return on shareholder capital, also known as equity, is more than 19 percent before taxes at utilities. For large corporations, on average, it is 6.7 percent, government data show.

Over all, the very biggest American companies earn an average profit of less than 10 cents on each dollar of sales. Entergy earned 17.5 cents thanks to the high rates it gets to charge customers, and other benefits, such as the more than $200 million taxpayers gave Entergy to repair damages to its equipment from Hurricane Katrina.

Indeed, of eight major electric utilities in 2007, J. Wayne Leonard ran the smallest by revenue and earned the smallest profit, but took home the biggest executive paycheck by far, the Web site entergypaywatch.org noted. That year Leonard was paid more than five times what the chief executive of PSEG, the New Jersey utility company of almost identical size and profit margin, was paid.

But back to Joe Seeber. Starting in 1988, his audits caught Entergy's Texas utility overcharging two Texas colleges, three cities, and the Texas Department of Transportation. The customers got the following refunds from Entergy:

Sam Houston State University	$155,000
Lamar University	$60,000
Beaumont	$100,000
Huntsville	$60,000
Orange	$31,000
Texas Department of Transportation	$280,000

In Louisiana, Seeber's audits prompted much larger refunds from Entergy, including:

New Orleans Sewer and Water Board (1992)	$1,000,000
City of New Orleans (1993)	$400,000
City of New Orleans (1994)	$1,800,000
New Orleans Centre (Superdome mall)	$70,000
Louisiana State University	$90,000

The U.S. Coast Guard got back $50,000 from Entergy thanks to a Seeber audit.

The excessive billing Seeber uncovered was not the result of some minor glitch or of a billing error made one month and then corrected soon after. He uncovered inflated Entergy bills going back years and in some cases decades. The patterns were so evident that Seeber followed them back in time—he compiled records on Entergy and its predecessor companies back to the 1800s. He's become convinced that overcharging was standard operating procedure at the utility from the start.

Seeber has examined the billing practices at many utilities, and TriStem audit teams have found utilities that charged more than they were entitled to in all fifty states and Canada. They've found meters that recorded a much greater flow of power than actually passed through them; customers billed at higher rates than those set by state public-utility regulators; and places where utilities installed two meters, making customers pay twice for the same juice.

The odds of finding such cheating are so high that Seeber charges clients only if he finds improper charges. That Seeber turns a healthy profit even though he bears all of the risk of an audit's upfront costs is a damning indictment of the corporate-owned electric-utility industry's dishonest practices. Utilities often overcharge the schools, libraries and other government services you support with your tax dollars. Few governments, businesses or individuals check their routine monthly bills. Out of some sort of blind faith, most just pay them without question.

That utilities overcharge local governments is no surprise to Ed Doherty, who spent more than twenty-five years as budget director and later commissioner of environmental services for the City of Rochester in western New York.

"Many street lights exist only on electric bills," Doherty said. "Charges for higher levels of service, nonexistent services and lamps that burned out or were removed a long time ago, are everywhere—and it's worse in the suburbs." That is because many suburban governments are lightly staffed and affluent enough that widespread overbilling for municipal electricity gets little attention. Most suburban towns miss streetlight overbilling because they use special lighting districts. "The only government people who review the bills are clerks who see their job as only converting the utility bill to a tax levy for the district—typically, no one 'owns' the charges and so no one takes responsibility for making sure they are accurate," Dougherty said. Without audits, overcharges can go on for months, years and even decades.

Streetlights are just part of the problem. Telephone, natural gas, water, and sewer utilities have been caught overcharging. In Oklahoma, Seeber once got the City of Tulsa more than $358,000 in refunds, partly from AT&T, which billed for unused telephone equipment. In Los Angeles an internal audit in early 2010 found that the city was being billed for twelve thousand telephone lines that were not in use. That cost $3 million per year, or about a dollar annually for each city resident. That may not sound like a lot, but a dollar here and a dollar there in bogus charges to governments and individuals adds up.

Auditing firms like TriStem thrive because cheating has become pervasive. The problem is exacerbated by automated bill-payment systems that states and municipalities are buying in the name of efficiency. That these vendors are often significant contributors to the campaigns of politicians who control budgets for acquiring such equipment is not surprising, but has received very little attention from the news media.

According to a *New York Times* report in 2007, every fifth dollar the state of New York pays doctors, hospitals and other providers is for care either not rendered or not needed. A lengthy investigation of state healthcare spending revealed how automated bill paying, which was intended to save money, enabled fraud. The state controller pronounced the newspaper's estimate solid.

What makes Joe Seeber unusual among utility-bill auditors is how he charges clients. Seeber's contract calls for a fee of just under half of any refund his clients collect for past overcharges. No refund, no fee. The clients' future savings are just that: pure savings to the customer. TriStem's competitors usually demand a piece of future savings, which gives them a predictable flow of income for two or three years as the clients pay smaller electric bills, and then a third or half of what they save to the energy auditor. But, Seeber says, that system makes it easier for the utility to negotiate not paying full refunds for past cheating, and that a focus on future savings rewards wrongdoing. And, Seeber adds, sustained overcharging is wrongdoing.

Seeber's opinion rankles utility executives. Entergy executives have told me and others that refunds corrected simple mistakes; they cite the costs of fighting in court over what they characterized as bogus claims of excess charges. Like other utilities, Entergy prefers to address only future billing, giving back as little as possible from past overcharges—and certainly not with interest paid in cash.

Marcus V. Brown, one of Entergy's lawyers, told me the company would like Seeber to just go away. He described Seeber as zealous and difficult to work with (auditors who do their jobs tend to be seen that way). Entergy once asked Seeber how much he wanted for his business, including a clause that would prevent him for starting a new a firm that would audit electric bills. Such a clause would ensure that Seeber retired from such auditing, and stay retired.

In what Seeber now concedes was an act of stunning stupidity and weakness, he gave Entergy a price in writing. Ever since, Entergy has argued that Seeber was trying to extort the company.

Why would Seeber respond to such an offer? Because, like all human beings, he makes mistakes. Seeber was tired of fighting to get paid, weary from battling an opponent that used its political power to reduce the fees he made and that forced him to divert a lot of time to dealing with their backroom efforts to avoid making refunds. He was at retirement age and thinking about selling when the offer appeared. That it might have been a trick should have been obvious, but Seeber just thought it was a way to get rid of all the hassle and to retire.

The company may or may not have been serious, but Seeber was obviously not thinking clearly when he responded with a price instead of ignoring the offer. But it is also true that Entergy has always had it in its power to make Seeber go away in an instant. Seeber's business would collapse if firms like Entergy just stopped overcharging its customers. If Entergy billed honestly, market forces would end Seeber's ability to make money auditing Entergy's bills.

Instead of ending its gouging ways, however, Entergy decided to get Joe Seeber put away over that broken light pole.

SEEKING TO JAIL JOE SEEBER

The effort was rooted in Seeber's 1994 audit of a City of New Orleans contract with Entergy to maintain and power 50,000 streetlights. Tri-Stem auditors found that Entergy charged the city for numerous bulbs at higher wattage levels than those it installed, as well as for 600 streetlights that did not exist. Entergy eventually reimbursed the city $6 million, about half of what Seeber said it should have returned. That 1994 audit did result in one reform, and the city and Seeber hoped that the new penalties clause specifying high penalty fees would deter future cheating.

In 2001, Seeber's firm audited bills that two Entergy utilities sent to the Louisiana Department of Transportation. He concluded that the state was due $5 million, a sum that included $3 million in interest. Most of the money was for streetlights paid for by local governments but for which the state also was being charged. In some instances, the double-billing went back a half century. Entergy said the TriStem estimates were out of line with actual overcharges. Entergy offered the state about $151,000, or three cents on each overcharged dollar.

Entergy also told state officials and a reporter for the *New Orleans Times-Picayune* that Seeber was merely a self-taught energy auditor. Seeber did not have credibility, Entergy said, and besides, he was really hard to deal with. An Entergy spokesman said that Seeber was just in it for the money.

Eventually the state transportation agency met Entergy more than halfway. A government lawyer wrote Seeber that the state "does not wish to pursue collection of interest" on any overcharges. The agency disputed neither the legitimacy of collecting interest nor the $3 million estimated interest charge, but, in the end, the state settled with Entergy for about fifteen cents on the dollar. Seeber went public with his criticism, saying the state gave away too much in looking out for the interests of Entergy to the detriment of Louisiana citizens.

The next year, Lillian Regan, the city public-utilities director, brought Seeber back to New Orleans to audit Entergy's streetlight bills again. Seeber found that, despite having been put on notice eight years earlier, Entergy had committed more billing abuses. According to Seeber, Entergy charged the city excessive amounts for the repair and maintenance work of its own power lines. And there were still plenty of phantom streetlights. Indeed, Seeber said he found that some of the imaginary streetlights that Entergy billed the city for in 1994 were still on the city's bills.

"Vindictive billing," Seeber called it. "The abuses were far worse than what we found in the first streetlight audit." Seeber calculated the overcharges, after eight years, at about $15 million. When the penalties negotiated under the terms in the 1994 deal were added in, the bill came to $25 million.

Mayor Marc Morial's aides said the figure could be more than $40 million, but they met with the president of the Entergy utility to work out a settlement. When the mayor got nowhere, the city took Entergy to court. The lawsuit charged that Entergy did not simply make mistakes, but engaged in systematic overbilling. When caught, the lawsuit said, Entergy refused to allow inspection of its records, a tactic the city described as "clearly calculated to obstruct a legitimate investigation of its actions and the failure of performance of its obligations to the city." Entergy claimed it was just protecting records that were not relevant to the audit.

In a front-page article, the *Times-Picayune* characterized the litigation as "the extraordinary step of filing suit against the city's electric and gas provider, a subsidiary of New Orleans' only Fortune 500 company." That a mainstream newspaper regards suing a vendor for overcharging taxpayers as "extraordinary" speaks volumes about what has become a widespread bias in the news these days. The gratuitous mention of Entergy as the only Fortune 500 company in town helps make clear the journalistic tilt toward the rich and powerful, rather than to their readers, the people forced to pay Entergy more than it was legally due.

Unmentioned in the news was the relative size of the dispute. At the time, the New Orleans city government budget was about $500 million a year. In 2002 the city was facing a $25 million shortfall between revenue and expenses. Even after paying Seeber's full fee, the city would have recovered enough to pay all of its bills for a week. Instead, the local newspaper left the impression that the $25 million was a burden to Entergy.

As the lawsuit proceeded, a new mayor was elected. A man with a deep understanding of monopolies, Mayor Ray Nagin had been the general manager of Cox Cable New Orleans, the local Cox cable television monopoly. He had many close ties to Entergy executives and even appointed a senior Entergy lawyer as New Orleans city attorney.

Nagin quickly fired Lillian Regan, the city official who had hired Seeber and been adamant that the utility should make a full refund on the overcharges. Regan found herself facing criminal charges in a taxi-license case, although the case was so weak that the judge who heard the accusations dismissed the charges. Regan's alleged crime had been to waive fifty-dollar fees for a handful of down-on-their-luck taxi drivers, including a cabbie whose leg had been amputated. In dismissing the case, the judge said in open court that he would have done the same thing had he been in charge of cab licenses.

Still, no one in New Orleans missed the message that was being sent by the mayor's office. Nagin, a native son who grew up to become a monopolist executive, would go after petty corruption with a vengeance. But for his fellow monopolists at Entergy, the biggest and most powerful company in town? A very lenient standard of justice awaited them.

Evidence of this was soon at hand: Nagin agreed to settle with Entergy for $6.7 million, ending the lawsuit. Entergy got to keep more than half of the overcharges. After the penalties that were waived, Entergy paid just twenty-six cents on each dollar owed to the city. Mayor Nagin explained that he settled because of the costs and risks of litigation, but he did not publicly lecture Entergy or speak of the company in the moralistic tones that he used in referring to Regan, who had been wrongly accused of petty corruption. That's solidarity among monopolists.

The big discount for cheating sent a clear signal to Entergy: overcharging pays because, even when caught, the company can still keep most of the money. What Entergy needed to do next was make sure that Seeber never came back to audit the bills it sent the city.

That Entergy wanted to make sure Seeber would not ever get another chance to audit its records became clear when Seeber obtained an internal Entergy report and posted it on the Internet. The report details an Entergy strategy to "eliminate the need" for the city to hire an electric-bill auditor. Entergy says the report should not have been released and that it should be interpreted as part of a plan to make sure all bills were proper, thus eliminating any need for independent audits. But Entergy had another strategy to keep the insistent Seeber from sniffing out the misdeeds in its big invoices to the City of New Orleans.

That brings us back to the light pole on Tulane Street.

Nathaniel Joseph had been a fruit seller with a stand on the sidewalk outside Charity Hospital. At closing time one day in March 1996, fifty-eight-mile-per-hour winds snapped the light pole at its rusty base, dropping 626 pounds of steel on his Joseph's head. He survived, but after several surgeries, he suffers constant pain and will require lifelong medical care for his disabilities. He sued Entergy, which had the contract to maintain the pole, and the city, which owned it.

Entergy denied any liability for the rusty pole, but the courts ruled otherwise, saying the contract Entergy had with the city made clear that it alone was responsible. Nathaniel Joseph was paid more than $3 million in damages and his wife, Kecia, received an additional $100,000 for loss of consortium, legalese for an inability to have sexual relations with her husband.

Entergy turned around and sued TriStem, claiming that Seeber should

have to pay Joseph for his injuries and medical care. Entergy argued Seeber's company, not Entergy, had been negligent. As the city's energy billing auditor, Entergy asserted, Seeber knew or should have known that
the light pole on Tulane Avenue was rusted. Entergy said that Seeber had
a duty to inform Entergy and had failed in that obligation. (Seeber's contract, by the way, contained no requirement that he review safety conditions; his brief was to identify excessive and unwarranted charges by
Entergy.)

An angry Seeber saw Entergy's strategy as payback: the company was
trying to punish him for repeatedly exposing their overcharges. So Seeber wrote to each of the company's directors and to J. Wayne Leonard,
the chief executive, complaining that Entergy was trying to ruin his
business with a baseless lawsuit.

Judge Kern A. Reese of the state civil court summarily tossed out Entergy's suit against Seeber. Before doing so, though, Judge Reese took
note of an Entergy complaint that, by writing those letters, Seeber, who
was acting as his own lawyer, was improperly attempting to influence the
litigation. A defendant should deal only with the lawyers of the company
suing him, Entergy argued. Since Seeber was acting as his own lawyer
the court rules applied to him.

Judge Reese ordered Seeber to never mention the fruit vendor's injury
case to anyone at Entergy, and specifically not to Leonard, the chief executive. Seeber protested that his business required him to have contact
with Entergy and the lawsuit could require him to make mention of the
fruit vendor's case, whereupon the judge designated two Entergy lawyers
as the only people in the company to whom Seeber could mention the
fruit vendor's case. The judge's action might seem like the government
imposing prior restraint on free speech, but the courts sometimes impose limitations on those appearing before them in the name of what
judges call the efficient administration of justice.

Entergy promptly appealed the dismissal of its lawsuit—still trying to
make Seeber pay for the fruit vendor's injuries—but then let the case sit.
If the appeals court ever held a hearing on it, the case would almost certainly be dismissed. By not pursuing the appeal, Entergy kept the case
technically alive. By chilling Seeber's speech, Judge Reese had given Entergy a powerful lever toward getting rid of TriStem, as Seeber discovered in 2007.

In his short book called *Wired for Greed* and in interviews with reporters, Seeber publicly called Entergy "the most crooked utility in the country." He also sent a 400-page report to the Entergy chief, detailing what

he said were two decades of fraudulent Entergy financial and other reports. He wasn't the only one questioning the integrity of Entergy's financial statements. A large Florida utility holding company, FPL Group, had called off a merger with Entergy in 2001. In a statement, the Florida company said the merger collapsed because of "discrepancies in Entergy's financial forecasts and Entergy's repeated refusal to provide financial documents."

Entergy seized on the letters alleging false financial and other reporting as a means of going after Seeber: though forbidden to do so, Seeber had in fact mentioned the fruit vendor case in his letters asserting fraudulent filings by Entergy. The company's lawyers claimed this was contempt of court and that the proper punishment was forty-five days in jail.

Seeber was ordered to appear before Judge Reese. Before the hearing began, I watched Marcus V. Brown, the Entergy lawyer, walking in and out of the judge's chambers—meeting with the judge without Seeber's lawyer being present. What was said could not be heard, but when the hearing began Judge Reese adopted a stern tone that left no doubt that Seeber was in trouble.

Two TriStem employees testified that Seeber had instructed them to make sure all references to the fruit vendor's injury case were removed from his report. Brown argued that Seeber should have personally reviewed the report to make sure his instructions were followed precisely. Judge Reese sided with Entergy, stating that Seeber's conduct was contemptuous and must be punished.

Seeber and his lawyer, Philip C. Ciaccio Jr., repeated that the two passages were simple mistakes.

"Inadvertent error," Judge Reese said, was no excuse because "when you are the captain of the ship, you are responsible for everything that happens to the ship."

Then Judge Reese paused and looked out at the spectator section of his courtroom. He asked a bearded man taking notes—the only person in the room not involved in the case—to identify himself. I stood up, gave my name and said I was a staff reporter for the *New York Times*. After our exchange, Judge Reese stopped hectoring Seeber and spoke in a tone that almost resembled neutrality.

After a break, Judge Reese ordered Seeber jailed for thirty days, not the forty-five days Entergy sought. Then the judge added that he would suspend all but seven days because Seeber had tried to remove any references to the fruit vendor's lawsuit from the 400-page report. Next the judge moderated his order further, saying he would drop even the week in jail on the condition that Seeber write a letter apologizing to J. Wayne Leonard for mentioning the fruit vendor case.

Seeber had arrived in court fully expecting he would be sent to jail. He walked out of the courtroom a free man, saying that he was sure that but for my presence the judge would have jailed him for forty-five days. Brown, the Entergy lawyer, looked panicked after failing to get the forty-five-day jail sentence the company desired. He told me bluntly that the court proceedings should not be covered in the *New York Times* and that I had no business being there.

Examining Entergy's behavior in light of the company's eleven-page "Code of Entegrity" is revealing. CEO Leonard writes on the first page that "if you are under the impression that ideals and standards don't have a place in today's business world, remember that they do, right here." He continues: "Like safety, integrity is not merely a 'sometimes' proposition. It is a constant. It is a touchstone that impacts everything we do. Here at Entergy, honesty and integrity are absolutely essential in everything we do. It's who we are."

As the deadly electrified Medusa of Tulane Avenue shows, however, for Entergy safety can be a sometime thing.

The alignment of Entergy's policies and conduct is also in question when it comes to the repeated revelations about overcharging customers.

And the attempt to silence—and even imprison—Joe Seeber is still another example of Entergy's failure to live up to its own creed. Six pages into the ethics code for which Leonard wrote the introduction is a legend in bold capital letters: **"RETALIATION IS NOT TOLERATED."** The document continues: "Entergy strictly prohibits retaliation against anyone for making a complaint or report, with reasonable belief, of a violation of the law, the Code of Entegrity or a System Policy. Further, retaliation is prohibited against anyone participating in an investigation or proceeding relating to an alleged violation. . . ."

Seeber remains furious at the retaliation he suffered from Entergy, but he is no coward. "They do not intimidate me," Seeber says, adding that he would love to go back to New Orleans to audit the city's Entergy bills again. Of course, since Seeber only gets paid when he proves overbilling, what chance could there be that he would catch the company yet again overbilling for millions of dollars?

After all, Entergy boasts, "We lead the industry with integrity."

Paying Other People's Taxes

The regulator cannot create a phantom tax in order to
create an allowance to pass through to the rate payer.

—Judge David B. Sentelle

8. **Wouldn't it be** marvelous if someone else paid your income taxes? Imagine all that extra money in your paycheck. You could pay your debts, set aside a few dollars, or splurge on something special. Of course, if someone else had to pay your income taxes it would not be such a good deal for them. They would have to pay their own income taxes *and* yours. You wouldn't want to be that person, would you?

Well, in a sense, you already are. There's a federal regulation that makes us pay someone else's taxes and, worse yet, that somebody is exempt from federal income taxes, meaning they pocket the tax money we give them as extra profits.

This policy comes from the Federal Energy Regulatory Commission. FERC sets the level of water behind hydroelectric dams and oversees electricity grids and wholesale electric markets whose initial rules were written by Enron and then adopted by government. FERC also sets the rates pipelines charge to transport oil and natural gas across state lines but which are exempt from corporate income tax.

As federal agencies go, FERC is small. Its budget amounts to about a quarter of a billion dollars a year, less than a tenth of a penny on each dollar in the federal budget. And its staff is modest, too, about fifteen hundred people.

Most federal agencies have struggled for years with flat or shrinking real budgets, but not FERC. Its 2010 budget was 9 percent larger than in

2009, which in turn was 10 percent more than in 2008. Congress approved these increases because the energy industry wanted FERC's budget to grow. That may seem odd, given how often we hear how businesses dislike being regulated. But FERC's funding is just one of its peculiarities.

As it happens, FERC's budget does not come from the taxes you pay to Washington. Instead, the commission is financed with fees paid by the industries it regulates, industries that get their money from you. Energy companies gladly pay those fees because they help ensure incredible profits, like those earned by pipelines.

To put this into perspective, tax records show that the 5.8 million corporations in America keep as profit about six cents on each dollar of revenue. The 14,000 largest do better, keeping as profit roughly a dime on each dollar of revenue. And how well do oil pipelines do? Their profit is forty-two cents on the dollar.

Measured against assets, the story of bloated profits is the same. American companies earned 6.7 percent on their assets in 2010, according to calculations done by the federal Bureau of Economic, Energy, and Business Affairs. But among the 175 interstate oil pipelines, three earned more than 30 percent, three more earned more than 40 percent and a pipeline owned by Sunoco made an astounding 55 percent.

One reason they did so well is that you paid these pipelines for corporate income taxes, both federal and state. Problem is, most pipelines do not pay the corporate income tax. That means the taxes you were forced to pay—but that never got passed on to government—were really just extra profits.

How do you pay this tax? You won't find it cited anywhere on a bill you get. Looking at your utility bills and gas station receipts, you would never know that the federal government lets pipeline owners drill a hole in your pocketbook. But if natural gas warms your home, if you use electricity that comes from a generation plant that burns gas, or you drive a car fueled by gasoline, chances are the fuels travel via monopoly pipelines, meaning you paid your piece.

If you have never heard about this tax-gouging rule, that's not surprising. The major news media have missed it completely. News outlets rarely cover FERC. When they do, the stories tend to be superficial and based on press releases. Without a watchdog to watch, much less bark, how are you to know you're being ripped off by an entire industry? The way this rule came about is a perfect example of how big companies use the fine print of regulations to enrich themselves unfairly at your expense.

THE PIPELINE PROFIT

Pipelines collect all of their revenues from their customers, the energy companies that produce fuels and natural gas. The money they collect pays their costs, from pipeline operations to expense-account lunches; what's left over becomes profits for investors. Since there is no competitive market to determine prices, government regulators stand in for market forces. In theory, the FERC holds hearings, gathers evidence, scrutinizes accounting records and then determines the prices, or rates, that can be charged for moving oil and gas through America's more than five hundred thousand miles of transport pipelines.

A simple legal principle— "just and reasonable"—is supposed to guide this process. On one side of the equation, investors are entitled to reasonable costs and a reasonable profit so that the business is viable and the service reliable. On the other, customers are entitled to just and reasonable prices so that they pay what they would in a competitive market.

Historically, calculations of what is "just and reasonable" were made on the basis of money actually spent. But FERC had a better idea: it decided you can be charged for fictional expenses, not just actual ones. The real world of costs and prices once defined the limits, but with fiction, there are no boundaries.

This shift to picking your pocket rather than settling for "just and reasonable" rates based on actual expenses began with a provision in the 1986 Tax Reform Act, which passed Congress with bipartisan support and which President Reagan signed. Many excellent aspects of that law looked to make the tax system fairer, but the legislation also harbored hundreds of subtle favors to industries and individuals. One provision— the one that, in time, would allow charging for fictional costs—didn't make the news. But it changed the way that partnerships, specifically *master limited partnerships*, are treated under the tax law.

Before 1986, any partnership allowing its shares to trade like a stock was subject to corporate income tax. That meant the partnership might as well organize as a corporation, in which the company is taxed on profits and then its owners are taxed again on dividends and gains on shares sold at a profit. This is known as the double taxation of corporate profits. But the 1986 law allowed shares of "master limited partnerships" to trade just like stocks, only without the partnership being subject to the corporate income tax. Investors in a master limited partnership, or MLP, escape double taxation because they pay only one level of tax, their personal income taxes, on profits.

Historically, corporations owned pipelines. But once the 1986 law changed, so did the structure of the pipeline business. Many corporations created master limited partnerships and put their pipelines into them. Nearly two hundred master limited pipeline partnerships existed by 2012.

With the resulting elimination of the corporate income tax, you might think that monopoly pipeline rates would go down. After all, their costs went down by the amount of the corporate income tax once it was eliminated for MLPs. And since only actual expenses are supposed to be considered when regulators set "just and reasonable" rates, then rates, in theory, should decline.

Yet, even in the absence of a corporate income tax, FERC permitted master limited pipeline partnerships to include a charge for corporate income taxes in their rates. The organization that represents the owners and developers of natural gas wells, the Natural Gas Supply Association, objected. It said that including fictitious taxes in pipeline charges amounted to an "under the table" rate increase. Consumer groups, few and lightly funded, let the issue slide.

From the point of view of a pipeline monopolist, charging customers the corporate income tax and then pocketing the money makes an already lucrative business extraordinarily profitable. Court records from a test case that challenged the nonexistent tax that one oil pipeline charged show just how much. For each dollar of after-tax profit earned under the old system of actual costs, pipeline owners could now pocket $1.75. That 75 percent boost in after-tax profits came out of the consumer's pocket.

The pipeline that first got approval to charge the nonexistent tax is called the SFPP. Its name comes from the initials of the former Santa Fe and Southern Pacific railroads, which merged a quarter century ago. During the one-term administration of George H. W. Bush, the first Texas oilman to become president, the Federal Energy Regulatory Commission let this pipeline charge rates that assumed it paid a 42.7 percent corporate income tax on profits. Two of the pipeline's wholesale customers, BP (British Petroleum) West Coast and ExxonMobil, appealed FERC's approval of the fictional tax to the federal district court of appeals in Washington, which hears challenges to regulatory actions.

The court reversed FERC's decision. Judge David B. Sentelle and two colleagues held that regulators "cannot create a phantom tax in order to

FORCING YOU TO PAY OTHERS' TAXES

Including the corporate income tax in partnership costs, even though partnerships are exempt from the tax, boosts pipeline owners' ultimate net income by 75 percent at your expense.

	CORPORATION Actual taxes	MASTER LIMITED PARTNERSHIP Actual taxes	MASTER LIMITED PARTNERSHIP Fake taxes
PRETAX PROFIT UNDER GOVERNMENT-SET PRICES	$175	$100	$175
Less 42.7 percent corporate income tax paid on profit	$(75)	$ 0	$ 0
Net pipeline profit after taxes	$100	$100	$175
Less owner's personal income tax at 35 percent	$(35)	$(35)	$(61)
Owner's after-tax income	$(65)	$65	$114
Increase in after-tax profit			$49
Percent increase in after-tax profit			75%

Source: Calculations by author from Federal Circuit Court of Appeals decision in BP West Coast Products v. FERC.

create an allowance to pass through to the ratepayer." Monopoly rates set by government cannot include "phantom income taxes [the MLP] did not pay." The court ruled that under the "just and reasonable" rule, including a nonexistent tax was, in short, inherently unjust and unreasonable.

That might have been the end of it. But by the time that case was decided a former oil and gas tax-shelter salesman, George W. Bush, had become president. His administration hustled to remake the regulatory landscape to the liking of the energy industry, especially Enron, which had been Bush's single largest source of campaign funds. His vice president, Dick Cheney, had created a secretive advisory panel that put forth energy policy proposals which, years later, were revealed to be almost word for word what Enron and other energy companies proposed. And which companies pushed hard for these new rules to include fictional corporate tax expenses in monopoly pipeline rates? Enron and Kinder Morgan Management, a pipeline company headed by a former Enron president.

Cheney's point man regarding pipeline regulations was a career regulator named Joseph Kelliher. He must have done a reliable job for Cheney because in 2003 Kelliher got a promotion to FERC commissioner. In 2005, President Bush promoted Kelliher again, this time to FERC chairman.

Kelliher and other Bush appointees wanted to restore the fake tax that Judge Sentelle struck down. They also wanted the matter resolved— and avoid years of regulatory litigation—before someone less in the pocket of the oil industry got to the White House or Admiral's House, where the vice president lives. A clever trick made things move quickly. FERC announced in 2005 it would develop a "policy statement" on whether to include "actual or potential" taxes in pipeline rates.

Most legal matters in America involve administrative and regulatory law. The regulatory system, however, doesn't ordinarily recognize "policy statements," only formal rule making. But by creating this regulatory twilight zone, the commission effectively suspended the rules on making rules. When the rules are in effect and a case is under way, private meetings between commissioners and parties to cases, such as pipeline lobbyists, are generally prohibited. Lawyers call these meetings "ex parte"—from one side only—because other parties are excluded, making the meetings inherently unfair and one-sided.

But in the invented world of "policy statements," no such limitation existed. Kelliher and other commissioners could, and did, meet privately with pipeline lobbyists while giving little or no time to those who did not share their inclination to allow pipelines to charge for nonexistent taxes.

The Bush appointees' fealty to the pipeline industry ran deep. Once they had heard all they wanted from pipeline lobbyists and lawyers, they allowed only a brief opportunity for comments on the not-yet-issued "policy statement." As for the customary practice of letting parties respond to what their opponents say, that went out the window. Each side was given only a few days to file, and no rebuttals were allowed before FERC adopted the policy statement. Then in 2007, Kelliher and the other commissioners relied on the policy statement in approving new rates for the SFPP, the same pipeline controlled by Kinder Morgan that had been the subject of the earlier federal appeals court decision. These new rates included the corporate tax even though, as a master limited partnership, SFPP was exempt from corporate income taxes.

This decision on the added tax was more than a little odd because the second President Bush had pledged never to raise taxes. Bush signed a no-more-taxes pledge much stronger than what Grover Norquist of Americans for Tax Reform bullied many other politicians into signing. "If elected president," Bush wrote to Norquist in 1999, "I will oppose and veto any increase in individual or corporate marginal income tax rates or individual or corporate income tax hikes." Since no major news organization covered the FERC beat, the broken pledge went unreported. Even so, it's a truism that even if a tax falls in the forest of Washington regulations and no one reports it, the tax is still there.

Technically, one could argue that the pipeline rule that makes you pay other people's income taxes does not violate the presidential pledge. That tortured reasoning runs this way: the rule does not raise your marginal tax rates or hike taxes, it just makes you pay a tax that the law does not impose.

After the Bush administration put the "tax" back in place, ExxonMobil and other oil companies that shipped their products through the 2,700-mile SFPP pipeline filed new challenges. Based on the earlier decision, it looked like an open-and-shut case since nothing substantive had changed. A fake expense was still included in monopoly pipeline rates, and Judge Sentelle had said that was not allowed.

This time Judge Sentelle, joined by judges Thomas Griffith and Brett Kavanaugh, took a different view. The decision made it clear that they disliked FERC's new policy of imposing fake taxes, as the judges suggested that ignoring taxes altogether in setting rates might be a good idea, certainly a better idea than including nonexistent taxes in rates. They wrote that rates based on a fictional corporate income tax charge "and the policy statement upon which they are based incorporate some of the troubling elements of the phantom tax . . . disallowed in" the earlier SFPP pipeline case.

But their decision then took an unexpected turn. Judge Sentelle and his colleagues ruled that chairman Kelliher and the rest of the commission had "justified its new policy with reasoning sufficient to survive our review." How did the appeals court stand its earlier decision on its head? Judge Sentelle wrote that it was not the court's place to decide what regulation was best or smart, but only to make sure it was "not arbitrary or capricious or contrary to law." This was the same legal reasoning that permits monopoly railroads to charge customers like the Lafayette Utilities System in Louisiana a monopoly price for hauling coal 1,520 miles

when there are parallel tracks for all but 20 miles of that journey. Whatever the flaws in the FERC's reasoning, Judge Sentelle said, the fake
tax could be charged to customers. He and his confreres made no mention of two obvious and essential questions: How can any fictional expense be fair to customers? And how can any fake cost be "just and
reasonable"?

In California, SFPP sought to impose the same corporate tax charge
for oil it moves within the state. There, rates are regulated by the state
Public Utilities Commission. An administrative law judge who heard
evidence in that case, which began in 1997, issued a proposed ruling de-
nying any allowance for a fake tax. But late in 2010 Commissioner Timo-
thy Alan Simon put out an alternative decision that included the tax.
Simon, who was appointed by Governor Arnold Schwarzenegger, is a
securities lawyer who worked for investment firms engaged with energy
businesses.

What happened next shows how a spotlight, even a small one, focused
on government can produce positive change. I wrote a column about Simon's proposal to impose this tax in *State Tax Notes*, a small public policy
magazine; the column was also posted at tax.com, its sister Web site.
That prompted several people to notify the commission that they wanted
to speak about it during the next public comment period. Rather than
hear them, the commission put off the vote. Six months later, with Simon
gone, the commission rejected the proposed fake tax.

The amount of money at stake was small, about $9 million per year or
twenty-five cents per resident. But that one brief article and the action of
readers who asked that their voices be heard will save Californians that
$9 million, inflation adjusted, which should give heart to those trying to
make government more responsive to people and less friendly to corporations.

The money taken from you by all of America's pipelines together is
too small to be worth any individual putting up a fight. I estimate the
charge for this nonexistent tax comes to about $3 billion a year, which is
about $20 annually per American household, something like a nickel a
day. But to the two hundred monopoly pipelines that stand to benefit, it
is a lot of money, enough to justify huge spending on campaign contributions, lobbyists and litigation.

Unless consumers rise up and fight this, one thing is certain: unelected
officials, backed by judges with lifetime appointments, will authorize and
then approve more ways to pick your pocket because of what judges Sentelle, Griffith and Kavanaugh did. In a clear miscarriage of economic

justice, they destroyed the legal principle that "just and reasonable" rates rest on actual costs, at least for pipelines. This fake tax may be extended to other utilities and to the railroads. Achieving this requires only a simple change in federal law. All that would be required is the insertion of a list of industries that can be owned through publicly traded master limited partnerships without being subject to the corporate income tax.

A prominent regulatory lawyer and former chief counsel for FERC told me he expects that is what will happen. Gordon Gooch joined FERC as a young lawyer, after clerking for a Supreme Court justice, and rose to become FERC's general counsel. Later, as a private lawyer representing ExxonMobil, he lost the case in which Judge Sentelle allowed fake taxes to be added as a cost in pipeline rates.

Gooch says that corporate-owned electric utilities are salivating at the prospect of getting out of paying corporate income tax while pocketing the money. Their trade association has already defended collecting income taxes from customers, monies that are never turned over to government. The industry trade association Edison Electric Institute basically said its members just do what the law allows. "The electric utilities would be master limited partnerships now," Gooch said, "except that when the law was changed in 1986 the Edison Electric Institute was uncharacteristically asleep at the switch."

If Congress amends the law, or some creative judicial interpretation effects such a change, then the cost to consumers of this fake tax would soar. Instead of being a nickel per day, each family of four could be hit for more than a dollar a day, and $400 annually for a family of four is real money. It is the weekly after-tax pay for a single worker at the median wage in 2010.

How many other rules like this one benefit the heavily subsidized energy industry but lie buried beneath layers of legalese? The answer is: plenty. Just ask Calvin Johnson, a professor of tax law at the University of Texas, who has devoted years to uncovering hidden tax favors. Hidden in the legal and regulatory fine print Johnson found an astonishing profits booster for independent oil and gas companies. They get extra dollop after extra dollop of tax breaks on top of the thick layers of official favors the energy industry already enjoys.

Consider two companies, each of which earns a 10 percent pretax return in the market, but one of which is an independent oil and gas company. Johnson showed how energy industry tax rules create an additional profit of 41 percent. The independent oil and gas company investors will earn 14.1 percent instead of the market profit of 10 percent.

Johnson and others disclosed their findings through the Shelf Project, which is published in *State Tax Notes*. Its goal is to show ways that Congress could raise more money just by closing loopholes, fixing flaws in tax laws, and undoing unjust decisions like Judge Sentelle's shameless gift to pipeline MLPs. So far Johnson and his colleagues have shown how Congress, by closing loopholes, could raise $1 trillion each year without *any* new taxes or tax rate increases. That would be enough to nearly balance the federal budget in 2013.

After the election of Barack Obama, FERC chairman Kelliher decided it was time to leave. But before going, he found one more way to gouge our wallets. During the first week of 2009 Kelliher announced that on Inauguration Day he would step down as chairman of FERC but stay on as a commissioner. He also announced that he would recuse himself from FERC business because he would be meeting with energy companies the commission regulates to "explore other career opportunities." In other words, Kelliher hung around for two months doing no work, but collecting a paycheck until he got a new job. Kelliher's new post? He became an executive in charge of the regulatory team at what is now NextEra Energy, a holding company that owns Florida Power & Light and, yes—you guessed it—pipelines.

Investors Beware

> How long can such schemes last before there is an
> implosion that will make Samuel Insull and his pyramid
> holding companies' implosion look innocuous by
> comparison?
>
> —**Gordon Gooch, former Federal Energy**
> **Regulatory Commission general counsel**

9. *Caveat emptor.* **Even** if pipelines held by master limited partnerships, the subject of the last chapter, sound like a wonderful investment, there's a flip side—a dangerous downside, you might say—to MLPs.

Yes, cover stories in *Barron's, Forbes, Investor's Business Daily, Money* and other publications tout the lucrative returns. And, indeed, these pipelines "operate in areas where there is little to no competition," which, *Barron's* notes, means large profit margins.

Where else, these investment publications ask, can investors get annual returns of 6, 8 or even 10 percent on their investment while paying little or no income tax? During an era when government has driven interest rates on savings to nearly zero and many companies pay no dividends, the promise of such high yields is certainly seductive. But those fat distributions of tax-free money are illusory. MLPs may well turn out to be disastrous for individual investors.

If you, a relative or a friend has been taken in by the siren call of fat returns by investing in pipeline MLPs, read what follows very carefully. What is often overlooked is the reason why MLP payouts are tax-free. So look at the flow of cash and what happens to pipeline assets. They're crucial to knowing the real value of pipeline partnership shares.

WHAT'S THE PROBLEM?

In short, those fat MLP payout checks sent to limited partners are not a share of profits. Rather than a return *on* capital, they are a return *of* capital. That is why the limited partners pay little or no tax: mostly they get their own money back.

Pipeline partnerships are part of a multilayered legal structure so complex it would make Rube Goldberg proud. The partnerships themselves are mostly paper enterprises, as Gordon Gooch, the former Federal Energy Regulatory Commission general counsel, tells anyone who will listen. Sure, there is that pipeline lying in the ground. But many of the partnerships have no employees. Many have no cash, either, except what they borrow. And the general partner controls the whole deal. Typically the general partner is not a person, but a big corporation like, say, Kinder Morgan, which was started by a former Enron president. Starting to get the picture?

I promise you it's a real chore to figure out who gets those fake taxes the FERC and Judge Sentelle let the pipelines collect. Usually securities disclosure statements bunch all the information about an issue, say for executive compensation, in one place. Not so MLP pipelines. Gooch figured out what happens at one pipeline company by connecting language on one page with a passage dozens of pages deeper in the document and then another still deeper in, and then to a fourth page near the end of the thousand-page document. These legal breadcrumbs mark the path the general partner takes as he sweeps up the fake taxes, something missed entirely by the investor magazines.

Where do the pipeline partnerships get the money to write checks to those who buy shares? A 2007 report by the investment bank Morgan Stanley revealed that for each dollar in new capital the MLPs need to develop and expand their pipelines, they pay out $10 to earlier investors. By following that creaky equation, pipelines take on ever more debt, in the form of bonds, and sell ever more partnership share units, diluting the interests of earlier investors.

If one or more pipelines get squeezed in the future, as happens now and then to all businesses, the logical action for the people who control the pipelines would be to put the partnership into bankruptcy proceedings. It would be easy for the parent company to reorganize a bankrupt MLP in a way that lets the general partner remain as *debtor in possession*, which would wipe out the individual investors in the master limited partnership and force lenders to take a haircut. This happens all the time in corporate reorganizations under Chapter 11 of the federal bankruptcy code. In other words, the general partner probably remains whole and you get wiped out.

Some experts on utility regulation describe MLPs as a variation of a Ponzi scheme. These are not cynical observations made in casual conversations, but in writing in formal regulatory proceedings. It is an argument to which FERC, the Securities and Exchange Commission and other regulators have paid no more heed than they did to the whispers that Bernard Madoff was running an actual Ponzi scheme. What distinguishes pipeline partnerships from Ponzi schemes is that pipelines are real businesses with steady streams of income from customers who want their natural gas or petroleum moved. What makes pipeline MLPs like Ponzi schemes is that those checks to investors come in large part from new investors, not from profits.

On their face, pipeline master limited partnerships do not appear to be capitalism, at least not classic capitalism, in which owners try to maximize their profits and build wealth. Capitalism is about making profits and building up assets by retaining earnings for reinvestment. Not so with master limited partnerships. They are about stripping capital out of the enterprise, while raising new money from new investors.

Kurt Wulff, who runs mcdep.com, a Web site that examines the finances of energy companies with a critical eye, described one pipeline deal not as a takeover, but a "take under" because the price paid was $29 a unit, far below the $40 per unit investors could have gotten by selling their shares on an exchange. Anyone reading just the press releases, though, would have thought this was a fabulous deal for the limited partners.

Wulff has shown that many pipelines pay enormous "performance" fees to the general partner, typically more than the pipeline profits and often even greater than the pipeline's cash flow. Wulff analyzed one pipeline deal by the Williams Companies and concluded that it was based entirely on borrowing more and more money. "All the GP [general partner] has to do is borrow to finance the acquisition of another asset," Wulff explains. "Then like a Ponzi scheme, the distribution would be paid from future financing." And like a Ponzi scheme perpetrator, Wulff notes, the general partner would be paid oodles of money "for little fundamental contribution" to the business.

What if the pipeline had trouble paying off loans whose proceeds had been siphoned off by the general partner? Wulff noted that fine-print contract terms provide that the general partner "would have almost no liability for debt repayment." In other words, if a pipeline company borrows until it collapses, it likely will be the lenders and the little investors who take the losses, while the corporate parent keeps control of the pipeline and the borrowed cash.

Another warning comes from Gooch, the former FERC general counsel. Gooch wrote to FERC in 2007 that, since master limited partnerships extract capital from their pipelines rather than building up capital, they are at risk of collapse if the flow of cash slows from customers or new investors. He pointed to the collapse of the Insull Trust—the Enron of the 1930s—and warned of dire consequences. It was the Insull Trust's collapse that plunged the economy into its darkest days in 1932, three years after the stock market crash of 1929.

We met Sam Insull earlier. He bought a small electric utility in Chicago at a time when multiple electric companies served neighborhoods, not cities or regions. Insull created an intricate legal structure through which he controlled electric utilities in thirty-two states. He financed it all with layer upon layer of debt that tied seemingly unrelated utilities together in a financial web that no one, perhaps not even he himself, understood. While today's electric utilities are typically half shareholder equity and half debt, Insull had just 6 percent equity and 94 percent debt, making his company highly vulnerable because it had to spend most of its profits paying interest on loans. With the stock market collapse in 1929, many people struggled to pay their electric bills; three years later enough of them failed to pay Insull's companies that he lacked the cash to pay his six hundred thousand bondholders their interest, plunging the entire nation further into the depths of the Depression. Insull became the most hated man in America, the Ken Lay of his day.

Gooch warned FERC that such a disaster could recur. The money paid out to pipeline master limited partnership investors, he wrote, is "raised by higher rates (and perhaps skimping on maintenance), by extensive borrowing, and by sales" of new partnership shares that dilute the interests of existing shares.

"How long can such schemes last before there is an implosion that will make Samuel Insull and his pyramid holding companies' implosion look innocuous by comparison?" Gooch asked the commissioners. His letter went unanswered.

Gooch also noted that in the past decade many private equity funds had bought electric utilities so they could "strip, flip and skip" out of town, leaving behind not a reliable provider of power, but a hollowed-out corporation. A pipeline, or any utility, stripped of assets lacks the money needed to invest in reliability and to prevent explosions, fires, toxic spills and other disasters.

Even if you never buy a partnership unit and no one in your family does, you will still be hurt when a pipeline is bankrupted. Why? Because the general partner is sure to ask the Federal Energy Regulatory Commission to approve new, higher rates. After all, if the pipeline went broke, then it must not be charging enough.

The net result? You pay for someone else's taxes at the gas pump and when you boil water. You pay for profits that are wildly beyond "just and reasonable." And if the pipeline is bankrupted you will pay new, even higher rates. And on top of all that, because the government never gets the corporate income tax money you pay, you will have to pay higher taxes, accept fewer government services or pay more interest to finance government borrowing.

Playing with Fire

It looked like a napalm drop.

— Anonymous

10.   **Among fly fisherman** in the Pacific Northwest, Liam Wood was a wunderkind. He started casting at age nine and was soon tying his own flies. Still in school, he got a part-time job at a sporting-goods store that outfitted fly fishermen. Five days after graduating from Sehome High School in 1999, Wood grabbed his waders and headed for Whatcom Falls Creek, hoping to hook rainbow trout. It was a perfect day for doing what he loved best. Until, that is, he took a deep breath of cool June air. Liam Wood, eighteen, collapsed and drowned.

Just upstream, Stephen Tsiorvas and Wade King were doing what many ten-year-old boys do, playing with fire. They had a blue butane cigarette lighter. It was spent, but when they flicked the flint, a tiny spark ignited 237,000 gallons of gasoline, killing every living thing for a mile and a half along the banks of Whatcom Falls Creek.

"It looked like a napalm drop," one resident said.

The explosion came minutes before the gasoline, gushing from a ruptured pipeline managed by Royal Dutch Shell, would have flowed under Interstate 5. A few minutes later it would have reached downtown Bellingham, where a high-rise apartment tower for the elderly and disabled stands just seventy-five feet from the water's edge. Because their normal boyish play saved hundreds of lives by igniting the gasoline before it reached downtown, Mayor Mark Asmundson called Stephen and Wade, badly burned and in agony, "unwitting heroes."

Outside the state of Washington, the blast was reported as a freak accident, worthy of a single sentence on the ABC *World News*, which reported a dead teenager and two boys with burns. Stephen and Wade died soon after the broadcast ended. Within days the boys were largely forgotten by the media, which focused on a sudden spike in gasoline prices, a consequence of the ruptured pipeline that was no longer delivering fuel along the I-5 corridor in Washington and Oregon.

A little more than a year later, the New Mexico desert erupted just before dawn. The blast awakened people twenty miles away. When Carlsbad firefighters reached the scene south of town, they found what appeared to be a gigantic blowtorch, as natural gas under high pressure shot from a thirty-inch-wide pipeline. During the fifty-five minutes it took for El Paso Natural Gas to shut off the flow of natural gas, the roar from the flames was so loud that firefighters could barely hear orders shouted directly into their ears. But the silence that followed was punctuated by the sound of wailing.

Rushing down to the Pecos River, firefighters found six horribly burned members of an extended family of twelve. Those not killed in the blast sought refuge in the waters after flames engulfed their campsite. One begged to be shot.

This second pipeline disaster also made a brief appearance in the national news, covered as the sad story of an unlucky family that happened to be in the wrong place at the wrong time. Within days, all twelve campers would be dead; along with the causes of the rupture, their story was lost in the rush to talk about how electricity prices in California soared because there was no fuel for the modified jet engines that generate electricity to meet peak demand on hot August afternoons. The pipeline repairs took nearly a year.

A decade later, on September 9, 2010, another thirty-inch natural-gas pipeline exploded, this time on the San Francisco Peninsula. This pipe operated at 1,000 pounds of pressure per square inch. A wall of flames hundreds of feet high shot skyward as evening fell on suburban San Bruno. To reach manual shutoff valves, Pacific Gas & Electric crews had to negotiate rush-hour traffic. One valve was more than thirty miles from the blast, and it took the crew an hour and a half to get there. The explosion—which left a crater forty feet deep—killed eight people, injured sixty more, and severely damaged or destroyed 120 homes.

Among the dead were Jacqueline Greig and her thirteen-year-old daughter Janessa. Ironically, Greig had worked for the Division of

Ratepayer Advocates at the California Public Utilities Commission in San Francisco as a natural-gas analyst for more than two decades. Her last assignment: investigating whether PG&E was spending enough money maintaining and inspecting its high-pressure transmission pipelines to make sure they would not explode.

These are just three incidents out of many, but the explosions in Bellingham, Carlsbad and San Bruno should serve as warning signs about an increasingly dangerous future, one in which an immensely profitable industry too often works quietly to thwart safety regulations.

IS ANYBODY WATCHING?

If you live in an urban or suburban area, you probably spend part of your day above or near a pipeline that moves massive amounts of pressurized natural gas, scalding hot diesel, jet fuel or gasoline. Due to the potential impact of a rupture, these areas are officially known as "high consequence areas," a euphemism for what might more accurately be called *death zones*.

Compared to automobile or even plane crashes, very few people have died from pipeline ruptures in the past two decades. A pipeline blast kills someone about every three weeks on average, while someone is burned every few days. Most of these are the result of preventable accidents, often due to a mistake by a pipeline worker or a backhoe operator hitting a pipeline. Though the numbers are small, as the pipeline industry emphasizes, this reflects luck more than serious safety planning. Open spaces where pipelines were laid decades ago are now being developed, but aging pipelines in the vicinity remain in use. The political push for less government means fewer inspections, increasing the risk of a deadly blast that one day might wipe out a block of homes, offices, stores or even a hospital or an elementary school.

High-pressure natural-gas lines run in to every big city in America. In Manhattan alone, high-pressure gas lines enter Battery Park at the southern tip of the island, at the mouths of the Lincoln and Holland tunnels, near the George Washington Bridge, on the Lower East Side, and near the vast apartment complex on the East Side known as Tudor City. That is a partial list.

Vincent Dunn, deputy chief of the New York City Fire Department from 1973 to 1999, says what no one wants to hear: when it comes to high-pressure pipelines, profits trump safety. "Industry and big business run the city," Dunn told me. "So if a fire department was asked how to control high-pressure gas lines, we would say don't run it through the big population centers, but we would just be overruled. We have to clean up and wipe up whatever the results are when things go wrong."

A gas industry study, adopted by the federal Department of Transportation, defined "high consequence areas" and estimated the damages from an explosion in an open area, like the desert death zone in New Mexico. The study considered a thirty-inch pipeline operating at 1,500 pounds of pressure per square inch of the pipeline wall and concluded that the likely death zone in the event of an explosion would extend 660 feet in every direction. Experience shows that the estimate is woefully inadequate. The El Paso Natural Gas pipeline that killed the Heady, Smith and Sumler families in August 2000 operated at just 675 pounds of pressure, so the consequences should have been felt in a much smaller area than 660 feet from the blast. The family members were 675 feet from the rupture.

In a city, buildings could help contain the blast zone, but that presents another problem: streets are flush with secondary fuel sources. Gasoline, diesel and compressed natural gas fill the tanks of cars, trucks and buses. Fuel oil tanks lie under buildings. Sidewalks feature canopies made of canvas and people wear clothes that would add more fuel.

Chief Dunn praised Consolidated Edison for its annual training of FDNY crews, but still warned that the rupture of a large natural-gas line in a densely developed city would likely cost many lives and many billions of dollars in damage. "The gas would burn until the gas company could shut it off from two directions," Chief Dunn said. "The heat would radiate up five or six floors and go through the windows, which don't stop the heat." Fires would start inside offices and apartments.

Once the electric power went off, either from the fire or a deliberate shutdown to prevent sparking, those in elevators would be trapped. People fleeing tall buildings would have to navigate emergency stairwells, a difficult-to-impossible task for the elderly and disabled. Even in buildings that did not catch fire, the smoke and heat from the streets could kill many.

Professor Glenn Corbett, a New Jersey fire captain who teaches fire safety management at John Jay College in Manhattan, told of a pipeline explosion in Edison, New Jersey, in 1994. More than six hundred manual turns of a valve were required to shut off the gas, a process that took six long hours. "There is no question you will ignite some surrounding buildings," Professor Corbett said about a natural gas-fueled fire burning for hours in an area of office or apartment towers. "The chance of this happening is very small, but if it does happen, the costs in life, in services being shut off for weeks or months, and in reconstruction would be enormous."

HOW SAFE IS SAFE ENOUGH?

No law required that any pipelines be inspected until 2002. Even now, with an assist from government officials whose job is to ensure safe operation of pipelines, the industry regularly obscures pipeline locations.

Most troubling of all, segments of pipeline are being given waivers from the very limited safety inspections required under the Pipeline Safety Improvement Act of 2002. The exact locations of these segments are treated as secret, although with enough determination and a surveyor's transit and chain, they can be identified. The industry also benefits from rules it promoted, rules that discourage repairing or replacing old, corroded pipelines. The corroded pipe that exploded near Carlsbad hadn't been tested for integrity since it was laid back in *1950*, when Harry Truman was president.

Pipeline safety is the responsibility of the federal Department of Transportation and two agencies under its umbrella. "Safety is the number one priority," department spokesperson Maureen Knightly told me. She said the agency conducts eight hundred to nine hundred inspections a year and "reviews all available data to determine inspection frequency and focus."

A very different view comes from Carl Weimer, executive director of the Pipeline Safety Trust. It is funded with $4 million of the penalties paid in the Bellingham disaster. Weimer considers the Transportation Department's safety-first claims almost laughable.

"The overarching problem with the current pipeline safety regulatory system is the undue influence that the pipeline industry has on every aspect of how those regulations are designed and enforced," Weimer said. "The industry deluges rule-making processes with their public relations people and lawyers, and most regulators have either come from the industry they now regulate or plan to go to work for that industry once they leave government service."

At pipeline safety conferences, Weimer said, he is often the only person present who is not an industry advocate or regulator. As far back as 1978, the investigating arm of Congress, now called the Government Accountability Office, issued scathing reports about incompetence, weak rules and ineffective enforcement by the Transportation Department's Office of Pipeline Safety. Pacific Gas & Electric was repeatedly found to have violated safety rules in its natural-gas pipeline system, yet was not fined once prior to the deadly San Bruno blast.

Even the American Petroleum Institute, which represents big oil companies, criticized the pipeline safety office over the poor quality of its accident records. Yet the industry as a whole has worked hard to make sure that not enough money is spent to properly inspect pipelines. Six months after the Bellingham disaster, the chairman of the agency that investigates pipeline disasters, the National Transportation Safety Board, told the Association of Oil Pipelines that its efforts to keep the pipeline safety office short of funds and unable to effectively regulate for safety would backfire. Safety board chairman Jim Hall said that "no American would want to use any transportation vehicle that would not be properly inspected for 48 years, nor should we have pipelines traveling through any of our communities in this condition." His words drew no applause. Hall said that to get the industry's attention, criminal charges and prison sentences might be necessary.

The pipeline industry lawyer whom the Obama administration made head of the federal Pipeline and Hazardous Materials Safety Administration, Cynthia Quarterman, said after the San Bruno blast that "we inherited a program that suffered from almost a decade of neglect." She is wrong about that. The neglect goes back long before the George W. Bush administration.

The entire federal and industry approach to pipeline safety stands in stark contrast to the way government and industry deal with airline safety issues, where the focus is on preventing crashes through the use of engineering, analysis and data collection. Rick Kessler, a pipeline engineer who worked on pipeline issues as a Capitol Hill staffer, now serves as a volunteer vice president of the Pipeline Safety Trust. How bad is the current system? Kessler told me that if the Federal Aviation Administration operated on the same rules as pipeline safety regulators, "I wouldn't get on a plane."

Inspecting pipelines for corrosion, faulty welds and damage from earth movements, both natural and by excavators, is one of the best ways to reduce the chance of rupture. Yet buried in the fine print are government rules that discourage shutting down pipelines to inspect, maintain or replace them before they fail, in effect shifting the risks of pipeline disasters from pipeline owners on to unwitting Americans.

Instead of replacing corroded pipelines, the owners just *de-rate* them. "De-rating" means reducing the maximum pressure allowed from, say, 1,500 pounds per square inch to 1,200 pounds. As corrosion eats through more of a pipeline's steel wall, the pressure maximum may be reduced again and again based on calculations estimating the rate of corrosion. In theory, if the engineers guess right about the rate of corrosion, the pipeline will keep operating at lower and lower pressures until it is no longer profitable and will then be replaced or abandoned. In the meantime, as if engaged in some sort of life-or-death power game, they bet on the balance of corrosion and pressure.

Water and other liquids often contaminate natural-gas pipeline flows, despite industry efforts to dry out gas before it is sent through high-pressure pipelines. Liquids speed corrosion, especially in low-lying segments of the pipe, where the liquid tends to pool. The NTSB found that salts, sulfur and other contaminants had rusted the Carlsbad pipeline at a low-lying spot. The deaths of the twelve campers show that engineers estimating the speed at which corrosion weakens pipeline walls sometimes get it terribly wrong.

Gordon Allen Aaker Jr., a pipeline engineer in Kingwood, Texas, who consults on safety issues both to pipeline companies and those who sue them, sees de-rating as a dangerous policy that sends the wrong message to the pipeline industry. "Allowing producers to de-rate the pipeline does not give them any incentive to maintain the pipeline," he said. Why, Aaker asked, would companies shut down a pipeline (and the flow of revenue) to make repairs "when they can just de-rate it?"

The safety factors built into pipelines are slim, according to Theo Theofanous, a professor of civil and chemical engineering at the University of California at Santa Barbara and director of its Center for Risk Studies and Safety. Theofanous served on a National Academy of Engineering committee that wrote a 144-page report in 2004 that focused on the risks of development coming to rural areas with aging high-pressure pipelines. Its recommendations were softened at the insistence of industry representatives, the professor said, muddling some issues and avoiding the exploration of others, including improving technology to detect corrosion and other damage.

Theophanous said the rules on corrosion and other damage to pipeline walls are not nearly stringent enough and allow unnecessary risks. Nor is enough margin of safety built into their design.

"[A] safety factor of two not uncommon in situations involving high pressures, even if the consequences of failure are modest," Theofanous said. A factor of two means that the pipeline must be twice as strong as the minimum needed to contain its maximum pressure. Yet many high-pressure pipelines are built with a safety factor of just 1.4, meaning they have only 40 percent more strength designed into them than is necessary, not twice as much strength as needed. Federal pipeline safety regulators routinely allow these safety margins to be weakened as corrosion eats into pipeline walls and pipelines are operated at lower pressures.

"Safety factors are employed to provide a margin of safety against unexpected causes," Theofanous said. "It is not good engineering practice to use them against known deterioration of the structure." Doing so means that after the pipeline has deteriorated, the safety factor will be even slimmer.

The federal officials whose responsibility is to keep us safe from pipeline explosions hold a very different view. They have been granting "special permits" for segments of high-pressure pipelines that are supposed to be inspected under the 2002 law. While the federal Department of Transportation calls them "special permits," that is just another euphemism for inspection-rule waivers.

In reading some of these waivers, I noticed that they seemed not to say what was presumably intended. Five safety waivers were issued to Empire Pipeline LLC, a subsidiary of National Fuel Gas in suburban Buffalo, New York, for nearly two miles of pipelines because of the difficulty involved in inspecting the pipes, which vary in diameter. As written, the permits set limits: Empire Pipeline may pump gas through when corrosion has eaten through 72 percent of the pipeline wall not covered by the safety waiver and, where the safety waiver is in effect, 80 percent along segments. After confirming with Professor Theofanous and others that the permit was actually intended to say the reverse—requiring repairs at 28 percent corrosion for the main areas and 20 percent for the waivered areas—I notified both Empire's president, Ronald Kraemer, and Secretary of Transportation Ray LaHood's office.

Kraemer told me that he did not understand. After I explained the error, Kraemer did not follow up; nor did LaHood's office. If the Empire pipeline ever blows up, what is reported here will almost certainly become a full-employment act for litigators, thanks to the studied inaction of both the company and the government when notified of this potentially lethal mistake.

PEERING INTO THE PIPES

The Empire pipeline segments with waivers aren't easy to find; although the pipeline safety administration that issues these permits discloses their location, the language is, at best, cryptic. Here is a typical description, for a third of a mile segment of the Empire State Pipeline in Western New York, that was given a safety waiver:

> Special Permit Segment 2—24-inch Empire State Pipeline mainline, approximately 1,715 feet in length, located in Monroe County, NY from Survey Station 4018 + 73 to Survey Station 4035 + 88; (MP 76.09 to MP 76.42)

Just where is this one-third-mile-long pipeline? Unless you know the proprietary mile marking system that the pipeline company uses, you cannot tell. Does it run through a wheat farm or along Church Street? Past a wooded lot or a hospital? If you request map coordinates, street intersections or street addresses at the start and end of the section, neither Empire nor Transportation Secretary LaHood's office nor his agency's Pipeline and Hazardous Materials Safety Administration will tell you.

The reason for this secrecy, LaHood spokeswoman Maureen Knightly told me, is official concern that terrorists might blow up the pipeline segments. Knightly was subsequently incensed when, in reporting this for the Web site remappingdebate.org, I paraphrased her words and cited Al Qaeda by name. "I never said 'Al Qaeda,'" an angry Knightly said, missing the point. With easily identifiable pipelines in places like Manhattan, media-savvy zealots who want to scare us into thinking their worldview is superior aren't likely to target a section of pipeline in the Finger Lakes region of New York. But this misguided secrecy on the part of federal pipeline safety regulators does mean that people along the Empire Pipeline route are ignorant of the fact that they are living, shopping, playing and going to schools near pipelines that have been given inspection waivers and are still allowed to operate when pipeline walls may be 80 percent corroded.

Although the means to inspect inside pipelines exist, the principal method of detecting gas leaks is to fly overhead and look for desiccated grass and trees (leaking natural gas kills plant life at the roots). That may be adequate for slow leaks, but not sudden ruptures in which tearing metal can create sparks.

Internal inspections are done using in-line inspection tools. So-called "pigs" employ lasers and magnets to identify corrosion, weak welds and other signs of wear and damage. Not only had a pig never inspected the Carlsbad pipeline, the San Bruno pipeline also went more than a half century with no internal inspection. Pacific Gas & Electric explained that was because the pipeline varied in diameter, preventing use of a pig.

San Bruno Mayor Ruane told me that PG&E's rationale troubles him. "We put a man on the moon decades ago and we can't build a pipeline pig that can measure pipelines of varying size?"

Professor Theofanous said the problem could have been solved long ago. "Yes, there are engineering problems, but the reason they have not been solved is a failure of will, not skill," he said. He explained that a prototype pig capable of moving through a pipeline of changing size is being tested, but is not yet in field use.

Even when pigs are used to check inside a pipeline, government rules allow inspections to be conducted as infrequently as once every seven years. Seven years is too long in the view of Theofanous and some other experts. The Transportation Department's Pipeline and Hazardous Materials Safety Administration agrees, at least in some of the safety waivers it grants. Some of them require external inspections every four years.

There are other ways to detect leaks, one of which could be a boon to consumers. The pipeline industry's rules allow 5 percent of natural gas to go missing between the wellhead and the consumer, who gets charged for the full 100 percent. In Texas the rules are so loose that up to 30 percent of gas can just vanish. The industry says these loose measurements are needed because of shortcomings in gas meters. While that may have been true at one time, it isn't with modern technology that can detect pinprick leaks.

In the Carlsbad disaster, the NTSB made other troubling findings. Prior to the explosion, the federal Office of Pipeline Safety found no flaw in El Paso Natural Gas training and procedures for dealing with corrosion; after the blast, the pipeline safety office determined that corrosion control was "not carried out by, or under the direction of, a person qualified in pipeline corrosion control methods. This is because [El Paso Natural Gas's] corrosion personnel have not received the informal or formal training necessary to perform the tasks required to implement the corrosion control procedures." So the regulators were clueless and the company lackadaisical. Neither suggests a vigorous focus on safety, much less basic competence.

That any pipeline inspections are required in our nation is only because of the insistence of people in Bellingham, including the parents of the three youths, who couldn't believe it when they discovered that no law required pipeline inspections. The local federal prosecutor, incensed over what he considered the pipeline company's blasé attitude, saw to it that the $4 million penalty paid by the pipeline company was used to create the Pipeline Safety Trust (pstrust.org). The trust lobbied for the

Pipeline Safety Improvement Act of 2002, which covers large-bore lines that convey fuels, but not the small-bore transmission lines that distribute natural gas to homes and offices.

Under the 2002 law, only 44 percent of liquid fuel pipelines and just 7 percent of natural gas pipelines are subject to safety inspections. "We thought it was a good start, but that it was just a start, and the safety regulations would be expanded and increased over time. We are still trying to achieve that goal," said Weimer, executive director of Pipeline Safety Trust.

The 2002 law requires that residents be told if they live near a transmission pipeline, but the notices I inspected were nothing more than inserts in utility bills, which most people toss out unread. Aside from boilerplate copy advising anyone with a backhoe to call 811 to locate pipelines before digging, the supposed warning notices read more like promotional brochures for pipeline safety.

The actual purpose of the pamphlets—to alert people who live near a high-pressure pipeline of its presence—typically gets a single paragraph deep in the pamphlet using that ill-defined term mentioned earlier, "high consequence area." Words like *death*, *blast* and *burn* do not appear, nor does any advice on what to do in case of explosion. None of the brochures I reviewed mentioned the size, age, condition or location of any pipeline.

Even when schoolchildren are at risk, the pipeline industry and the government put obfuscation ahead of safety warnings. One colorful six-page pamphlet sent to schools by the pipeline industry states on its fifth page that "you are receiving this information because pipeline infrastructure is located near schools or facilities in your district." There is no useful information in the brochure about where pipelines are located, what precautions or plans are appropriate, or anything else that might help school officials or parents. This utterly useless document comes from the Pipeline Association for Public Awareness, an industry group, with official approval from the federal Office of Pipeline Safety and its Pipeline and Hazardous Materials Safety Administration.

The federal government has done no studies or surveys or convened any focus groups to see if these pamphlets are effective. But the proof that they do not work is this: Mayor Ruane said San Bruno fire and police officials did not even know of the existence of the pipeline that exploded in 2010. The mayor said a second pipeline came to the city's attention only because of plans to build a structure—a tot lot, a park for small children—directly atop that pipeline.

When the next pipeline disaster occurs, how well prepared will pipeline companies be? Paul Blackburn ran Plains Justice, a public interest law firm that was in Vermillion, South Dakota, on the border with Nebraska. Earlier in his career Blackburn worked as an energy regulatory lawyer in Washington. Because he is engaged in several public interest actions aimed at dealing with damage from pipeline ruptures and efforts to make a proposed new pipeline from Canada into the United States safer, he filed Freedom of Information Act requests for pipeline company safety planning.

"I expected detailed emergency response and evacuation plans, including emergency contact numbers and an assessment of firefighting resources," Blackburn said. Instead, "I found there was almost nothing in the file. It was pathetic." Blackburn said the files show that "the government basically rubber stamps industry documents" with little to no evidence that it questioned, much less challenged, anything the companies proposed.

Utility workers across the country have told me that customers are being put at risk by cost-cutting that they say began with the deregulation of gas distribution. "All the gas utility companies are basically playing the odds," said Charlie D. Rittenhouse, president of the Utility Workers Union of America, Local 98 in West Virginia. "They've cut the workforces and cut the workforces and cut the workforces while at the same time keeping the CEOs' and top executives' wages going up and up and up. A major concern for our group and many other groups we deal with is that there's not enough people there to do the work."

Rittenhouse and others say their greatest concern is with the rebuilding of compressor stations serving pipelines laid three or more decades ago. "The compressor stations have been refitted to handle higher pressure and higher volumes of gas," Rittenhouse said, "so you would think that means more and more careful supervision, but just the opposite . . . has happened. Now in compressor stations, fewer people are utilized and more reliance is put on computers. Fortunately we have not had a major disaster at a large compressor station for some time, but when we do, I believe it will make the pipeline explosions look like small fireworks."

"Fact is, pipeline safety and regulation for compressor-station manning has not kept up with the times; the companies are pretty well allowed to handle the manning any way they see fit," he said.

Rittenhouse recalled what a federal Occupational Safety and Health Administration official once told a gathering of union members concerned about the risk of a compressor blowing up. "Once there is a major disaster," the OSHA official said, "then there will be all kinds of regulations regarding compressor stations. Until then, as the companies tell us, we should not worry because it hasn't happened yet."

Prior to protests from parents and the prosecutor that followed the Bellingham disaster, the federal Office of Pipeline Safety was so badly run that it did not even have maps locating pipelines. In 2006, four years after the very limited safety inspection bill became law, the *Houston Chronicle* showed that some pipelines did not even appear on official maps for East Texas and Louisiana. Other pipelines noted on the map were far from their actual locations.

The bottom line is this: America's 2.4-million-mile network of pipelines is aging and corroding. About 300,000 of these pipeline miles are high-pressure natural-gas transmission lines like the ones that blew up in New Mexico and California. Another 200,000 miles of pipelines move diesel, jet fuel and gasoline, like the one that ruptured in Bellingham. While experience so far has been that pipeline explosions killing more than one or two people are rare, past performance is no indicator of future outcomes.

There's a final irony. The pipeline monopolies whose prices are regulated by the government get to include in their rates the cost of insurance to pay for losses from pipeline disasters. As pipelines age and as more people live near pipelines, the risk of disaster increases—and so does the cost of insurance. But because pipelines are monopolies, they get to add the higher insurance costs to the rates they charge. So you get to pay more even as you are put in greater danger.

Draining Pockets

What we did not know then, but realized later, was that they planned to double our water rates about every three years.

—Connie Barr, Felton, California

11. **Connie Barr figured** three dozen people might come to the Felton firehouse in 2002 to learn about the stealthy takeover of their water supply by a giant German corporation. When a hard rain started falling, Barr expected half the seats to go empty.

Instead, the room quickly overflowed with people. So many came that the fire trucks had to be moved into the street, allowing an audience of 120 people to crowd into the empty bays. Several dozen latecomers stood outside, intent on hearing even as the cold night rain pelted them.

The story of that night, and what happened over the next four years in Felton, may well be repeated in your town. Water companies are doing their best to win ownership or control of reliable, low-cost municipal and community water systems. They know that, over time, they can make big profits by jacking up water rates.

We tend to take water for granted. It flows from the tap instantly, pure enough to drink and cheap enough to water our lawns. About 275 million Americans get their water from piped systems; some 240 million of those are served by nonprofit operations. Water provided by cities and other nonprofit systems typically costs less than half a penny per gallon. Even in Atlanta, which has perhaps the costliest municipal water in America, the price runs only about a penny a gallon.

Corporate water costs more. A 2006 study for the American Water Works Association (AWWA) found that, in New York State, the six largest water companies charge 25 percent higher rates than nearby municipal systems. The association represents mostly municipal water systems and the companies that sell them equipment and services.

In Wisconsin, corporate water costs on average 49 percent more than municipal water, according to Wisconsin Public Utility Commission data.

In California, where about 140 corporate water suppliers serve 6 million people (a sixth of the state population), corporate water, according to a 2007 study by the national consulting firm Black and Veatch, cost on average 20 percent more than public water. Three years later, American Water filed to raise rates in seven California systems it operates by 31 percent, at a time when wages were flat to falling and inflation the lowest in living memory.

How high can it go? In the lettuce-growing town of Chualar, an hour's drive from Felton in neighboring Monterey County, some people saw their water bills jump 500 percent after American Water bought their system in 2002.

GOING PRIVATE

Monopolists protect their exclusive franchises with targeted campaign contributions, seeking to acquire the allegiance of elected officials, who then put in place rules that mean ever higher prices for water. But that is not all. These monopolists can get laws changed to make it harder to buy them out (that would let people get water at lower prices).

Typically, these monopolists don't talk about the profits they plan to make when they seek to acquire publicly owned water systems. They talk about easing tax burdens, staying mum about rate hikes. Sometimes they appeal to the beleaguered taxpayer, proffering a big cash payment. To local governments facing a budget squeeze, that big cash payment looks like a great deal. But compared to the stream of costs that will follow, it is probably a mirage. The corporation will recover that upfront payment through higher rates; it's no gift to the community, but an advance that must be paid back—along with what studies show is typically an 11 percent profit.

Corporate owners employ more expensive executives than municipal water systems, adding to the pressure to hike water rates. The corporation pays dividends to its shareholders, unlike municipal systems that can return any surplus to the community through lower rates or by reducing local tax burdens. If a holding company sits atop the water utility, which is the case with all of the big operators, the corporate income taxes embedded in water rates may never make their way to government. And the holding company may borrow most of its capital, making its real rate of return to shareholders double or triple the officially authorized rate of return.

Increasing the cost of all the piped water Americans use by just a penny a gallon taps an extra $96 billion from consumer pockets per year. That penny would increase the total price that households would pay for piped water from about a billion dollars a week to nearly three billion.

In Felton, California, people fought to avoid having their pockets drained by a distant water corporation and to regain control of a water system that, more than a century earlier, the town fathers built as a perpetual benefit for the community.

The Feltonians succeeded, despite a 1992 law the state legislature passed at the behest of corporate utilities to insulate the companies from municipal takeovers. Before 1992, California law assumed that public takeovers of water utilities were in the public interest; but the new law, sponsored by an association of corporate water providers, required that communities trying to buy out a corporate utility prove the action was a necessity.

That 1992 law was just one brick in a nationwide wall that monopoly corporations are building with their campaign contributions. What the people of Felton and some other California towns did to fight back provides a template for stopping price-gouging monopolists and their allies in government.

In addition to their corporate opponents, the people of Felton faced open hostility from the California Public Utilities Commission. In the sixties and seventies, corporate utilities regarded CPUC as the toughest regulator of its kind in the nation, a guardian of public interests that wrought many reforms, including addressing phantom taxes related to water billing. By the dawn of the new millennium, however, the good reputation of the commission had deteriorated.

After passage of the 1978 property tax limit known as Proposition 13, political power in California concentrated in Sacramento as taxing power and responsibility shifted to the state from elected county and municipal officials. By the time the Felton fight began, two of the five utility commissioners came from utilities, and staff members of a third commissioner openly mocked consumers for challenging what utility companies wanted. Hardly anyone knew this, however, because only one major newspaper, the *San Francisco Chronicle*, retained a journalist who frequently covered utility issues.

Yet the prospect of costly water in Felton ignited unexpected interest. Felton is an idyllic hamlet, with a covered wooden bridge and a small-gauge steam railroad attracting tourists and picnickers. The business district parallels the San Lorenzo River, which flows beneath steeply raked mountainsides studded with giant redwood trees that drink from the morning fog. Nestled among the redwoods are a few hundred cottages and some sprawling modern homes that overlook a two-lane road that wends through the coastal mountains until the asphalt, along with the river, flows into the seaside resort of Santa Cruz, six miles away.

Felton is home to some five thousand people, an amalgam of Silicon Valley commuters, entrepreneurs, artists and small-business owners like Connie Barr. She arrived as a widow escaping crowded Southern California and kept busy for a decade running a children's clothing shop. I know Felton well. For a year, starting in 1967, as a teenager I earned the minimum wage reporting for the weekly *Valley Press*. Later six of my children attended school there.

The place began as a logging town after the Civil War and supplied many of the materials used to rebuild San Francisco after the 1906 earthquake. In the 1880s, the townspeople had created a water company to "hold, in trust, the water works of Felton, for the use and benefit of that village forever."

Over the years, Felton's population dwindled, along with the biggest redwoods, until in 1923 the water company was sold to a developer. He kept water prices low, as did the local owners who followed. In 1961 Citizens Utilities, a Connecticut operator of water systems, paid about $1,785 per customer in 2012 dollars for the Felton water system, but the price was in line with its value and did not require raising rates.

This long history of good service and low water prices evaporated in 2002 when American Water Works' CalAm (California American Water) subsidiary bought a number of little California water utilities from Citizens Utilities, including Felton's. American Water Works soon became one of more than eight hundred subsidiaries of the German company Rheinisch-Westfälisches Elektrizitätswerk Aktiengesellschaft (the name means North Rhine-Westphalia electric power plant joint stock company).

RWE is one of the largest publicly traded companies in Germany, a global leader in turning water from a public-service commodity into a private-profit center. At the time it acquired Felton's little water utility, RWE had 2.6 million water customers just in North America, and its executives boasted of their plans to wring huge profits from water systems. In the case of Felton, however, they faced unusual opposition.

Under California law, when a utility is sold, customers and local government officials must be given notice. That gives them a chance to object to the buyer and raise questions if the price implies future rate hikes. No one in Felton remembers getting notice. Connie Barr learned of the sale as president of the Felton Business Association, when Jeff Almquist told her. He was the Santa Cruz County supervisor whose district included Felton. Almquist told her that the notice of sale to American Water Works had, apparently, been sent to the wrong county office. By the time it reached Almquist, it was too late to challenge the sale or the price.

Barr and others describe the letter as misdirected accidently on purpose, but what alarmed Almquist was the high price American Water paid. It was 67 percent more than the value of the Felton water system assets. He guessed that a price so much above book value meant the new owners would seek a big rate hike. His hunch was right, as the rates promptly went up a whopping 74 percent. The new German owners also signaled their intent to seek annual rate increases.

"What we did not know then, but realized later, was that they planned to double our water rates about every three years," Barr recalled.

Hundreds of letters were sent to the Public Utilities Commission, and 1,200 people signed a petition asking that the neighboring San Lorenzo Valley Water District take over the Felton water works. Supervisor Almquist and the newly formed Friends of Local Water, or Felton FLOW, wrote to oppose the rate hike.

The Public Utilities Commission agreed to hold three public hearings in Felton. Several hundred people jammed the community center, its windows opened so those standing outside could hear the hours of complaints lodged with an administrative law judge. Connie Barr, like everyone else, thought the commissioners were giving their views due consideration. They thought wrong.

"After one of the meetings I was in the hall talking to a couple of the girls who worked for the judge," Barr recalled. "I said this was pretty dramatic testimony about poor quality water and lack of repairs and the company asking for big rate increases." Then Barr wondered aloud how long it would be before the results of the meeting would be known.

"One of the judge's girls just looked at me," Barr remembers.

"They don't have to do anything," the woman told Barr. "This is not that kind of process. This is the ability for people to come and speak. It goes nowhere."

The administrative law judge did cite the public statements in his report, but nothing in his decision suggests that those statements resulted in a lower rate hike than the one he granted. Meanwhile, American Water Works, which had bought itself back from RWE, was busy trying to sabotage Felton FLOW. It got a bill introduced in Sacramento to make it harder to use government's power of eminent domain to force a buyout. American Water Works sent out two flyers asserting that people in another California town, Montara, had been unhappy after winning control of their water system. The flyers omitted mention of the community celebration held a year after the takeover and the fact that all of the Montara water board members won reelection. There were other reported shenanigans by the company: Mark Stone, then a Santa Cruz County supervisor, said that an American Water Works official told him that if he did not back off and support their continued ownership of the Felton system, they would make sure he lost his reelection campaign in 2004. The company supported a lawsuit brought against the Felton FLOW organizers. In neighboring Monterey County the company tried to get a law passed exempting it from any local regulation. When a Felton resident whose water supply suddenly stopped took photographs of an American Water Works crew, the company called the sheriff. And the company gave an antitax group money to produce another flyer, one opposing the takeover by showing hundred-dollar bills burning. The flyer made no mention of the fact that water rates had more than doubled in three years and that more increases were pending.

Then, in 2005, a measure to raise taxes and sell bonds to buy out American Water finally got onto the ballot. It passed with 74.2 percent of the vote. American Water works was subsequently bought out for $13 million, of which about $11 million was cash.

Was the price fair? Was it, as utility law requires, "just and reasonable"? American Water bought several small water systems at about the same time, its reports to shareholders show. The company paid on average $1,540 per customer. At $13 million, Felton residents paid almost $10,000 per customer to be free of American Water, more than six times what American Water Works paid others to acquire their systems.

"Buying out the water company was a huge victory, even though we got robbed blind," said Jim Mosher, a veteran lawyer who was the volunteer legal coordinator for FLOW. "Even when you add the higher property taxes to pay off the bonds and the water bills we now pay, people still save money every month. Had the company won we would be paying the huge future water rate increases the water company was seeking and be much worse off. When the bonds are paid off after thirty years, this will be a really great deal."

For its part, American Water Works says the price it got for the Felton system was only half what it deserved. Comparing what the company got for the Felton system to what it paid for small water systems elsewhere is basically nonsense, Kevin Tilden of American Water Works told me. "Each water system is unique," he said. A difference such as location or age of the system "makes an apples-to-apples comparison nearly impossible."

Tilden has a point. A water system with new pipes and pumps and other gear is worth a lot more than one that has been run down, leaks and needs upgrades.

So what shape was the Felton water system in? "The system was one step short of awful," said James Mueller, the general manager of the municipal water system that serves the rest of the San Lorenzo Valley and who is in charge of upgrading and modernizing the system that American Water let fall apart. After the takeover, he says, "the company pretty much stopped maintenance." That means the $10,000 per customer buyout price was actually higher as the system had to be rebuilt and upgraded after years of corporate neglect. (See table on page 126.)

A WIN FOR AMERICAN WATER

While people in Felton won their fight, some New Jersey customers of American Water were not so fortunate. American Water's New Jersey subsidiary remains the dominant supplier of water in the Garden State with 2.5 million customers in thirty-eight towns. It also sells water wholesale to ten municipal water systems.

The company reported that the typical New Jersey residential customer paid $38.21 per month in 2007. It got a 12.5 percent increase that year and 15.2 percent the next and in 2010 was seeking a further 14 percent increase. Add it all up, and the average customer wrote a monthly check for $56.44. That's a nearly 48 percent increase in three years when inflation ran just 5.3 per cent.

Raising monopoly water prices nine times faster than inflation is a surefire way to make company executives and shareholders wealthier while damaging local economies. The increase in water rates alone means that each New Jersey community of 100,000 people has $8 million less money to spend each year.

Despite these enormous rate increases, all approved by the New Jersey Board of Public Utilities, American Water in 2010 wanted to cut benefits to its workers. The company said it just could not afford them. It demanded that the workers pay 52 percent more in health insurance premiums for their families. The American Water workers in New Jersey earned an average wage of $24 an hour, according to the Utility Workers Union of America, which represents many of them. That's about $48,000 per year.

Customers of American Water Works, who have no choice but to pay its rapidly escalating prices, have helped it produce stellar performance for investors even as it cuts back on investments in its water systems. The company reported that the volume of water it sold in 2010 increased only 2.4 percent over 2009, while operating profits soared to more than four times the 2009 operating profit. Customers can expect even bigger and faster rate hikes because, as the company disclosed in the fine print of its annual Form 10-K statement, management has "continued its focus" on getting rate increases approved faster.

Taxes are another story. American Water paid just 6 percent of its profits in 2009 taxes, far below the 35 percent tax rate set by Congress. In 2010, when profits quadrupled, it paid nothing. Instead the company got back $30 million from the government, making its real tax rate negative 4 percent.

The company's statements to investors show it intends to squeeze customers for more and more money. It told investors in its 2011 annual disclosure statement that "water and wastewater rates in the United States are among the lowest rates in developed countries; and for most U.S. consumers, water and wastewater bills make up a relatively small percentage of household expenditures compared to other utility services."

Another pattern is easy to discern. American Water lets its systems run down, then demands huge rate increases to fix them up, not unlike the problem Pacific Gas & Electric customers will face because the company is replacing power poles that last fifty years on a 700-year cycle. Despite rate hikes approved or being sought everywhere, American Water sharply cut spending in 2009 and 2010 to improve its water systems. It also told shareholders that in 2011 investments to maintain and improve the systems would be "at the lower end" of its budget.

The rates customers paid American Water Works bought them more than $1 billion of capital improvements in 2008; but in 2010, when rates were much higher, this spending fell 24 percent to $766 million.

As at corporate-owned electric, natural gas, telephone and cable systems, American Water's captive customers can expect more of the same—higher rates, minimal spending to improve the system, and a decrease in the compensation of its rank-and-file workers.

All this adds up to a very good deal for the company and its owners, but what about the customers? Fortunately, most water in America is still distributed by nonprofit systems administered by cities, counties, special water districts or cooperatives. These systems do not pay multimillion-dollar salaries to their executives and do not operate corporate jets that the executives can use to fly off to play golf. But Wall Street is busy promoting private takeovers of municipal water systems that give governments a one-time slug of cash. Politicians like Governor Mitch Daniels of Indiana promote these sales as a way to ease taxpayer burdens. But the relief is illusory. The cash infusions the government gets must be paid back through higher rates, while commonwealth property is transferred to private hands.

Local governments that are smart about their water systems not only

FELTON WATER BUYOUT SAVES MONEY		
CORPORATE-SUPPLIED WATER, ANNUAL PRICE AFTER RATE HIKES		$2,017.76
COMMUNITY-OWNED WATER SYSTEM BILL	$484.50	
TAX INCREASE TO BUY OUT AMERICAN WATER WORKS*	$535.00	
TOTAL COST OF COMMUNITY-OWNED WATER SYSTEM		$1,019.50
SAVINGS PER YEAR		($998.26)
* Bonds paid off after 30 years		

maintain them, they charge prices high enough to cover part of the city budget, a surplus that reduces the need to raise money through sales taxes, property taxes and fees.

People tend to use more water as their incomes grow; this behavior is mildly in accord with the ancient principle that the greater one's economic gain, the greater his burden to sustain the civilization that made his gains possible. It's a better model than the monopoly.

How We Beat the Garbage Gougers and Their Stinking High Prices

I was searching for my perfect Donna Reed neighborhood.
Sidewalks, streetlights, family life. Pleasantville.
—**Melinda Goldberg, Brighton, New York**

12. **Your monthly bill** to have your garbage hauled away has been rising faster than inflation. Even during the Great Recession, when we had less money to spend and less trash, prices kept rising. And they'll continue rising if executives of the big garbage companies have their way.

The explanation has nothing to do with growing demand or even a shortage of landfills. Indeed, some landfills are actually shrinking—and sinking; that's what happens when you spray water onto them and let bacteria silently dine on the buried trash. But your trash-hauling bills are on the rise because of a long-term strategy by the biggest garbage haulers to reduce competition, thereby handcuffing the invisible hand of Adam Smith's competitive marketplace. In fact, executives of the two largest garbage companies, Waste Management and Republic Services, have touted their shares to Wall Street analysts as lucrative investments *because*, they boast, they have defeated the power of the market to hold down the prices customers pay.

Republic Services says it has about 18 percent of trash-hauling revenues. Waste Management has 26 percent. Two companies controlling 44 percent of a $47 billion industry describes not competition, but oligopoly. Competition is good for consumers and the economy overall as it promotes efficiency, tends to hold down prices and encourages innovation. Oligopoly is good for owners because it helps them escape the rigors of market competition so they can jack up prices, earn bigger profits than a competitive market allows and expend less effort managing their assets.

Later in this chapter, we'll look in more detail at the stranglehold these two companies have on their industry. First, though, some good news: you can fight the garbage gougers and win. The path to lower prices may surprise you: paying higher taxes lowers the cost of garbage collection. In my neighborhood in upstate New York we agreed in 2006 to raise our property taxes. The next year we started saving money and since then the savings have grown. Every extra dollar of tax I paid in 2011 meant $1.80 more in my pocket.

The truth behind such tax calculations has come under such vicious attack for the last three decades that many Americans have a blind spot, refusing to consider how expedient this strategy can be in cutting costs and maximizing services.

TRASH TALKING TAXES

At one time, a wide cross section of Americans understood that taxes could save money and help grow the economy. The principle has been largely forgotten since the modern antitax movement got going with the 1978 passage of Proposition 13, the ballot initiative that froze basic California property taxes at 1 percent of a property's value.

According to the now dominant narrative, lower taxes are the only path to prosperity. Americans have been told for more than three decades that higher taxes equal less money to spend, that lower taxes equal more. As President George W. Bush liked to say about his tax cuts, "With my policies, you'll keep more of your money in your pocket."

That higher taxes are inherently bad has become the default rhetoric of politicians from both parties, an unassailable truth trumpeted by network and cable television news personalities. The best newspapers and opinion magazines implicitly embrace the belief that higher taxes must always cost individuals more. The result is that almost everyone accepts that the only way to keep more of their money is to cut taxes.

That narrative is so utterly false one might call it economic garbage. The people spewing it both in Congress and on the political trail, as well as in the news media, are largely people with less understanding of the economics of taxation than vote-getting savvy. So let's take a fresh look.

Higher taxes can make you richer or they can make you poorer; ditto for lower taxes. What matters in both cases are three factors:

- What is taxed.
- How the tax is applied.
- What the tax money is spent on.

The story from my neighborhood about taking out the trash illustrates how a well-designed tax can save you money.

I live on Council Rock Avenue in the Town of Brighton, five blocks outside of the city limits of Rochester, New York, the home of Kodak and, back in the 1820s, the town whose rapid growth made it the place first described as a "boomtown."

The asphalt of Council Rock Avenue runs for two long, wide blocks lined with leafy trees; it is named for a big pockmarked boulder at one end. The boulder was deposited by the last of several dozen mile-thick glaciers that covered the area in eons past. Our rock is one of several "council rocks" where, long before the Europeans came to the New World, delegates to the first known democracy met. According to some of the Haudenosaunee people, better known as the Iroquois Indians, who occupied much of what is now western and northern New York state, their democracy began three thousand years ago—five centuries before the democracy of ancient Athens. Because of a solar eclipse told of in Iroquois history, we know for sure that their democracy existed on August 31, 1142, long before self-governance in Europe.

For today's Council Rock Avenue residents—mostly doctors, lawyers, executives, and other professionals—the higher taxes that save them money started after Melinda Goldberg bought her dream home there in 2005. Rochester is one of the lowest-cost housing markets in America. Spacious homes here sell for about a tenth of what an identical property costs in the fancy communities of the Boston-Washington corridor or urban West Coast. While much of America is house poor, Rochesterians tend to be house rich because a smaller share of their money goes to buying shelter.

Goldberg chose a sturdy blue-gray, center-entrance colonial built decades ago on a large landscaped lot with graceful shade trees. It came with a bathroom for each of the five bedrooms and a home office big enough for her husband, Ron Turk, who sells the cab portion of tractor-trailer rigs.

"I was searching for my perfect Donna Reed neighborhood," Melinda

Goldberg recalled. "Sidewalks, streetlights, family life. Pleasantville." But on their very first morning in their dream home, the couple was awakened by a diesel engine revving and metal clanging as a garbage truck mashed a neighbor's trash.

In the years after a century-old wheat field became Council Rock Avenue in 1926, families hired their own trash haulers. There were white trucks and green trucks, red ones, even lilac ones named for the lilac gardens in a city park designed by Frederick Law Olmsted. Every weekday was trash day for someone. Trash cans and recycling bins lined the curbs, along with bundles of flattened cardboard boxes and the occasional old chair or worn-out appliance. In spring and summer, the trash detracted from the colorful flowerbeds and neatly trimmed hedges; in winter trash piles marred the white mantle of fresh snow.

Goldberg could not stand it. "The early morning clanging noise in my perfect neighborhood that awakened me five days a week, along with the ugly aesthetics of the trash cans that lined our otherwise beautiful street, led me to make a few phone calls." She found out that the neighborhood could create a taxing district to finance trash collection on a single day of each week. When she met another resident, Tess McFarland-Porter, and found common cause in the noisy, smelly garbage trucks, they decided to act.

"I had lived in four other houses in town and all had refuse districts," Goldberg said. "So I thought we would benefit from creating one. We talked to people and explained the benefits. Everyone was for it except two neighbors, who were just against paying any more taxes."

They recruited a third neighbor, retired judge Dick Rosenbloom, to notarize signatures on a petition to create the Council Rock Refuse District and, despite the minor opposition, the neighborhood dumped the individual market system of buying trash removal retail and replaced it with one harnessing the collective buying power of the tax system for common benefit. For trash companies, stopping at every house on a street meant more efficient use of labor and equipment. A company could charge less and profit more. In 2012 dollars I had been paying about $575 annually for trash collection. The winning bid for the new system came in so low that my trash-hauling cost for 2010 fell 62 percent to $221.

So much for the rhetoric that higher taxes are always and everywhere a bad idea. Those higher taxes mean nearly a buck a day more money in my pocket. The $221 more in taxes my wife and I pay means we are buying improved service and spending only thirty-eight cents for each dollar we used to spend privately.

The winning bidder, currently Waste Management, must be making enough money to justify this piece of business because the price we pay has been going down, dropping by 12 percent from 2009 to 2010—even as Waste Management and Republic Services were jacking up prices elsewhere in America.

Until 1998, Republicans outnumbered Democrats in my town. Yet counter to almost universal Republican rhetoric, we embraced higher taxes for decades when it saved money or made good sense for other reasons. Brighton taxes us for other services that many people in other towns pay more for because they buy them individually. The town picks up leaves, branches and other plant material left curbside and takes them to a municipal compost heap year-round. When the maples, oaks and birches turn yellow, orange and red and shed their leaves in the fall, the town quickly hauls them away. At year's end, it takes away dried-out Christmas trees, too. All of that is paid for with taxes. Those taxes save us money compared to the cost of having to haul away this detritus individually.

Our extra taxes also add convenience and safety beyond trash and yard waste removal. Goldberg and McFarland-Porter persuaded us to raise our taxes to start a second service, one particularly valuable to people who live in areas like the Finger Lakes region of New York where the snowfalls can be deep and the cold enduring. We created a sidewalk snowplowing district that, like trash hauling, is put out to bid.

"I wanted to live in a suburb that had sidewalks," explained Goldberg, who grew up a few miles away in a neighborhood of mid-century homes without sidewalks. When the first snow fell, she found she had to walk in the street because not everyone promptly shoveled their sidewalk. Some people never did. Goldberg thought to herself: "This is ridiculous, this is dangerous. There are cars in the street!"

Sidewalk snowplowing cost me $35 in 2009, thus creating a double bargain for my bank account and my health. The price under the winning bid rose to $37 in 2010. Still, for a bit more than $7 per snowy month, I escape the drudgery of hours spent shoveling or the expense of an infrequently used snowblower. I also avoid the increased risk of a heart attack that comes with shoveling snow. (For men in top condition, that risk doubles after shoveling snow; it increases a hundredfold for men who are out of shape, according to a 1993 study in the *New England Journal of Medicine*.)

Of course, raising taxes does not always lower costs or prevent heart attacks. Higher taxes can leave you worse off, depending on what is taxed and, more important, how the tax money is spent. But, as Melinda

Goldberg and Tess McFarland-Porter showed their neighbors, paying well-structured higher taxes can drive down costs.

THE OTHER KIND OF TAX SAVINGS

The demonstrable fact is this: taxes are not an absolute economic evil, despite their simplistic portrayal as such by the antitax movement. Television personalities and actual reporters who lazily accept antitax comments without checking them help spread this lie; politicians who only know economics through talking-point memos reinforce the distortion. The truth is that, often, taxes harness the buying power of the many to save money and improve society through joint purchases. We may take these benefits for granted, but examples of money actually saved by taxes abound.

Think about the cost of police we hire with our taxes. Now compare that with a society with few or no police, a society where citizens bear the individual expense and risk of guarding their property and their lives. Think of those third-world cities where people live behind high walls topped with broken glass or barbed wire, prisoners in their own homes. An extreme example is the wealthy in Rio de Janeiro: even cars with armor plating and guards in vehicles running in front and behind don't always provide enough protection, so the very rich travel by helicopter. America is not immune to urban dangers: there are neighborhoods where thousands of homes are equipped with heavy steel security contraptions and iron bars cover ground-floor windows. Such ugly security measures are a warning sign about what happens when society fails to create enough jobs to keep people busy and fed, fails to fund programs that keep teenagers occupied and fails to instill in children a conviction that study and hard work will be rewarded.

The urban dangers in America should remind us that taxes, per se, are no more dangerous than a gun in a locked box, no more helpful than a book sitting unread on the shelf. What matters is how we use our taxes. That is the crucial issue on which we need to focus: *what we spend our taxes on.*

We need to look at taxes both for what they buy for us *and* the price we pay when we let others reduce or escape taxes. Known to economists as *tax expenditures*, tax favors are tax breaks and subsidies that encourage various behaviors, ranging from home ownership to charitable giving to spending on renewable energy. Tax breaks for independent oil and gas companies, gifts of tax money to Walmart and Warren Buffett, tax exemptions for new factories and office buildings, and lowered tax rates for golf courses and amusement parks are tax favors for the few—but a form of taxation for the rest of us. They shift the burden of taxes from those who get these deals on to those who do not. In short, lower taxes can cost you more money.

The economic health of our society can suffer when we fail to properly fund basic services. Criminal and civil justice systems, for example, are central to a stable society. When we neglect to fund them properly and encourage people to turn to private vengeance instead of adjudication we add to our costs. We incur costs for more police and prosecutors and, especially, prisons, all of which consume tax dollars. And when we fail to achieve what our Constitution calls "domestic tranquility," we pay in a reduced quality of life, as well as a risk of the loss of innocent life from stray bullets, drive-by gang shootings, and the inability to walk safely outdoors in some neighborhoods after sunset.

Taxes spent to make sure children grow up to become productive adults who work for decent wages reduce the need for taxes to address social pathologies. This is by no means a new insight. Aristotle warned 2,500 years ago that extreme inequality produces strife and violence.

Consider another area where socializing a cost through taxes saves us money. Getting rid of your local fire department would reduce your taxes, but the loss of general fire protection would soon enough cost considerably more in both property and lives. Politicians and pundits who complain that taxes make us poorer seldom mention how successful socialized fire departments have been at saving everyone a lot of money.

One community in Tennessee learned a lesson about the wrong way to finance firefighting in September 2010. A teenager burning trash in a barrel was not attentive and the flames spread. First his grandfather's shed caught fire; pretty soon the house was ablaze. But the firefighters in nearby South Fulton, Tennessee, would not put out the blaze because homeowner Gene Cranick had not sent in his $675 annual fee. Cranick insisted he had always paid and that this nonpayment was just an error of omission, but the firefighters stood by and watched his house burn, killing a dog inside.

Once fires routinely burned down whole cities or blackened vast neighborhoods. People acting individually could do little to stop it. The fire that legend attributes to Mrs. O'Leary's cow knocking over a kerosene lantern on the evening of October 8, 1871, destroyed a big swath of Chicago and took about 250 lives. That same night a much greater fire several hundred miles to the north engulfed the Wisconsin town of Peshtigo, killing as many as 2,400 people.

During the nineteenth century, most fires were fought by volunteer brigades. Some scholars attribute the original organization and training of such brigades to the inventive Ben Franklin. Today in rural and suburban areas, where buildings tend to be just one or two stories high and not very large, a volunteer fire department may be sufficient. But not so in urban and industrial areas where construction is dense and buildings rise many stories. Without taxpayer-financed fire fighting, urban life would at times literally be consumed by infernos.

Imagine the costs today had we not socialized fire-suppression measures and mandated preventive ones. We taxpayers invested in training and studying how best to put out all sorts of fires in all sorts of buildings. We bought fire trucks and installed water mains. We invested in research that transformed building codes, making buildings less likely to catch fire and slower to burn. Some of those codes imposed private expenses, such as requiring sprinklers in large buildings, more costly construction materials or an end to central staircases that acted as chimneys when a ground-floor fire broke out, spreading flames quickly. Those regulations can be seen as a form of tax because the spending is mandated for those putting up structures. But the savings in lives, in property and in heartache is a huge social dividend made possible by taxes and well-designed government regulation.

How about schools? Parks? National defense? Bridges across mighty rivers and tunnels beneath bays?

Taxes are also a key reason why people are less likely to die in accidents than they were a century ago. The rate of death from accidents today is less than half what it was in 1902, despite the remarkable mobility that characterizes our lives. Exclude automobiles, and the accidental death rate in our time is about a third of what it was a century ago. Back then a greater share of the population worked in factories and on farms. That meant more people used equipment that could crush hands or whole bodies, relied on unsafe wiring that caused electrocutions, and were forced to work using dangerous construction and mining techniques. That accidental death toll has been slashed because we spent tax money on safety rules and regulations and on research and development for safer manufacturing, construction and mining techniques.

The idea of requiring employers to invest in safety equipment was denounced a century ago as morally and politically wrong, just as it is today. Business owners said the government had no role in deciding what equipment they bought or how they used it. But as unions, progressive politicians and engineers who believed in safety worked on these issues, laws were enacted to address worker safety. In time both accidents and deaths declined.

The 1911 Triangle Shirtwaist Company factory fire in New York City helped advance the idea that worker safety was a problem to be addressed through taxes. Just before closing time one Saturday afternoon, fire spread through the top three floors of a Manhattan building where immigrant women labored at sewing machines in a sweatshop. The workers had been locked in to make sure none slipped away early. When the fire broke out, some women jumped to their deaths rather than wait for the flames. In all, 146 workers died; the photographs of their bodies laid out on the sidewalk provoked public outrage. The workers' compensation tax on your paycheck is one of the legacies of that unnecessary tragedy.

Taxes have advanced the benefits of specialization, which improves efficiency. Adam Smith tells the story in *The Wealth of Nations* of how pins—ordinary straight pins, like the ones that come stuck into a new blouse or shirt—went from being the province of the rich to cheaper than cheap, providing the classic illustration of this principle. The trick was to switch from having each pin maker fashion a complete pin to breaking the work into eighteen or so separate tasks. Smith wrote:

> One man draws out the wire, another straights it, a third cuts it, a fourth points it, a fifth grinds it at the top for receiving the head; to make the head requires two or three distinct operations.

The result? Ten workers who could not hope to make 200 pins in a day churned out 48,000 pins every day. The price of pins plummeted until even the poor ceased to worry if they lost a no-longer precious pin.

That same principle of specialization applies to government services. Instead of workers leaving the mill or assembly line to become volunteer firefighters and shutting down production, the workers kept to their tasks. Taxes were levied to pay firefighters, who could be highly trained, more efficient, and more effective. In education? Instead of parents teaching their children as best they could, taxes paid for teachers who were trained in what and how to teach at what were known as "normal schools." This vastly improved reading, writing, and arithmetic skills. More taxes were spent to develop public universities, advancing human knowledge and fueling economic growth. With an educated workforce, the United States led the world in developing new technology and services. But maintaining that lead depends on continued investments of tax dollars in education and research.

Few taxpayer investments have paid a greater return than the G.I. Bill, which made it possible for one in seven World War II soldiers and sailors to go to college. Taxpayers spent about $59 billion in 2012 dollars from the end of World War II until 1952 to provide more than 2.2 million soldiers and sailors with a college education. Millions more got other education and training.

The G.I. Bill paid for the educations of 450,000 engineers, 240,000 accountants, 238,000 teachers, 91,000 scientists, 67,000 doctors and 22,000 dentists, among others. In today's dollars that was about $26,000 per student. The higher incomes those college graduates earned, and the advances their education made possible in every field from astrophysics to zoology, laid the foundation for today's advances in medicine, biology, software, materials and every other field in which increased human knowledge has made people better off.

Taxes also lengthen lives. American life expectancy at birth in 1900 was just 47.3 years. One century later it had been extended to 77.2 years, a 63 percent gain. The biggest single reason for that change: public health measures financed by taxes. Publicly funded projects provide clean water and sanitary sewer lines to take away wastewater and treat it. In 1906 the Pure Food and Drug Act and the Meat Inspection Act launched a food safety revolution.

Opponents of each of these measures in their time said that the costs would be ruinous. They were wrong in every case. The costs of *not* taxing ourselves would have been ruinous, both in the quality of life and its duration. Diphtheria, pertussis (whooping cough), and measles are still around, but they rarely kill, unlike a century ago when every parent feared them. Polio no longer cripples, putting its victims into braces, wheelchairs, and iron lungs. Smallpox is gone. Tax dollars were central to the development of vaccines, blood plasma, lifesaving drugs, and new diagnostic and surgical techniques. All of this came about because of taxpayer spending to improve the common good through research, education and infrastructure.

Taxes have made Americans safer on the job and while traveling. They have made us healthier, better educated and more productive; they've reduced misery and lengthened lives. Those are big things. But on Council Rock Avenue, we appreciate the small ones, too, as increased taxes have bought us six quiet mornings each week while putting more money in our pockets.

Rising garbage removal bills are an individual problem mostly in suburban areas, where about half of Americans live, and rural areas, where another fifth of Americans live. In urban centers, though, where the other third of Americans resides, businesses and large apartment buildings often hire cartage firms, and in many cities refuse removal is a basic municipal service.

The public health and aesthetic reasons for this are more obvious than the economics. Rotting garbage attracts rats and other vermin. It only takes one family that does not, or cannot, arrange for garbage collection to make the whole neighborhood stink on hot summer days. But the economics also favor this approach, as universal service through government lowers costs compared to having competing trash-hauling companies. More trash is collected per mile, per hour of labor, per gallon of diesel fuel. It is also cheaper to prepare and send one bill than many thousands of individual bills.

In suburbs and rural areas, garbage removal is more often a business in which homeowners and small businesses contract individually with a cartage company. In a competitive market, the ease with which customers could move from one company to another would tend to hold down prices. Any company that unilaterally raised prices would lose customers, or so economic theory holds. But that theory has been buried at landfills owned by the biggest garbage companies.

The $47 billion that garbage removal costs annually nationwide works out to about $150 per person each year, figures disclosed by the two largest trash-hauling companies indicate. When only residential removal costs are counted, the monthly household bill often runs $40 a month in suburban and rural areas, or $480 annually, plus sales taxes.

Your garbage bill will typically have add-ons for the costs of fuel and for dumping the trash at a landfill, even when the company that hauls your trash away owns the landfill. Your total bill can easily run $50 a month to have two cans of trash emptied each week and your sorted recycling hauled away.

These prices should not be climbing, based on what the big trash companies tell the Securities and Exchange Commission and their shareholders. Waste Management wrote in its annual report to its shareholders and the SEC in 2010 that "the solid waste industry is very competitive."

But that is hardly the impression one gets when the garbage industry is out touting its stocks to investment advisers for mutual funds, where much of your 401(k) money is probably invested, and to managers of public pension plans, which are backed up with your tax dollars. The garbage company executives talk in the arcane language of the investment industry, but their jargon can be easily translated into plain English.

Consider what two top executives of Republic Services, the second-largest garbage company, said at a series of conferences for stock analysts in 2009 and early 2010. "[The industry] generates very predictable cash flows," said Tod Holmes, the chief financial officer. "That's really the underlying strength of this business, the cash that's spinning off out of these companies."

"Predictable cash flows" means the company experiences a steady stream of dollars that, after paying its expenses, goes into its bank accounts. Cash flow is often larger than profit because profit comes after all costs, including depreciation, which is the declining value of machinery and buildings as they are used up. Wall Street watches cash flow much more closely than profits, which under modern accounting rules can be manipulated, as we have seen from Enron, MCI, Tyco and the recently bailed-out banks.

In a competitive market, the flow of cash from customers to company coffers generally would be shallow. Adam Smith wrote that in a competitive market, companies should make just enough profit to justify staying in business. Competition would also permit customers to move freely from one trash-hauling company to another, resulting in occasional floods of cash flow and periodic droughts.

In a market with two big companies, however, competition is diminished. Typically the giants have more power than their customers and their small competitors, even if there are thousands of mom-and-pop operations. When the big guys have this "market power," they possess the ability to raise prices even when there is no outside force, such as increased amounts of trash to be hauled or general inflation, affecting prices. Even in a weak economy, in the absence of real competition, market power can be wielded to keep prices high, and even raise them. This is most often true when the service provided is an essential one—like hauling garbage before the stink becomes overwhelming.

CFO Holmes also explained that the big garbage companies managed to raise prices in the face of myriad small competitors by "rationalizing the market" over the past five to seven years. That's business-speak for avoiding direct competition by carving up markets to minimize competition. That is, the two big companies swapped routes and landfills and also "rationalized" other assets so that each could dominate in particular areas and avoid the competition that would result in stable or lower prices.

Holmes's boss, Jim O'Connor, CEO of Republic Services, told a conference hosted by Credit Suisse in 2010 about these deals. O'Connor said that in "rationalizing the business over the last five or six years, we've done a significant amount of asset exchanges with, at that time, Allied and Waste Management to improve the profile of the business in various marketplaces."

At the same forum Holmes boasted that the company was able to raise prices by more than the rate of inflation. Two years earlier, he had told another conference that "pricing's the key driver and the key thesis here."

In December 2009, O'Connor told another investment conference that the ability to raise prices in real terms was the reason for Republic's takeover of Allied Waste Industries. O'Connor said Republic was also able to raise prices because the largest trash company, Waste Management, also raised prices.

O'Connor said flat out at one meeting for stock analysts that lack of competition was the major reason his firm could raise prices, even in a weak economy:

And today, and, actually, for the last almost four years now, we've seen pricing flexibility in the marketplace, even in light of a bad economy, and a lot of that due, again, to that consolidation at the top and a different perspective of the major companies to the marketplace.

Having two companies dominate the garbage-removal business is not the only reason they are able to gouge customers. Another factor is ownership or control of landfills. Small competitors often have to pay the dominant companies to use their landfills; in some places those sites may even be closed to the competition, forcing smaller concerns to go farther to dispose of trash. Economists call this a "barrier to entry," the very phrase O'Connor used as he told stock analysts about plans to keep raising prices. Republic's "business platform is much stronger today because of the disposal network," he said. "And, really, the strategic reason that we did the merger with Allied Waste was to merge both of our disposal assets to what I call securitize the cash flows of the business and the future cash flows of the business, because, again, that's the barrier to entry, and that will also be the foundation for continued pricing in the sector," he added.

Holmes frequently tells stock analysts how predictably lucrative trash removal has become. So what makes it lucrative? "We're focused on pricing," Holmes has said over and over in various ways.

To stock analysts, "pricing" means higher prices for consumers, which can be translated into rising prices for the shares of a company's stock. There is nothing wrong with raising prices when market forces are at work. But that is not what the garbage-hauling business is doing. Instead, its strategy is to escape competition, which tends to hold down prices.

At another conference, Holmes described how his company encouraged higher prices when it "bought out" a local Waste Management franchise in Cincinnati, leaving just "two predominant players," Republic Services and a local family-owned company named Rumke Consolidated. Holmes said the two were very much alike and boasted that Republic was helping Rumke make bigger profits by encouraging it to raise prices higher than it would otherwise. "Maybe they don't go quite as far as we do in terms of moving our pricing up," Holmes said, "but they're certainly riding this wave and I think they're enjoying it."

It's surprising, isn't it, how many underlying economics lessons there are to be found as we take out the trash.

Fee Fatigue

The fundamental rule in our national life—the rule which underlies all others—is that, on the whole, and in the long run, we shall go up or down together.

—**President Theodore Roosevelt to Congress, 1901**

13.   **In the fall** of 2011, word leaked out that Bank of America planned to charge millions of customers $5 a month to use their debit cards. Combined with existing fees for customers who did not keep at least $1,500 in their checking account every day of the month, that would bring the monthly charges for a Bank of America checking account to as much as $240 per year.

That sum is equivalent to what a single worker, at the median wage, takes home, after taxes, for two and a half days of work.

Other big banks had or were testing similar debit-card fees. But these debit-card fees quickly died because the news media gave huge play to the story, including several nights of coverage on the network news shows. Demonstrations held outside some banks spurred coverage. So did the timing of the fees, which came just three years after the bailouts. Bank of America, which got $45 billion in the first bailouts in the fall of 2008, was cast as a corporate ingrate. The bank's decision to back down was an excellent (and extraordinarily unusual) example of the power of news coverage to affect big business. Unfortunately, the coverage focused more on the hole than the donut—and it is a very big donut.

The usual suspects in the financial press defended the bank fees, blaming them on a 2010 law often cited in the news as the Dodd–Frank Act, lopping off the crucial rest of its name. The law, in full, is the Dodd–Frank Wall Street Reform and Consumer Protection Act. Banking industry apologists at *Forbes, Investor's Business Daily*, Rupert Murdoch's *Wall Street Journal* and their like provided the usual coverage from the point of view of bank executives, ignoring or belittling bank customers unable to keep what, for the median wage worker, would be nearly four weeks of net pay in a checking account.

Lost in the coverage was another fact: retailers were also complaining of being gouged with debit-card fees by banks. The retailers understood that it cost banks far less to digitally process debit cards swiped at a checkout terminal than processing paper checks does. So why were they required to pay more?

The journalists writing from the perspective of the banks warned that other costs would go up—that banks would not make loans. That was utter nonsense, of course, since banks must make loans and handle transactions to stay in business. The fact that the six largest banks had a much larger share of all bank deposits after the bailouts than before it also suggested that, at least for the six largest banks, government was a generous friend, not an antagonist or even a referee.

Before President Obama signed the Dodd–Frank Wall Street Reform and Consumer Protection Act in 2010, retailers paid an average of forty-four cents in bank fees each time a customer swiped a debit card. That may not seem like much unless you know that the profit margin in retail is often 3 percent or less on sales, so on a $10 debit-card swipe, the bank fee was significantly larger than the profit margin of perhaps thirty cents. Under the Dodd–Frank Wall Street Reform and Consumer Protection Act, the charge to swipe a debit card could be no more than twenty-four cents (once, that is, the rules implementing the new law were put into effect nearly two years later). Only the smallest banks were exempt from these limits. Retailers said the price cap would help hold down retail prices and improve economic efficiency, which *Forbes* in particular dismissed with the gusto to be expected not of financial journalists looking out for investors, but of partisans cheering for bankers to rake in fat fees.

A loss of two dimes in revenue per transaction may not seem like much money. As with the oil pipelines, however, where a penny per day per American in fake taxes adds more than a billion dollars a year to the bottom line, the banks knew better. The bankers said losing those two dimes would be ruinous. Visa and Mastercard say they have issued more than 521 million debit cards, more than two per adult, and that they are used for more than 40 billion transactions per year. At two dimes per purchase, that would add up to more than $8 billion of revenue in a year—more than a dollar per day for each adult in America. Bank of America said losing those two dimes on each debit-card swipe would make its revenue ($93.5 billion in 2011) slip by $2 billion annually.

Aborting the $5 monthly debit-card fee was a victory for consumers; so was the reduction in swipe fees. Yet these were but skirmishes in a much larger war that consumers are losing.

A FESTIVAL OF FEES

Fees everywhere—often morbidly obese ones—are being imposed on bank customers unless they have large savings, checking or loan balances at the same institution.

Consider, for example, the growing practice of charging a fee to issue a check when consumers take out a loan. The idea that a lender would charge you to hand over money you are borrowing may seem bizarre, but it is exceptionally lucrative. So long as this practice remains largely unobserved it will flourish.

Sallie Mae, which makes loans to students, charges some borrowers $300 to issue a $7,000 check to their school. Sallie Mae's practice is to issue checks by semester or quarter rather than once per year. So a student lent $14,000 for fall and spring semesters will get dinged for $600 in fees as two checks are cut. That $600 disbursement fee comes to more than 4 percent of a $14,000 loan, which in turn inflates the interest rate on the amount actually lent because the student is paying a posted percentage rate for ninety-six cents on the dollar, not the full dollar. A student on a quarter system with fall, winter and spring quarters pays even more in check fees.

Here is the fine print footnote in which Sallie Mae discloses (or more accurately, obscures) this charge for sending loan proceeds directly to a college or university, known as disbursement:

> Interest rates for the Fixed and Deferred Repayment Options are higher than for loans with the Interest Repayment Option. APRs for borrowers attending non-degree granting institutions range from 8.00% to 13.76% with an origination fee up to 5.00%. Origination fees mean application or disbursement fees.

Banks need, of course, to collect enough from customers to justify staying in business and earn a profit. In the long run, only healthy banks can supply the rivers of cash that keep an economy flowing and growing.

The historic rule about how much banks needed to service the economy was 3-3-3—borrow at 3 percent, lend at 3 percentage points above that and hit the golf course by 3 p.m. A bank that can borrow at 3 percent and lend at 6 percent should be profitable as long as it makes sound loans that customers pay back. Of course with the rise of credit-card lending in the last half century, the bigger banks got hooked on fatter margins, borrowing at, say, 5 percent and then lending at 14 percent, a margin of 9 percent, or three times the traditional spread between interest out and interest in.

Most banks do not get that spread, however. That is because each month they bundle all of their credit-card accounts and sell them to Wall Street, which gets the 9 percent spread. And unlike banks, the Wall Street system is part of a growing shadow banking system that is unregulated and largely obscured from oversight. Transparency is always the friend of markets and consumers, opaque practices the secret ally of price gougers, monopolists and thieves.

Bankers have learned that they can slap on fees, especially fees that were big enough to be lucrative, but not so big that customers would go through the complexities of closing their accounts and moving to another bank. Moving to a new bank is much harder in 2012 than a decade or two earlier. The task is made more difficult with the spread of electronic bill-paying services in which the consumer must keypunch every account name, number and address into her personal computer if she switches banks. And since most banks charge the same, or nearly the same fees, what gain is there in switching? The consumer shrugs and says, *The next bank will just gouge me, too.* The result has been a climate in which there is little incentive for lowering fees, so fees tend to rise in unison. And that, as shown earlier, is another sign of oligopoly instead of competition.

Other fees abound. Many banks charge a fee for using a competing bank's automated teller machine, a device that, when introduced, consumers were told would lower their cost of having a checking account. There are charges for using paper checks and getting copies of checks, as well as annual credit-card fees.

The biggest pile of gold comes from fees for overdrawing an account. Charge a $5 item when your account has $4.99 and the overdraft fee can easily be $40. Some banks no longer let customers use their savings account to cover overdrafts, but instead require the use of a credit line. M&T Bank, a Warren Buffett bank, charges customers $10 even if they go online and move money in advance of a shortfall from their overdraft account to their checking account. The cost to the bank for such a transfer? The best indication that the cost is infinitesimal is this: moving money from checking *to* the overdraft account is free of charge. So is moving money from, say, a home equity line of credit to checking, which is free at M&T.

Overdraft fees nationwide totaled about $20 billion in 2011, according to the Consumer Financial Protection Bureau, the federal agency created by Congress to deal with gouging by banks. A much larger estimate, more than $38 billion, was made by Moebs Services, a private research firm used by the banking industry, for 2009. It found that such fees doubled between 2000 and 2009 as banks raised overdraft charges and more customers incurred them. But as the economy ebbed, so did overdraft fees, down to $31.6 billion in 2011 by Moebs' estimate.

Moebs Research also made a finding that raises questions about how well many banks are managed. It found that nearly half of banks imposed overdraft fees larger than their net profits in 2010. That means, in short, that without overdraft fees, the banks would have lost money.

Consumers could respond to the imposition of these fat fees with political action, which would certainly unsettle bankers. They could demand that members of Congress enact laws to regulate banks in the public interest. A license to run a bank is not a right, but a privilege, one that politicians could limit to those banks that do not gouge customers with high fees. The Federal Reserve policies that let cash-short banks borrow as much as they need are also a privilege, not a right. That privilege could be denied to banks that charge fees that can generate profits of *hundreds of thousands of percent*, as is the case when the marginal cost is a penny and two charges are imposed (as is Bank of America's practice), assessing total fees of $47.

Here, however, the banks have proved politically astute. The banks designed fee systems, like the two Bank of America charges that it slaps on some customers who innocently deposit a bad check, to hit younger people (under age thirty-five) and those with modest incomes. These people tend also to be less sophisticated and have less access to politicians. Four out of five bank customers surveyed by the American Bankers Association said they paid no overdraft fees in 2009. More customers than that overdrew their accounts, but their bank waived the fees in many cases. Moebs Research estimated that just 10 percent of bank customers pay 90 percent of overdraft fees. Some customers, research by Moebs Research and others shows, pay more than $125 a month in overdraft fees month after month. The banks would shun them as customers except for the fees they generate.

Designing a system so that the people who pay the fees are the very people with the least capacity to get government to listen to their concerns makes sense from the bankers' point of view. It also shows the nation's growing disregard for the least among us, a trend exacerbated by the decline of private-sector unions and reductions in money for government consumer advocacy agencies. Vanderbilt University political science professor Larry Bartels has shown that political influence is concentrated at the top. The bottom third of Americans have zero direct political influence on roll call votes, and the next third have almost next to none. Thus it is not surprising that the burden of bank fees falls on the most vulnerable.

REWRITING RULE 23A

What should trouble all taxpayers is how Congress and the regulatory agencies are so deeply in the embrace of the bankers' point of view that they permit not only unconscionable fees, but banking practices that put all taxpayers at risk of having to cover overdrafts by the banks themselves, not for a day or two but permanently. The danger is in how the Federal Reserve interprets, and fails to enforce, Rule 23A of the Federal Reserve Act.

The Federal Reserve is the "lender of last resort." Any member bank can borrow whatever cash it needs overnight to avoid overdrawing its own accounts. Banks do it all the time. Bankers don't have to check their account balances to see if they can cover the funds to be disbursed to you for, say, a new car purchase. No, the bank just makes the loan and, if it needs to cover the cost, it borrows it from others, including the Federal Reserve.

To make sure banks do not just loot the Federal Reserve, the Federal Reserve has rules. One of them, Rule 23A, requires that banks hold, and pledge as collateral, valuable paper, such as mortgages, on which the balance owed is much less than the value of the property. Bonds will do, too, those issued by cash-rich and profitable companies, as will stocks in blue-chip companies. By demanding quality collateral, the Federal Reserve should be able to collect on its overnight loans even if the cash-short bank fails.

The Federal Reserve has the power to waive its rules on the quality of the collateral it accepts for loans from cash-short banks. It can, under Rule 23A, accept pretty much any piece of paper as collateral, not just valuable paper like mortgages on which the balance is much less than the value of the property or bonds from cash-rich and profitable companies.

In recent years, the Federal Reserve has taken less valuable assets as collateral, as you can see by going to www.federalreserve.gov/boarddocs/ legalint/FederalReserveAct/xxxx. Just replace the four Xs at the end of the Web address with the year you want to check.

Among the borrowers allowed to pledge speculative (and perhaps worthless) paper to get cash were Bank of America, Citigroup, General Electric, Goldman Sachs and J. P. Morgan as well as Deutsche Bank (a major force in financing illegal tax shelters) and the British banks Barclays and HSBC. (The initials used to identify the last of those, the old Hong Kong and Shanghai Bank, are understood among its employees to stand for Hugely Successful British Corporation, though in recent years its success is thanks to the largesse of American taxpayers in bailing it out.)

Nearly all of this dubious collateral was in the form of credit default swaps. Those are promises to make a lender whole if a borrower does not repay a debt. This makes them a kind of financial insurance. But the premiums charged were not nearly large enough to pay off the debts of others if many of them failed to pay back their loans. This makes credit default swaps a kind of gambling, betting that borrowers will not default because if more than a few do the swap will not pay off.

Historically, speculative credit default swaps did not qualify as proper collateral for overnight loans because, as a kind of gambling, they didn't meet the standards for good collateral. But in the fall of 2011, Bank of America quietly began shifting these derivatives contracts from the books of its Merrill Lynch stock brokerage to its bank, where the Federal Deposit Insurance Corporation (FDIC) guarantees deposits up to $250,000 per customer. So did other big banks, including J. P. Morgan. Bank of America's Merrill Lynch had more than $50 billion in derivatives contracts. That movement from brokerage to bank might seem to be internal shuffling of no interest, or concern, to the public. It's easy for bank publicists to suggest it is no different from moving money from Bank of America's left pocket to its right. But it should be of deep concern to every taxpayer. The reason is that credit default swap losses in the Merrill Lynch pocket will cost Bank of America shareholders, but losses in the bank will cost you.

A borrower pays a small fee to a bank, which then guarantees that the debt will be repaid even if the borrower does not. As long as nearly all debts are repaid as promised, the fees mean profits. It is like selling life insurance on children and young adults. When hardly anyone dies, the insurer makes few payouts and gets to keep not only most of the premiums paid for the insurance, but the income from investing the premiums as well. However, if an epidemic kills many children or a war takes the lives of many young men, the insurer might not have enough money to pay the promised death benefits to survivors. Credit default swaps work the same way. They generate easy profits until a financial collapse means many borrowers cannot repay their debts and suddenly there is not enough money to pay off the unexpectedly large amount of unpaid debt.

The United States Comptroller of the Currency reported that 97 percent of bank derivatives at the end of 2011 were credit default swaps, the very instruments that made the flow of cash on Wall Street freeze just three years earlier (more on that shortly; see chapter 15, "Giving to Goldman," page 165). More than 40 percent of these were rated below investment grade. That is, they were speculative investments, some as risky as you placing money on a number at the roulette wheel (though without the prospect of a 35:1 payoff if the marble happens to settle on your number).

The move from brokerage to bank came during summer 2011 as the credit ratings agencies began issuing downgrades on Bank of America bonds. Those downgrades warned bondholders that the risk of not getting their principal back was on the rise—a valid concern given Bank of America's huge risks of loss and minute profits in 2011. That year the bank operations lost money but Bank of America turned a paper profit of more than $1.4 billion because of tax rebates from years past. As its bond ratings began to slide, Bank of America started moving its Merrill Lynch derivatives contracts to the bank. That means it could use some of the $1 trillion it holds in deposits from bank customers to pay off those contracts if need be and, in turn, that the government would have to pony up cash to make checking account and savings account customers whole. That is where Rule 23A comes in.

By waiving Rule 23A requirements and accepting potentially worthless credit default swaps as collateral for loans, the Federal Reserve can keep Bank of America from dying. The dubious Merrill Lynch credit default swaps are given to Bank of America's bank, which then uses them as collateral to borrow billions from the Federal Reserve. Think of it as trading toilet paper for greenbacks.

The larger reality is that Bank of America has become a zombie bank, kept alive by infusions of cash. But those loans from the Federal Reserve also menace everyone else's wealth. Maybe, with enough infusions of cash, Bank of America will come back to economic life as a profitable enterprise without government help. But as the bond rating agencies warned, the risk of failure is growing, not diminishing.

What makes the Rule 23A waivers astonishing is that it was the separation of risk from reward that brought about the Great Recession in 2008. The relaxation and removal of sound laws took more than two decades of campaign donations and favors for politicians. As chairman of the Senate Banking Committee, Phil Gramm of Texas did all he could to remove laws and regulations that ensured prudent conduct and protected taxpayers. Gramm then left office and became a vice chairman of UBS, the big Swiss bank whose tax-shelter salesmen came onto American soil to sell their criminal products.

Laws weakened over many years changed America from a land where bank failures were almost unheard of from 1945 until the early years of Reaganism. With prudent rules and actual regulation fading into history, we began to get the bill. You know the headline story: just weeks before the George W. Bush administration was to end in January 2009, Treasury Secretary Henry (Hank) Paulson demanded that Congress give him $700 billion, no questions asked, so he could bail out the firm he had run before coming to Washington. Although Goldman Sachs and other banks had acted imprudently, they were deemed too big to fail.

Congress gave Paulson the money, but not entirely unfettered, and we got the bill. The Bloomberg news agency, after analyzing a mountain of arcane documents, concluded that the Wall Street bailouts put taxpayers at risk for $14.7 trillion. That is roughly one year of all the work, all the profits, and all the other economic activity of the entire nation. And while the ultimate costs will be in the hundreds of billions or a few trillions (but certainly not a profit, as Wall Street and Washington claim), it should not have happened. Sound regulation would have prevented the need for the bailouts.

Capitalism without the failures of bankrupt enterprises is not capitalism at all. It is not market economics. It is rather the proof that Congress has turned the United States into a land of corporate socialism in which gains are privatized and losses are socialized. Self-regulation as espoused by Chicago School economic theories (see page 241); the ideological marketing by the Heritage Foundation and others; and decades of campaign contributions and favors for politicians taken together have enabled a system by which the few steal from the many with no risk of prosecution and a virtual guarantee of lavish riches. By wrapping the whole in complicated terms few understand, and by making piecemeal changes, the plunderers have made themselves appear to be beneficiaries of circumstance, not thieves.

The first time we had a disaster brought on by undoing sound regulation we got the savings and loan crisis of the late 1980s. At that time, a banking regulator named Bill Black understood what was happening and was in a position to make sure others understood. Because of Black's diligence, more than three thousand people were convicted of felonies, more than a thousand of them high-level insiders at savings and loans that were in many cases criminal enterprises posing as financial institutions. In 2009 through 2011, prosecutions for financial crimes fell to less than half the numbers in the 1990s, Justice Department data show.

Black has a phrase to describe what happens when the head of a corporation runs it not for profit, but plunder. He calls it "control fraud." That's essentially what the Mafia does when it takes over a business from someone in too deep with loan sharks. The mob orders all the supplies it can to be delivered as quickly as possible, carts them out the back door and then the torches the place. The vendors never get paid. Crooked bankers just use accounting rules to mask their crimes and then either put the business into bankruptcy or get the government to rescue it with taxpayer money.

The Chicago School economists and other promoters of the idea of regulation that favors corporations all insist that control frauds are rare and thus not significant. That position remains plausible as long as officials insist that no one saw, or could have seen, the 2008 collapse coming; as long as law enforcement is kept busy not looking for criminal conduct. But achieving this requires blinders, what we might call wishful denial of obvious facts.

One set of those blinders was applied to the usually prying eyes of the FBI by the Mortgage Bankers Association (MBA). In 2004 the FBI announced that it had identified mortgage fraud as an epidemic. It identified two kinds of mortgage fraud. One involved people who borrowed money to buy a house they could not afford, hoping they could flip it for a profit before their inability to pay became apparent. The other involved people borrowing to live in a house they could not afford until they were evicted. The FBI also announced that its partner in identifying such frauds was the Mortgage Bankers Association.

What the FBI missed was that it was banks that were creating the frauds, including some members of the MBA. The fox got the watchdog to look at the eggs instead of watching the chickens, which were being eaten by the fox family. Bank agents were helping buyers fabricate loan documents. At Countrywide Financial in suburban Los Angeles, the largest source of fraudulent mortgage loans in the country, people fabricated documents to justify loans, making up wage and business profit statements. Loan officers put people with solid credit into mortgages that would force them to make big future interest payments because selling such toxic mortgages paid the officers three times the normal fee.

Why would any bank make loans it knew could not be paid back? They would not—unless it did not matter to the bank whether the loan was paid back. Thanks to Gramm and other politicians, reward (fees and stock options) had been separated from responsibility to make sure borrowers repaid the loans. Once a loan was issued, it was sold in a package with thousands of other loans to Goldman Sachs and other Wall Street firms, which then sliced and diced the loans and sold them to investors as investments. Among the biggest buyers were state and local government pension funds, which were told the mortgage loans were all top rated and sure to be paid back. When that proved false, the resultant losses to the public employee pension funds meant higher taxes to make up for the money lost to Wall Street.

The two institutions that resisted the easy profits in packing and selling off these loans were Freddie Mac and Fannie Mae, the two government-sponsored mortgage agencies that right-wing Republicans and Rupert Murdoch's *Wall Street Journal* try to blame for the housing crisis. In 2006, as the coming collapse should have been obvious to anyone in banking regulation, the two loan giants were under pressure from Wall Street stock and bond rating analysts plus politicians in both parties to stop being stodgy and get in while the getting was good. Fannie Mae and Freddie Mac did, but with so little and so late that their loan loss rates were much smaller than Wall Street firms like Goldman Sachs.

Alan Greenspan, the Ayn Rand acolyte (he was executor of her estate) who headed the Federal Reserve during the years when the bubble was inflating, insisted he never saw a housing bubble forming. Greenspan is famous for poring over financial and economic data, often in his bathtub, yet like Claude Rains's Captain Renault in *Casablanca*, he claimed to be unaware there was gambling going on.

Many people saw the housing bubble forming, including me. And if I could see it, how could Greenspan not? Even though real estate was not my beat, I wrote two articles in the *New York Times* in 2004 to have a record I could cite when the collapse took place. Housing prices were growing faster than economic conditions could justify by 2002. Way back in 1993 George Akerloff, who won the Nobel Prize in Economics in

2001, and Paul Romer wrote a seminal paper after the savings and loan crisis titled "Looting: The Economic Underworld of Bankruptcy for Profit." Anyone who read it could see the pattern that arose in the housing market starting in the late 1990s.

Criminologist Bill Black, who is now a professor of law and economics at the University of Missouri–Kansas City, testified widely about how the lessons of the savings and loan crisis should be applied to the housing bubble. Black gave speeches, promoted his book *The Best Way to Rob a Bank Is to Own One* and appeared on national television. He did everything he could except yell *Thief!* in a crowded bank. But hardly anyone listened. The White House, the Justice Department, and the banking regulators all failed to seek his counsel.

Instead of the thousands of prosecutions we saw after the savings and loan debacle, there have been less than a handful of prosecutions of bankers in the mortgage frauds. Angelo Mozilo, who made more than $600 million as head of Countrywide, escaped not only prosecution, but also civil liability. His $47 million in fines—modest compared to the costs Countrywide imposed on society—was paid mostly by insurance companies. Mozilo insists he did nothing wrong. So do the prosecutors and regulators who settled with him. Mozilo is another example of how thoroughly those at the top are insulated from accountability while those at the bottom are pursued in modern America.

"Wells Fargo Will Take Your House"

I didn't read, I just signed.

—Judge Richard Posner

14. **Barbara Keeton's old** blue truck started leaking so much oil she knew she needed a new set of wheels, fast. Keeton lives in the nation's capital with its modern subway and plentiful bus routes, but the system is designed to serve office workers, not people like Keeton, a former army cook who drives a school bus. She must get to the bus barn by six in the morning, just a half hour after the subway starts running, too little time for her to bundle up her little ones and get them to day care.

So one July day in 2005, the army veteran stuffed some pay stubs in her purse and drove across the Potomac River to one of seventeen used-car lots run by Easterns Automotive Group, which advertised heavily on television. Their commercials convinced Keeton she could count on a fair deal on an affordable car.

Keeton figured she could handle a $200 car payment. The Easterns salesman convinced her that she needed a better car than $200 a month would buy. Easterns put her into a four-year-old Mazda Tribute, a sport utility vehicle priced at $19,955 plus taxes and fees. Wells Fargo Bank financed the deal with a six-year loan at $389 a month for a total cost of more than $28,000.

Before long the Tribute stopped dead in traffic. The ignition system, one of those modern ones with electronic coding in the keys, had failed. Easterns fixed it, replacing the keys. Then the ignition failed again. Soon numerous other flaws became apparent. Between towing bills, repair bills and a car payment nearly twice what she had budgeted for, Keeton knew she was falling behind. Then she was placed on temporary disability, which meant her income dropped.

"My doctor put me out of work because I was forty-two and pregnant," Keeton recalled. Knowing she could not make more payments, Keeton said she "asked them to take the car back, but they refused. So I went to my credit union because I knew you could refinance a car, and when the credit union said it was only worth $8,800 my heart sank."

Wells Fargo repossessed the car and sold it—for $6,100, less than a third of what Easterns had charged Keeton for it. Then Wells Fargo called Keeton and demanded $13,368.95, the difference between what it got for the car and the loan balance.

Keeton said that from the first call, the Wells Fargo collection agent was menacing. "She was very belligerent," Keeton recalled. "She said 'How much can you pay?' and I said a hundred dollars a month, and she said, 'We will come back for an increase in three months,' and when I said I could not pay more, she said, 'Fine, Wells Fargo will take your house.'"

Terrified that Wells Fargo, a Warren Buffett bank, would take her home, Keeton began a frantic search for help. She found her way to a legal clinic run by the law school at American University. The first students on her case took the car dealer and Wells Fargo to court. That was a mistake. The judge dismissed their case with prejudice, meaning no further action could be filed on Keeton's behalf. The judge did so because Keeton's purchase contract said she agreed she could not sue over any dispute, but must instead go to arbitration.

Unless you are one of the working poor, this may not seem like a case that matters much to you. Maybe you know how to negotiate the price of a car and you have a decent credit score. If you pay cash for your cars, this may seem like just another tale of a gullible single mother who didn't stand up for her own best interests, but let a salesman sweet talk her into a clunker of a car at a premium price.

What happened to Keeton, however, shows how Congress and the Supreme Court are systematically destroying a crucial tenet of commercial law. The process encourages inflated prices and shoddy goods, and leaves consumers with little or no recourse. The lesson is broader than you may realize: bad law makes for bad conduct. And I'm not talking about Barbara Keeton's.

ARE YOU AT RISK, TOO?

As the law now stands, you are at risk every time you buy a car, an appliance, furniture or many other goods. Open a bank account, deposit funds with a stockbroker or open a credit line and you could end up in the same jam that Keeton found herself in. The reason is that all of these transactions, and many others, are done using boilerplate contracts with a clause, often buried deep in the contract, requiring that any dispute regarding the contract be resolved through arbitration, not through the courts.

The beginnings date to a 1925 law, the Federal Arbitration Act. Congress enacted it so that disputes between corporations in different states, with their different laws, could be resolved quickly through binding arbitration. The record from 1925 shows no intention to apply the law to consumers and workers, only to corporations that negotiated mandatory arbitration clauses for their mutual benefit. Despite this limited purpose, the courts have now stretched the law into a parody of its original intent. In doing so they have encouraged misconduct by all businesses, but especially those with unscrupulous owners and managers.

This trend is encouraged by the refusal of Congress to increase the number of federal judges to keep pace with the demands of a larger, richer and more complex society. Not having enough judges makes those who sit on the bench eager to find ways to shed cases. Enforcing contracts that deny access to the courts and require private arbitration of disputes is an easy way for overworked judges to get rid of cases without considering their merits.

In arbitration a panel of private individuals, who may lack training, decide a case and their decisions, generally, cannot be appealed to the courts.

As reinvented by the Supreme Court in a series of decisions, the 1925 arbitration law now applies not just to disputes between corporations, but to consumers and workers. Worse, the courts have applied it in ways that eliminate consumer and employment rights in favor of business interests; impose costly barriers to obtaining redress; and ignore the Constitutional right to jury trial in civil disputes, all without any knowing consent by consumers and workers.

Margaret L. Moses, who teaches at Chicago's Loyola University School of Law, has studied how courts have perverted this law. She wrote that if a bill that included today's court interpretation had been placed before Congress in 1925, it probably would not have garnered a single vote.

Keeton's path to the threat of the loss of her home began with the contract she signed for that overpriced Mazda.

Sales agents routinely present us with "standard form" contracts. "Initial here and sign there," they say, and often we do as we are told without bothering to read the fine print. One of the greatest legal minds of our time, Judge Richard Posner of the federal appeals court in Chicago, told a 2010 legal conference that when he took out a home-equity loan, he was shown innumerable pages of documentation. "I didn't read, I just signed," Posner said.

Lawyers call these "contracts of adhesion." The term means that the contracts are one-sided in favor of the company that presents the contract to you. Typically, the contract will require of the company few obligations beyond delivering the house or mortgage or whatever else you bought or rented. In law, the contract generally stands as valid unless its terms are found to be so unfairly one-sided that it shocks the conscience. But even the doctrine of the unconscionable is under judicial attack.

You, the weaker party, must adhere to the terms of such contracts. If all goes well, as it usually does, this is an efficient way to do business. For example, if you join a car-rental frequent driver plan, you can pick up a rental car by just showing your driver's license. But if something goes awry, you will find yourself at a severe disadvantage because virtually all contracts of adhesion require you to give up your right to sue. Instead, they require that disputes go to binding arbitration. In arbitration you will not have the same rights you would in a court of law to make the other side reveal evidence, especially evidence that may show you were wronged.

In arbitration you will have to pay fees to file, and the arbitrator may require you to travel to another city or state for his convenience. The arbitrators may not even be lawyers, who understand legal principles, but former executives of the industry. Then you must pay half the cost of the arbitrator, who may charge $400 per hour. Then again, maybe you will pay more than half.

That is what happened to Ernestine Strobel, known as Mabel. She worked as a government secretary starting in 1944 and, after going to college at night, did drafting work for the navy. She never married. Having to support herself, Strobel lived frugally, saved and bought real estate. In 1998, when she was seventy-nine, she put more than $645,000 into the hands of a Morgan Stanley broker. Her broker then persuaded her to sell her real estate and entrust the half-million-dollar proceeds to Morgan Stanley, too.

Now you might think the firm would have bought some blue-chip stocks that paid dividends or a lot of bonds paying interest for the retired Strobel. Instead, Morgan Stanley put the old lady's money into risky technology stocks and into Morgan Stanley mutual funds that charged a load (translation: commissions for the broker). Her accounts soon lost $281,000. In contrast, court records show, had the money been conservatively invested 15 percent in stocks and 85 percent in bonds her accounts would have grown by $11,000.

Strobel demanded recompense. After a five-day hearing before an arbitrator she was awarded just $5,000 in damages, with no explanation of how that figure was determined. But what was revealing about that award was how the three arbitrators, none of them lawyers, split the costs of the arbitration. Strobel was ordered to pay $10,350 in fees, more than twice the damage award, but Morgan Stanley paid only $6,900 in fees. This looks a lot like mitigating the damages award by shifting more of the arbitration fees onto Strobel. Morgan Stanley called the outcome a "fair and complete arbitration."

Strobel did not agree and hired Jeff Lendrum, a San Diego lawyer who specializes in such cases, to get the arbitration award overturned as unconscionable.

The federal judge who heard the case, Roger T. Benitez, wrote that he was "troubled by the severe disparity" between the huge loss and the tiny damages the arbitrators awarded. The judge also dismissed Morgan Stanley's claim that Strobel was rich and sophisticated and could ride out a ten-year slide in the markets. He also rejected as irrelevant Morgan Stanley's suggestion that rather than being a frugal government employee who saved, Strobel had struck it rich in a rising real estate market.

Judge Benitez said he would award Strobel the entire $281,000, but the law did not allow him to do that. Indeed, he showed that he had only a very limited power even to review the case. He sent it back to the arbitrator. Eventually a settlement was reached, its terms confidential at Morgan Stanley's insistence.

None of this would have happened had Strobel not had enough money to hire Lendrum. He believes brokers should have to put advice in writing and be held to a duty of loyalty to the customer, putting their interests ahead of their fees. Lendrum said he has seen many cases of elderly people who were put into speculative stocks and mutual funds that rewarded brokers with fat sales commissions instead of conservative portfolios appropriate to their age and need for income.

Strobel was disillusioned. "Before this happened, I thought that Morgan Stanley was a company that is fair and honest. And I don't trust arbitration anymore, believe me."

She was lucky in another sense. Lendrum has San Diego-area clients in their seventies and eighties who have had to go, at their brokerages' insistence, to Las Vegas or Phoenix for arbitration hearings, adding travel costs as well as risks for those not in good health. He sees distant forums as just another way to discourage complaints and challenges for recompense.

Paul and Pamela Casarotto got a costly taste of this after they bought a Subway sandwich shop franchise in Montana. They opened their Missoula eatery in 1988 at a location that was not the best, but one they agreed to when Subway's franchising agent promised that when a better location became available, they could move. But when they tried to move, Subway said no. The Casarottos then sued Doctor's Associates, the Connecticut firm that owns the Subway name.

Montana law required that any mandatory arbitration requirement be "typed in underlined capital letters on the first page of the contract." Subway disclosed the requirement for arbitration on the ninth page of fine print.

The Casarottos also complained that they should not be required to go to Connecticut to have an arbitrator hear their case under Connecticut law because the travel posed an unreasonable and costly burden on their small business. They said Montana law should prevail and the case should be heard in Montana. The case worked its way through the courts until it came before the Montana Supreme Court in 1994. Subway's lawyer, Alan G. Schwartz, opened his argument with a casual remark that unwittingly helped make the Casarottos' case.

"It is a pleasure to be here in Montana after my trip from Connecticut," Schwartz said, introducing himself to the court.

"Was it a long trip, counselor?" Justice Terry N. Trieweiler asked.

"A very long trip," Schwartz said.

"Well, counselor," Trieweiler responded, "that's how far these plaintiffs would have to travel to have their case heard by an arbitrator."

The Montana Supreme Court ruled against Subway because it did not disclose the arbitration requirement prominently on the front page of the contract, as state law required. When Subway appealed to the United States Supreme Court, which takes only a tiny minority of the cases presented to it each year, the court took the case. Its ruling? Eight to one in Subway's favor.

Justice Ruth Bader Ginsburg held that the Montana law requiring the front-page disclosure was invalid. Why? Because the disclosure require-ment applied only to arbitration and not to all types of disputes, making it discriminatory and thus invalid. The decision invalidated similar no-tice laws in Georgia, Iowa, Missouri, Rhode Island, South Carolina, Tennessee, Texas and Vermont.

Business lawyers hailed the decision—it obviously enhanced corpo-rate power in such disputes—but not so consumer advocates. Deborah Zuckerman, a lawyer for the American Association of Retired Persons, which filed a brief in support of the Casarottos, described the decision as an "unfortunate ruling for consumers" because "the Montana statute at issue in this case is merely an attempt to ensure that parties are aware that a contract contains an arbitration clause."

This decision illustrates how the Supreme Court focuses on legal for-malism without context and often without recognizing how the law oper-ates in the real world. It is part of a long line of decisions that skew economic power toward corporations that use contracts of adhesion. It also erodes the ancient legal concept that courts must look out for the interests of less sophisticated, less informed and weaker parties if the law is to be merciful and thus widely respected. Ginsburg, a liberal long known for taking a sharp look at discrimination, in this case hurt many buyers not as sophisticated as she is about discrimination.

Justice Trieweiler got another chance to express his views when the case came back to the Montana Supreme Court. He went right to the heart of the issue—unequal power between a big corporation and its cus-tomer.

"What I would like the people in the federal judiciary, especially at the appellate level, to understand," Trieweiler wrote, is that they make a "na-ïve assumption that arbitration provisions and choice of law provisions are knowingly bargained for" when in fact "these procedural safeguards and substantive laws are easily avoided."

He added that "any party with enough power over the other" can "stick . . . an arbitration provision in its preprinted contract and require the party with inferior bargaining power to sign it."

Justice Trieweiler wrote that the idea that "people like the Casarottos have knowingly and voluntarily bargained and agreed to resolve their contractual disputes or tort claims by arbitration, is naïve at best, and self-serving and cynical at worst. To me," Trieweiler continued, "the idea of a contract or agreement suggests mutuality. There is no mutuality in a franchise agreement, a securities brokerage agreement, or in any other of the agreements that typically impose arbitration as the means for resolving disputes. . . . These provisions, which are not only approved of, but encouraged" by federal judges and others, "subvert our system of justice as we have come to know it. If any foreign government tried to do the same, we would surely consider it a serious act of aggression."

Plain and simple, that is the issue—mandatory arbitration is being used to enhance the power of corporations over people, and in ways that make it likely corporate power will prevail.

DID I SAY THAT?

The Casarotto case revealed another problem—that the law allows corporations to make promises they have no intention of ever fulfilling and, further, to use those promises to induce people to do all sorts of things, from buying a sandwich shop franchise to accepting a buyout package from a job.

A company can put promises in writing and then not fulfill them—without consequence. Curtis Bridgeman and Karen Sandrik, law professors at Florida State University, call this "promissory fraud." Unless one can prove "a positive intention to deceive, not just a lack of an intention to perform," Bridgeman and Sandrik wrote, corporations and their agents can make promises to induce people to do business with them and then simply not perform as promised.

"It is possible to make a promise without having an intention to perform or not to perform," they note, and yet under the law not commit fraud. That is because fraud requires "an intention to deceive" when the promise is made. Unless you can prove that the company or its agent intended to defraud you, the company and its agents "will not be liable for promissory fraud in courts today."

How are you going to prove, though, what the company's agent intended? How can you establish what the courts call a scheme to defraud? It can be done, but it is extremely difficult unless you can afford, and get a court to approve, subpoenas for company records and you have the time and resources to go through what could be a huge pile of unsorted raw data. Even then, you would likely need to turn up something damning, such as an e-mail boasting about a plan to deceive. Absent such a smoking gun, a company and its agents can explain that they never intended to deceive you, they just did not do what they promised.

Buried in the fine print of many agreements are the promises about what a company will do and when, but look even deeper and you'll often find that the company reserves the right to change the terms of the agreement any time it wishes. Bridgeman and Sandrik call these "pseudo promises." Read through the notices you get from your bank, mutual fund company, insurer and others and you will almost always find language that says the company reserves the right to change its policies and the terms of its agreement with you. After reading over innumerable such notices, I have yet to find one that grants *you* an equal right to change the terms.

ARBITRATION GONE AWRY

There are many significant issues of unfairness when customers are forced, often unknowingly, into mandatory arbitration. Let's take a quick look at two of them.

One arises from the acceptance by the courts of arbitration clauses that require that each case be heard separately, even when the facts are basically the same. Imagine, for example, that a company promised free oil changes every four thousand miles for as long as you own a car bought this year. Then next year the company reneges. The situation is the same for everyone who bought a car from them, but if the contract used to sell each car says each dispute must be handled individually, then you must spend hundreds and perhaps a few thousand dollars to go to arbitration. Nobody is going to do that for oil changes, not even if they plan to keep the car for fifty oil changes.

Requiring separate arbitration for each and every small case is an open invitation to the unscrupulous to steal modest sums from many individuals, none of whom has enough at stake to justify the costs of arbitration, but all of whom, acting together, might. Only instead of the penny or three the pipelines collect from each of us every day for a tax they do not owe, this technique can be used to steal any sum lower than the cost of hiring a lawyer to fight individually. This is another example of how the courts generally, and the United States Supreme Court in particular, favor corporations over people.

The courts are increasingly hostile to class actions, taking their cue from the Supreme Court, especially under Chief Justice John Roberts. When a class action case brought on behalf of 1.5 million women workers at Walmart came before the Supreme Court in June 2011, it was rejected in a 5-4 decision. The court ruled that the women's cases did not have a common thread, but needed to be adjudicated individually. The majority opinion, by Justice Antonin Scalia, said that the women could not achieve "a common answer to the crucial question, *why was I disfavored?*" because millions of decisions were involved and they lacked "some glue holding the alleged reasons for all those decisions together."

Scalia relied heavily on the fact that Walmart had a written policy against discrimination at its 3,400 stores, while also giving each store manager broad discretion. Scalia called this "the opposite of a uniform employment practice that would provide the commonality needed for a class action." Justice Scalia wrote, "It is a policy *against having* uniform employment practices." His interpretation favors discrimination by companies that adopt Walmart's written policy and toss in a few words about giving each manager discretion.

Scalia also wrote that statistics showing discrimination in pay were not worth considering because managers in different stores may have been faced with potential workers who had very different skills and work habits.

What the Court did was force individual actions, which are much less likely to come about because the stakes for each woman are small. It has taken a similar stance in arbitrations; at best, in the eyes of the Court, it's class arbitrations, *bad*; individual cases, *maybe*.

Now let's look at how arbitrators get paid. Judges, paid by taxpayers, have no financial interest in cases before them. In contrast, parties pay the arbitrator. You might think that if each side pays half, the arbitrator is economically neutral. Not necessarily.

The problem is that while you might go to arbitration once in your life, the auto dealer or bank or stock brokerage on the other side of the table is a frequent customer. Arbitrators who rule for consumers tend not to get picked for future work. This record on how arbitrators tend to decide in accord with their stream of income is quite consistent, as studies have found examples of arbitrators who issued dozens of decisions in a single day, all in favor of the businesses who repeatedly hired them.

Economists call this the "repeat player" problem, and it brings us back to Barbara Keeton because it was one of the issues she faced in her dispute with Easterns Automotive and its egregious pricing on the unreliable Mazda it persuaded her to buy. Her court case seemed dead when it was picked up by two new American University law students, Natalie Huls-Simpson and Sheri Strickler. With help from Professor Elliott S. Milstein, who oversees the university's legal clinic, they devised a creative new approach.

To Huls-Simpson, who grew up in much better circumstances than

Keeton, the difference between the car's price and value "was a bit of a shock. I just did not realize that car dealerships would take advantage of a consumer to this extent."

The clever argument the students devised was that, because the court case had been dismissed with prejudice, it was a final order and therefore Keeton was entitled to appeal whether that decision was fair. The trial judge had never considered whether it was fair or unreasonable that Keeton had to pay half of the arbitrator's $200 hourly fee or that Easterns got to pick who would hear the case. The students also noted that the contract had a provision that gave Easterns a stronger hand than Keeton. While the contract forced Keeton into arbitration with no right to sue in court, Easterns retained the right to go to court against her. All of this and more, the student lawyers wrote, showed the contract was unconscionable and therefore unenforceable.

With the help of her enthusiastic young counselors, Keeton won the appeal. Wells Fargo could have gone back and fought the case. Instead it stopped trying to take her house and, to make the case go away, paid her some money, though it insisted the sum be kept confidential.

While Keeton came out all right in the end, the case did not help anyone else. This is another shortcoming in the law—even when systemic problems are identified, they can be hushed up with settlements. The *Seattle Times* in 2010 published a superb series about judges who improperly sealed court cases, putting people in danger from dangerous drugs and unsafe caregivers and helping suspected thieves hide their conduct. Any newspaper in the country could find similar abuses if it tried. Putting an end to sealing cases, especially commercial cases filed in public courts, is a much needed reform.

The reality is that consumers continue to be at risk of being forced into costly private arbitration where the rulings will come from arbitrators whose financial well-being lies in making awards that please those who decide whether they will get hired again in the future. That is not justice. But, once again, it helps explain why the haves do so much better in arbitration and in class-action court cases than the have-nots.

Giving to Goldman

> Our word was our bond, and good ethics was good
> business. That got replaced by liar loans and "I hope I'm
> gone by the time this thing blows up."
>> —**Gordon Murray, former Goldman Sachs managing director**

15. **Of all of** the bailed out banks, the sweetest deals were given to the derivatives trading house of Goldman Sachs. Goldman grew famous as an investment bank, marshaling vast sums of money from investors to build factories and all sorts of new enterprises; but in recent years, investment banking has accounted for just a tenth of its business. Instead, most of its profits come from trading in its own accounts and derivatives. In short, Goldman Sachs is less an investment bank than a new kind of casino.

The derivatives Goldman dreams up and sells are mostly zero-sum bets. One side bets the value of an asset or basket of assets will rise, the other that it will fall. These are actually worse than zero-sum games because the fat fees Goldman charges mean the final result is less than zero for the two parties to the deal. Goldman also places lots of these bets itself. And make no mistake, that is what most derivatives are— gambling. These bets are also a form of unregulated insurance. The premiums charged were not big enough to pay claims because no one thought they would ever actually have to pay off.

Most of these derivatives were credit default swaps, a kind of insurance against the risk that someone who owes money will not pay his or her debts. Against $15 trillion of U.S. mortgage bonds in 2008, Wall Street marketed credit default swaps with a face value of $67 trillion. Worldwide, traded swaps at their peak equaled $670 trillion or $100,000 for every person on the planet, vastly more than all the wealth in the world. Those numbers made it a mathematical certainty that the swaps were mostly speculation, not commercial hedging.

When the time came to pay up and firms such as Lehman Brothers and Bear Stearns could not, the giant flow of cash that is Wall Street froze solid. No one knew who was holding more bad bets than they could pay. No one wanted their money in anyone else's hands, even for a second, in case they shut down, as Lehman did. This was a mess that Alan Greenspan and many other top officials insisted no one saw coming, especially not the part involving mortgage securities. But there were at least a dozen journalists who got it right and alerted people. There were economists and critics who issued warnings, too. The handwriting was on the wall for those who, unlike Alan Greenspan, cared to pay attention.

When the Bush administration decided to rescue Wall Street, instead of letting the market do its job, one firm was favored above all others: Goldman Sachs.

FAVORITE SON

Taxpayer dollars paid off Goldman's losing bets with AIG, the insurance giant. That cost you $13 billion or so. Goldman had told the government it was willing to take a loss on the deals, but gladly accepted one hundred cents on the dollar for bets that might have paid off in pennies.

Treasury Secretary—and former Goldman Sachs chairman and CEO—Hank Paulson arranged this and other deals. At a key moment, he also met with government officials about the bailouts. In the room was one outsider, Lloyd Blankfein, who succeeded Paulson as Goldman CEO.

In October 2008, Paulson invested $10 billion of your money into Goldman. He made the deal three weeks after Warren Buffett had also invested in Goldman. How did the deals compare? Buffett got a $500 million annual dividend. You invested twice as much, but got the same dividend. Buffett got the right to buy 11 percent of Goldman for $115 per share. You bought the right, for almost $7 more per share, to buy just 2 percent of Goldman. That was obviously a bad deal for taxpayers, but just how bad?

Using textbook valuation techniques, Leon Potok, the financial adviser to the United Steelworkers Union, compared the deals. What he found, in plain English, was that American taxpayers made a gift to

Goldman Sachs worth $5 billion. It amounted to more than $16 for every American, $64 for a family of four.

Later the Obama administration let Goldman buy back the securities. Goldman issued a statement saying taxpayers made a 22 percent annualized return on their money. That figure is correct, but it ignores three key facts. One, Goldman got to pick when to buy out the federal government's investment, which would not be when it reached maximum gain. Two, the 22 percent return was not commensurate with the risks taxpayers took, especially compared to the deal Buffett made. Three, it ignored the $13 billion Goldman got from taxpayers when they paid off its bad (and possibly worthless) bets with AIG. All in all, taxpayers lost a bundle, the government saved Goldman from facing the rigors of the market for its mismanagement, and you were left with less while Goldman enjoyed more. And Goldman did not even thank you for your generosity.

As an extraordinarily profitable concern, Goldman should not have needed any help at all. Goldman made $39 billion in pretax profits in the three years 2009 through 2011. For every dollar that came in the front door, Goldman rang up an astounding twenty-nine cents as profit, triple the rate for large businesses overall. Even more astounding was how profitable Goldman was compared to American business as a whole during that three-year span. Goldman's pretax profit in 2009 accounted for 1.5 percent of all the pretax profits earned by all six million corporations in America. For the three years 2009 through 2011, it reported close to a penny out of each dollar of pretax profit in America.

Even bigger than Goldman's profit was the money paid in bonuses to its executives and traders. In those three years Goldman bonuses came to $44 billion. That is an average bonus of close to half a million dollars. For each dollar of pretax profit, the company paid out $1.12 in bonuses to executives and traders. Add the pretax profits and bonuses together, and sixty-one cents of each dollar that came in the door at Goldman stayed as profit or bonus.

In 2009 alone, Goldman bonuses accounted for three-tenths of one percent of all the salaries, wages and bonuses paid in America. Now a fraction of a penny may not sound like much, so let's put it in context. Nearly 117 million people reported earnings from a job in 2009, but just 35,000 of them worked at Goldman. The average 2009 Goldman bonus represented more than a decade of work at the average wage earned by the 99 percent of Americans who make under $200,000 annually.

These riches meant Goldman could build a new corporate headquarters in Lower Manhattan that opened eight years after 9/11. The new headquarters is remarkable for several reasons. It is two blocks long and forty-three stories high, every one of its 2.1 million square feet occupied by Goldman, including six trading floors. The address is simply 200 West Street. Nowhere is the Goldman Sachs name emblazoned on the building.

Thanks to its political connections, Goldman got taxpayers to pick up much of the tab. Goldman says the building cost $2.1 billion. It took out a mortgage for $1.65 billion, financed with Liberty Bonds, which were supposed to help stimulate the economy that Goldman had done such a fine job of crashing. Goldman's share came to almost a fifth of all the Liberty Bonds available to rebuild Lower Manhattan after 9/11. Investors who bought the bonds get their interest free of federal, state and New York City tax. Because the bonds are tax-exempt, the interest rate Goldman paid was reduced, saving it about $175 million over thirty years. As usual, you will make up for that savings in higher taxes, fewer government services and more government borrowing. Think of your share as another part of your gifts to Goldman, adding to each family of four's $64.00 another $2.16.

Tax-free financing was not the only tax benefit Goldman got. The state and city lavished at least $66 million of tax breaks on Goldman, for example, not requiring it to pay sales tax on all its new furniture the way a homeowner or small-business owner must. Then there was $49 million in job-training grants from government, welfare not for workers but for Goldman owners and executives. Meanwhile, many smaller businesses in Lower Manhattan said they could get little more than the time of day from the government as they tried to rebuild after the attacks on 9/11.

Greg LeRoy, who runs Good Jobs First, a small Washington nonprofit that uncovers subsidy deals and tries to get news coverage about them, considers the Goldman Sachs building "one of the most lavish giveaways in U.S. history." That's a big claim in the context of massive gifts in the past to politically connected businesses like the railroads, defense contractors and many others.

LeRoy explains, "After twenty years documenting outrageous subsidy deals, I thought I'd seen it all"—until he saw Goldman with its $39 billion in pretax profits over three years "hogging 9/11 reconstruction funds while small businesses languish." Moreover, he observed, the "approval process is rushed and secretive, mocking taxpayers' right to review and comment."

Taxpayers are not the only ones Goldman abuses. Consider its role in

the $21 billion takeover of the El Paso Corporation, the owner of the
pipeline that killed the twelve campers in New Mexico. A Delaware
judge, Leo Strine, called what Goldman did in facilitating the sale "disturbing." In the past, Goldman had been accused of having a conflict of
interest involving Kinder Morgan, the owner of the pipeline. When
founder Richard Kinder took Kinder Morgan private by buying out
other shareholders, Goldman Sachs was his partner. Their tactics were
such that the shareholders who were forced out sued. Goldman paid $200
million to settle the claim but, as has become standard, Goldman neither
admitted nor denied wrongdoing.

In the deal before Judge Strine in early 2012, Goldman advised El
Paso, recommending it accept Kinder Morgan's offer for its shares. Some
big El Paso shareholders thought they should get a lot more for their
shares and they sued, too. In fact, Goldman had a huge interest in giving
its client (El Paso) bad advice to sell itself cheap: Goldman owned almost
one-fifth of Kinder Morgan and had two people on the Kinder Morgan
board. The less El Paso shareholders got, the more Goldman's Kinder
Morgan stake would be worth. This is about as clear and obvious as any
conflict of interest can be.

We're not done. Douglas Foshee, the El Paso chief executive who personally negotiated the sale with Kinder Morgan's Rich Kinder, wanted to
carve out part of the property for himself in a later deal. The lower the
price Kinder Morgan paid El Paso, the less Foshee would have to pay
later to get the property he wanted. Goldman knew about this blatant
conflict of interest, too, but went ahead anyway, advising El Paso shareholders to accept the lowball buyout offer from Kinder Morgan.

When these conflicts of interest became known, a second adviser was
brought in—the banking firm of Morgan Stanley. The terms of its fee
did not suggest it would be independent. Morgan Stanley was to be paid,
the judge explained in his opinion, only if El Paso was sold to Kinder
Morgan. If any other deal was reached, Morgan Stanley would get nothing. That, of course, created an incentive for Morgan Stanley to look favorably on a deal for which it would get $20 million versus any other deal,
lest it be paid nothing. In this, Judge Strine noted, Goldman had nar-
rowed the range of advice Morgan Stanley was likely to offer to only that
which benefited Goldman.

Judge Strine's word for all of this—"disturbing"—seems much too
mild. But it also fits the judge's decision merely to speak harshly of what
he saw and then let the deal go through to the detriment of El Paso
shareholders, who thus received neither unfettered advice nor the best

price. The El Paso case serves as a reminder that the ancient principle of sale to the highest bidder is too often set aside.

A LECTURE FROM MR. SMITH

Just days after Judge Strine issued his ruling in February 2012, Goldman got slapped again, this time by one of its own. Greg Smith quit Goldman Sachs after twelve years. His resignation letter came in the form of an op-ed column for the *New York Times* in which he wrote that, at Goldman, "the interests of the client continue to be sidelined in the way the firm operates and thinks about making money." He described a toxic environment in which callous "talk about ripping clients off" was so accepted that in e-mails, executives referred to Goldman clients as "Muppets."

Smith wrote of "derivatives sales meetings where not one single minute is spent asking questions about how we can help clients. It's purely about how we can make the most possible money off of them. If you were an alien from Mars and sat in on one of these meetings, you would believe that a client's success or progress was not part of the thought process at all."

Gone from the 143-year-old firm was a culture of "teamwork, integrity, a spirit of humility, and always doing right by our clients," Smith wrote. In its place was one concern: making money. "This alone will not sustain a firm for so long. It had something to do with pride and belief in the organization. I am sad to say that I look around today and see virtually no trace of the culture that made me love working for this firm for many years. I no longer have the pride, or the belief."

Goldman issued a damage-control statement belittling Smith as just one of twelve thousand Goldman employees, though one with the title of vice president. He was in fact head of Goldman's United States equity derivatives business in Europe, the Middle East and Africa.

A decade before Smith quit in disgust, Nomi Prins did the same. A Goldman analyst who specialized in highly complex mathematics and derivatives, Prins became vexed when she was asked how to design derivatives to help turn a profit for people who had invested in the life insurance policies of AIDS patients. The development of new drug regimens let people live longer with the disease, wiping out profits from those who had placed bets that AIDS patients would die soon. That left Prins disgusted. But what finally drove her to quit was the reaction on Goldman's oil trading desk on 9/11. No one she was with quite understood what was happening, but they knew that all the phones at the World Trade Center were dead. Once the traders realized the first plane had hit one of the Twin Towers, their reaction was to debate what trades would make Goldman money. As people who knew they would die tried to make cell-phone calls to their loved ones before time ran out, the question of the day at Goldman Sachs was "how do we trade this?"

No business sector can do more damage to an economy and a society than finance. The potential losses are virtually unlimited, as shown by the simple fact that in 2008 the stated value of all derivatives far exceeded the net worth of the entire planet. By wrapping unsound financial products in fancy names like *credit default swap* and *collateralized mortgage-backed securities*, the wizards of Wall Street can practice modern alchemy—until one of their formulations blows up. But just as the philosopher's stone never turned lead into gold, the mortgage-backed securities turned out to be as toxic as lead, and the implications for the average person very real.

The 2008 meltdown cost every thirty-fourth person in America his or her job. Then the federal government compounded the irresponsible greed of the financiers by committing what, in the worst case, would have been the entire economic output of the nation for an entire year to rescuing the very same derivatives trading houses and failed commercial banks whose alchemy had just been exposed as bankrupt.

Phil Angelides, the California businessman and politician who headed the Financial Crisis Inquiry Commission, has a warning about all of this. On a budget of less than $10 million, the commission produced a solid, 545-page report so well done that no critic has identified a single factual error. The budget was a fraction of what was spent investigating President Clinton's lying about sex with an intern, an indication of Washington's confused priorities when it comes to spending taxpayer money. The response to Angelides's report made clear that Congress did not want to know what really happened and that it didn't want to stem the flow of campaign money, private jet trips and lucrative jobs for those leaving office. Congress would not even pay to have it archived on the Internet, which is why the report and supporting records are at Stanford University's Web site. Washington effectively threw it in the trash can.

Angelides says failure to heed what the commission found is not without its risks. His blunt assessment of what to expect unless we change our ways: "It's going to happen again."

Please Die Soon

The company knows that if I don't get the medical care I
need I will die sooner. That is their strategy. They want me
to die.

—Bob Manning

16.   **Bob Manning enjoyed** a wonderful life in northern New York.
He grew up near the border with Quebec in a land of lush green sum-
mers, colorful falls and winters deep with snow for frolicking. Manning
married well. At age twenty-six, his wife Helen had borne one son and
was carrying a second. Manning secured a job as an electric power lineman, which kept him outdoors where he could work his long, lean mus-
cles. It even paid well. He made union wages and winter storms ensured
a fair amount of overtime pay.

One freezing February afternoon he was working twenty-five feet up
a pole near the St. Lawrence Seaway, the system of locks that lets large
ships move between the Great Lakes and the Atlantic Ocean. As the soft
light of a short winter day began yielding to darkness, Manning's boss
hollered up that it was time to come down. Just then a bolt of electricity
flung Manning into the air. Manning hit the pavement head first, snap-
ping his neck between the fifth and six vertebrae.

Manning was desperately looking for someone to help him collect his
workers' compensation benefits when we met in 1997. He fell in 1962.
While a thirty-five-year fight by a paralyzed man to collect benefits to
which he was entitled may seem extreme, it is unusual only in how long
it continued. Manning had won more than thirty orders to pay him his
benefits, yet he hadn't gotten satisfaction.

The cruel reality that would emerge in the years after we met was that, for Manning, the worst was yet to come.

STAYING SAFE

American workers in every state are supposed to be protected by laws that provide both medical care and income if they are hurt on the job. That is one legacy of the tragedy of the Triangle Shirtwaist Company fire in 1911 that killed those 146 young women and so shocked the public conscience that reforms began across America. Some reforms dealt with worker safety, including fire-escape drills now common to workers in office towers. Fire departments began making inspections, including checking that exit doors opened.

A century ago, the factory's two owners paid the families of the 146 dead less than $1,000 each in today's money. The fire insurance company paid the owners more than five times that much, allowing the factory to reopen. Two years later one of the owners again locked his workers in (recall that the locked doors in 1911 had accounted for most, perhaps all, of the deaths). This time no one died. The fine assessed was less than $200 in today's money.

In 2004, retail giant Walmart admitted that, for fifteen years, some managers had been locking workers inside its stores after closing. A Walmart vice president explained that it was for the workers' own safety in high-crime areas, but workers told different stories. Some said they worked at stores in areas with hardly any crime, suggesting that Walmart's famous strategies to squeeze more profits, rather than protection from burglars, was the real motive. Others told of being trapped inside Walmarts and Sam's Club stores after heart attacks, after accidents or as hurricanes approached; one man told of being unable to leave when his wife went into labor. Shortly after reporter Steven Greenhouse of the *New York Times* began asking around about lock-ins, the company changed its policy. Walmart headquarters did not end the lock-ins, but it did make sure night managers had keys to unlock fire-escape doors.

While luckily none of the locked-in Walmart workers died, a Texan named Rolan Hoskin wasn't so fortunate. He worked at McWane Inc., a privately owned maker of cast-iron water and sewer pipes, at its factory east of Dallas.

In the eight years from 1995 through 2002, McWane, which employed

5,000 workers, reported 4,600 workplace injuries, though there is good reason to believe the actual number of injuries was much higher. Nine McWane workers died on the job. The safety record at McWane was far worse than all six of its competitors combined.

On the day he died, Hoskin, who made less than $10 an hour, was at work deep inside a giant machine with a conveyor belt, which the law required to have a suspenders-and-belt safety system. Not only were safety catches required, but the machine was supposed to be turned off when someone was working on it. There were no safety devices, however. When the conveyor started up, Hoskin was caught in it and crushed. He was forty-eight.

Only after a joint investigation by PBS's *Frontline*, the Canadian Broadcasting Corporation and the *New York Times* were prosecutions of McWane's executives begun. In 2006, four were convicted of multiple felony charges based on evidence showing that safety rules at the plant were routinely flouted and reports falsified.

A similar story unfolded at the West Virginia coal-mining firm Massey Energy Company, where twenty-nine miners died needlessly in the Upper Big Branch mine explosion in 2010. Much later prosecutors sought two low-level indictments over what they said were determined management efforts to obstruct enforcement of the mine safety laws, including falsifying records and disabling equipment that detects explosive gases. Documents and testimony also made clear that Don Blankenship, Massey's CEO, fought safety efforts because he believed they reduced profits, which in turn would reduce his income (he was by far the highest-paid person in that poor Appalachian state, making more than $20 million in some years).

Government safety inspectors, at least some of them, knew what was wrong and tried to act at both McWane and Massey and no doubt many other companies where worker safety was compromised. But there are too few inspectors. In the name of shrinking government spending, the ranks of job-safety inspectors have been continually cut, and those who remain are overwhelmed with complaints, weakening enforcement. Without backing from the ever-changing political appointees at the top, real correctives are becoming rare.

When a safety inspector does decide to get tough, many companies can call on their political connections, as the Massey coal case shows. In 2006, CEO Blankenship vacationed in Monte Carlo on the French Riviera. He shared meals and fine wines several times with his friend Spike Maynard and the single men's female companions. At the time, Massey

had a $50 million case on appeal before the West Virginia Supreme
Court, whose chief justice was Spike Maynard. A year later Justice Maynard voted in favor of Massey. Few knew then about the French
connection—only after photographs emerged of Blankenship and Maynard partying (ten other photos were filed under court order, leaving us
to wonder what frolicking they depict) did Chief Justice Maynard recuse
himself from a rehearing in the case. But that was not the end of the
machinations.

Massey Energy contributed more than $3 million to help elect Brent
Benjamin to the West Virginia Supreme Court, an amount far greater
than any other in West Virginia campaign history. The money was used
against another candidate whom Blankenship feared would vote against
Massey in the same case. When that case resurfaced before the court, the
duly elected Justice Benjamin did indeed vote in favor of his political
donor. This resulted in a suit and, eventually, a U.S. Supreme Court ruling on the propriety of Benjamin's conduct. In 2009, the Supreme Court
found that Justice Benjamin should have recused himself. The impropri-
ety here is so obvious that it is hard to understand why the ruling was 5-4
instead of unanimous.

The dissenting opinions are revealing. Justice Antonin Scalia belittled
the majority. "In the best of all possible worlds, should judges sometimes
recuse even where the clear commands of our prior due process law do
not require it? Undoubtedly. The relevant question, however, is whether
we do more good than harm by seeking to correct this imperfection
through expansion of our constitutional mandate in a manner ungov-
erned by any discernable rule. The answer is obvious."

Of course there is an obvious rule: elected judges should not participate in cases where any party before them has donated to help them or
hurt their opponent.

Far more troubling was the dissent by Chief Justice John Roberts, who
saw nothing amiss because the Massey funds went not to Justice Benjamin's campaign but to an "independent" organization working against
his opponent. In this dissent we got a broad hint of the decision that, a
year later, would become the notorious *Citizens United* decision permitting corporations to spend unlimited sums to influence elections as long
as they do not hand cash directly to candidates.

In the Massey appeal, Roberts wrote: "It is true that Don Blankenship
spent a large amount of money in connection with this election. But this
point cannot be emphasized strongly enough: Other than a $1,000 direct
contribution from Blankenship, Justice Benjamin and his campaign had

no control over how this money was spent. Campaigns go to great lengths to develop precise messages and strategies. An insensitive or ham-handed ad campaign by an independent third party might distort the campaign's message or cause a backlash against the candidate, even though the candidate was not responsible for the ads."

What chance, you may well ask, does a solitary victim like Bob Manning have in a rigged system in which someone as intellectually corrupt as John Roberts sits as chief justice of the United States?

SEEKING COMPENSATION

We've all seen exposés on local television stations showing a cop, a firefighter or some other worker on disability laying bricks or wielding a shovel in his garden despite an allegedly debilitating back injury. That is cheating and should be pursued. But it is penny-ante abuse compared to the injustice of cases like Bob Manning's.

First, a little background. Workers' compensation insurance is tremendously profitable. In California, for example, insurers made more *profit* than they paid out in *benefits* to injured workers and the families of dead workers' in 2004 through 2007. According to official data from the California Workers' Compensation Insurance Rating Bureau, benefits paid totaled $26 billion versus profits of $28.2 billion. One implication of such profitability is that insurance rates are too high, but another is that profits are high because of improper denials of service.

Keep in mind what an insurance company is. Basically, it is just like a bank, with one crucial difference. Both banks and insurers take money from customers; these payments are called deposits at banks, premiums at insurers. The difference is in payouts. Banks return money on demand, insurers pay on event. And by arguing about the events, insurance companies can delay and deny claims, thus enhancing profits.

What happened to Bob Manning was, in essence, a denial of payment. The same thing can happen to you, even if you work in an office that you imagine is a safe place. If you get hurt at work and your employer dodges its legal duty to pay, as in Manning's case, you and your family will have your suffering compounded. Even if you avoid such terrible luck, others will not. As many as seven workers a day suffer permanent spinal injuries needing lifelong medical care, yet resistance to paying benefits appears to be increasing. When companies refuse to pay for the medical care they are legally required to provide, the costs get shifted to the taxpayers.

That means the insurers' profits are shielded and your taxes are diverted. By the time I met him, Bob Manning's medical costs were in the millions of dollars.

In theory, each employer buys insurance, either in the marketplace or from a state agency. The benefits are modest, but that is because they are supposed to be awarded without the need for litigation, in which lawyers who win claims rake in a large share of the money. In a no-fault workers' compensation system it should not matter if the injury was the result of employer misconduct, bad luck or even a mistake by the worker. As Bob Manning learned, though, the reality can be quite different.

When I met Manning he was sixty years old, living in Sacramento, California, in a ranch-style home with extra wide doors for his wheelchair. An aging van, modified to lift his wheelchair inside, sat in the driveway. His sons were grown, one of them an airline pilot entrusted with more than a hundred lives every day he worked. When some relatives died, leaving three children orphaned, the Mannings took them in and raised them as their own. The Manning home was as neat and clean as it was happy, filled with well-mannered grandchildren, cousins and kids from the neighborhood.

Manning was remarkably cheerful. But he also told me several times that he believed his old employer, the Niagara Mohawk electric utility, and its insurance carrier, Utilities Mutual, wanted him to die so they could escape the cost of keeping him alive. He recited details of what he felt was deliberate medical mistreatment and denial of care vital to keeping him alive, such as the insurer refusing to supply enough sterile catheters to help him urinate without getting an infection. "I understand what's going on," he said. "The company knows that if I don't get the medical care I need I will die sooner. That is their strategy. They want me to die."

At the time we spoke, I regarded those as the angry words of a man imprisoned in a body over which he had almost no control. But as I would learn a few days later, and again years later, Manning wasn't imagining things.

Back in New York, I spoke with two lawyers who were trying to help him, Samuel Spalter and James D. Harmon. Both said Manning was spot on in his assessment that Niagara Mohawk and Utilities Mutual wanted Manning to die as soon as possible to cut their costs. The lawyers also pointed out that they had won several dozen administrative and judicial orders that Manning be paid and yet they could not collect. But let's turn the clock back and revisit the beginning of the story.

Niagara Mohawk and nearly three dozen other corporate-owned utilities had formed their own insurance company to pay workers' compensation claims. This nonprofit insurer was called Utilities Mutual.

In 1962, soon after Manning fell, Utilities Mutual started paying him a weekly benefit. There was no provision for automatic cost-of-living adjustments, though, so Manning knew that in the years to come his benefits would lose value. On the advice of a lawyer, he sued the old New York Telephone Company, then part of AT&T, which had half ownership of the pole from which he fell. In 1968 a jury awarded him $750,000, out of which his lawyers took a big chunk.

The award also meant that, under New York State law, Utilities Mutual was permitted to stop payments and to force Manning to reimburse the insurer the $129,000 it had spent over the years on him for financial support and medical care. Utilities Mutual took the position that it would not have to pay any more until the award from the telephone company had been exhausted, even though it did not help Manning win his case against the phone company.

By 1975, the money from the New York Telephone award was gone. Most of it had been placed with a neighbor, a stockbroker who traded the nest egg into the ground. Manning then sought a resumption of payments from Utilities Mutual. The company refused. Its lawyer was Philip J. Rooney, who argued an unusual theory about why Utilities Mutual should not have to pay for anything except some minor items. Rooney said Helen Manning was required to care for her husband without being paid.

Rooney explained that, in his judgment, it was the law that a spouse is not entitled to payment for services provided to her husband in the course of her household duties. "If I, as a mechanic, for instance, fix my wife's car, she is not obligated to pay me for doing so if I do it around the house." He insisted this was not his idea, but the policy of both companies.

Rooney also told me he was "deeply hurt" by the idea that he or his clients would want Manning's life to be shortened. "Nothing could be further from the truth. I personally have deep sympathy for Mr. Manning, but I sincerely believe that there is a legitimate legal issue here and until it has been decided by the highest court in New York, the [insurance] carrier really is not obligated to make any payments at all."

Subsequently, I met again with Spalter, who had become the lead lawyer for Manning. He called the theory on wifely duties "outrageous and contrary to the law." So did other lawyers I consulted.

Helen Manning had her own take. She was a registered nurse. She said that if she had worked outside the home, Utilities Mutual, under its own theory, would have had to pay nurses to care for her husband because she—her husband's caregiver—was away. Rooney told me he was not so sure about that.

Even when Manning needed outside nurses because Helen Manning could not give him care, Utilities Mutual refused to pay. Spalter once asked that nurses be hired for two months to care for Manning and the state Workers' Compensation Board ordered Niagara Mohawk and Utilities Mutual to pay. The companies refused on the grounds that the New York Telephone award had not been exhausted. Spalter complained, but the Workers' Compensation Board said, in effect, that it had no power to enforce its own order.

The Mannings struggled until 1988 when, after a bit of saber rattling by one hearing officer got Rooney's attention, Utilities Mutual began voluntarily paying $350 a week. The rates were roughly those settled on in the first award back in 1962, even though inflation had reduced the value of a 1962 dollar to less than a quarter in 1988. Manning kept pressing; Rooney pressed right back.

Then in 1995, Manning finally won a $1.2 million award to cover the care his wife had provided at roughly $42,000 annually. The problem was that he could not get a check out of Utilities Mutual. By the time I got involved in 1997 more than thirty orders to pay had been issued, but not enforced.

Niagara Mohawk positioned itself as the good guy. A spokesman said the company had voluntarily provided lifetime medical care for Manning's wife and children and had even given the family a color television. Niagara Mohawk insisted that it had absolutely no role or responsibility in the case because the workers' compensation claim was in the hands of the Utilities Mutual insurance company. There was a small problem with that argument. Utilities Mutual was created by three dozen corporate-owned electric utilities, including Niagara Mohawk. For many years during Manning's fight its president was William J. Donlon, who some of the time had doubled as chairman and chief executive of Niagara Mohawk. Plus, Utilities Mutual earned phenomenal profits, regularly paying its member utilities huge dividends. So ability to pay was never an issue, just willingness to comply with the law.

At last, one Niagara Mohawk spokesperson had the integrity to acknowledge what the case was really about—the cost of keeping Manning alive. "No one expected him to live this long," the executive told me.

FRONT-PAGE NEWS

I wrote a story about Manning that ran on the front page of the *New York Times*. I got a call within hours from then-governor George Pataki, who said the case was a disgrace. The state attorney general and other officials weighed in, too. But Rooney was unmoved.

When I told him that Pataki was clearly angry and had assured me that he would see to it that Manning got paid, Rooney was nonchalant. "He's just a politician, not a court." And then Rooney said that, even though an appeals court had issued an order barring any further appeals to delay payment, his reading of the court decision suggested grounds for many new appeals.

Fortunately, executives at Niagara Mohawk recognized the damage an angry governor or a nosy attorney general could cause a utility, even when those officials were well-known friends of business. Utilities Mutual soon assigned a new lawyer, who read over the unbroken string of decisions ordering payment. He told Manning's counsel Spalter that the company would pay. A fight that had gone on for thirty-five years was over. Within ten days of the *Times* article, the Mannings had a check that, before legal fees and costs were taken out, came to nearly $2 million.

But the foolishness *still* wasn't over—for Manning or for you. Utilities Mutual continued its tactic of not paying Manning's medical bills. That meant that each time Manning needed to go to Sutter Hospital in Sacramento, the admission staff would perform what is known as a "wallet biopsy." They would learn that Manning had insurance from Utilities Mutual, and get the insurance company approval to admit Manning. When the bills came due, however, Utilities Mutual would refuse to pay.

You might think that this would prompt more litigation. But at Sutter and every other hospital I have spoken with about such circumstances, the standard practice with totally disabled people is to submit the bill refused by workers' comp insurers to Medicare, which pays without question. One hospital administrator was perplexed when I asked about pressing the insurer for payment. "Why would we get into a fight with the workers' comp carrier when Medicare will pay?" the administrator asked.

The better question is, Why doesn't Medicare go after the workers' compensation insurer? Manning for years got on the telephone to Medicare officials, members of Congress, medical economists and anyone else he could get to listen to ask why Utilities Mutual and other insurers were allowed to get away with shifting their costs onto Medicare. "It's stealing," Manning said.

Finally he got a lawyer to bring a lawsuit. It was not easy. For starters, the federal government had to grant permission to sue, which it was reluctant to do. Then a federal appeals court restricted the lawsuit so that only a small fraction of the bills Utilities Mutual shoved off onto taxpayers was recovered. This is typical of what happens in a system with not nearly enough judges to hear all the cases on their docket, a way that the push for smaller government creates not just injustice, but helps rich companies like Niagara Mohawk and Utilities Mutual shove their costs onto unknowing taxpayers.

Niagara Mohawk announced in 2000 that it was selling itself for $3 billion to a British company, National Grid. Soon after, Utilities Mutual was sold to Cologne Re, a reinsurance company. And right about then, a nurse started ingratiating herself into Manning's care at Sutter Hospital.

Bob Manning told me that he instinctively did not trust this nurse. His doctor, Stanley Chew, also found the nurse's interest odd. "She introduced herself as a home care specialist contracted by the workers' comp insurance company, which was Cologne, to monitor his care," Dr. Chew said. "At first she made a few simple suggestions regarding his seat cushion. In retrospect those comments were made to gain our trust in her. I also recall our meeting in my office in which she was extremely probing about Bob's prognosis, wanting to know just how long he was expected to live." The questions, Dr. Chew said, were entirely out of line—especially for an agent of a company with a financial interest in Manning's dying as soon as possible.

Cologne Re is a Warren Buffett company. By buying Manning's workers' compensation claim, and all the other obligations of Utilities Mutual, Cologne Re was making a bet. If Manning and others like him died soon, the deal was more likely to prove profitable. But the longer Manning lived, the smaller the profit. If Manning and others like him lived long enough, the result would be a loss for Buffett's Berkshire Hathaway holding company.

Soon the nurse said she wanted to inspect the Manning home, which workers' compensation laws allow. The Mannings thought her approach was anything but that of a caregiver because when she visited, her primary interest seemed to be in questioning why Manning would want to go on living. When she got to Manning's bedroom, her purpose became clear.

"Why don't you have a DNR order on the wall?" she asked. A do-not-resuscitate order is an instruction people who know they are dying may give to indicate that no resuscitative care should be provided. But Bob Manning had no interest in dying; after almost forty years of living with almost complete paralysis, he was a remarkably vital man.

As Dr. Chew noted when he told me about this incident, end-of-life decisions are a fit subject for a physician to discuss with a patient. But this nurse was not a caregiver; she was an agent of a company that would lose money if Manning went on living and would profit from his death.

"She was asking me to die," Manning told me.

Dr. Chew agreed: "She wanted Bob to have a DNR order and was quite insistent."

The nurse turned out to be an employee of a medical advice company called Concentra. When I asked Tom Fogarty, the doctor who is a co-founder of Concentra about this, he did something unusual. Unlike the top executives who will not come to the phone or who speak only through written statements, Fogarty set out to find out what happened. When he got back to me he was guarded about what he shared, but he made it clear he was aghast that any medical professional representing a financial interest in someone's life would even inquire about a DNR order. He also volunteered that after a brief spell, his company had gotten out of the line of business that the nurse had been part of. How much better American business would be if we had more chief executives who dealt forthrightly with issues instead of hiding behind publicists and lawyers, not to mention squads of burly security guards.

Now, to be clear, I do not think for a moment that Warren Buffett knew that the nurse working for his Cologne Re insurance company was going to ask Bob Manning, in effect, to die the next time he had a medical emergency. But that does not mean Buffett is free of responsibility for what happened. Buffett often says that his style is to let his managers run their shops, as long as they make their numbers, meaning their expected level of profit. His management style is widely praised in news reports and in profiles of the "Oracle of Omaha." By giving managers the freedom to run their business units as they see fit, Buffett takes on a duty to demand the highest ethical standards. That would not, in my opinion, include gouging customers on coal shipping rates as his BNSF railroad does. Nor would an ethical chief executive allow anyone in his employ ever to suggest that anyone should die to bolster a company's profits. But that is what happens under the Buffett style, in which by his own account he focuses on whether managers, some of whom resort to immoral conduct to give their billionaire boss what he demands, "make their numbers."

The reality is that what Manning had been saying all along, even before we met in 1997, was true. The insurance company wanted him to die. They had made it difficult for him to get care, they had for years refused to replace the crane Helen used to hoist him out of bed after the gears were stripped, they made it hard for him to get supplies to avoid infections. And finally a nurse hired by a Warren Buffett company came right out and asked him, in effect, why he was not going to die the next time he had a medical emergency.

Bob Manning lived until 2009. To this day, his family says they are still owed money to which he was entitled. They are owed more than that.

Your 201(k) Plan

Workers tend not to use them to full advantage, and
employers don't always follow best practices in designing
them.

—CFO Magazine

17. **Jim Mehling's career** was humming. As president of Monitor
Capital Advisors, his team was minting money for its owner, the immensely successful insurer New York Life. In effect, Mehling was an
internal financial adviser for New York Life, the largest life insurance
company in America owned by its customers and known therefore as a
mutual insurance company.

One March day in 1997 Mehling's boss gave him a glowing review, a
raise and a $147,000 bonus. Six days later Mehling was fired.

To anyone who has a 401(k) to save money for their old age, the story
of Jim Mehling and New York Life matters because it opens a small window on some of the many subtle ways your retirement funds get nicked
with dubious fees.

Mehling's offense was refusing to look the other way when he found
out that New York Life gouged the 401(k) and pension plans of its own
workers. He told his bosses the gouging had to stop. In a lawsuit filed
three months later, Mehling and lawyer Eli Gottesdiener sought the return of special bonuses paid to the executives and the return of hundreds
of millions of dollars in profit that New York Life made by charging the
pension plans as much as twenty-five times the market rate for investment management services.

New York Life offered up a revealing public defense to Mehling's accusations. Executive Vice President George J. Trapp invited me to the

company headquarters, an ornate forty-story temple of wealth that oc-
cupies an entire block on Park Avenue in Manhattan. Should its size, location and polished marble interior fail to make the point, atop the 1926
skyscraper rests a golden crown, a gilded melding of church spire and
Egyptian pyramid.

Trapp and Stephen M. Saxon, a pension lawyer, insisted that all fees
New York Life charged to its own retirement plans were within the law.
Trapp added that Mehling was fired for good reasons that had nothing to
do with the accusations that New York Life charged too much for services to its own retirement plans. The five plans had $4.1 billion of assets
at the time.

Even if excess fees had been charged, Trapp and Saxon said, they could
not imagine a cause of action against the company or its executives. They
noted the solid returns and that the company's defined-benefit pension
plans had $2.7 billion, including a surplus of $900 million, a robust 50
percent more than the $1.8 billion in benefits owed to New York Life
employees and agents at the time.

Of course this was also 1999, when the stock market was soaring beyond any values justified by profits, as investors would learn the following
April when the Internet bubble collapsed and $7 trillion of paper wealth
was lost to those who had not yet cashed out. More important, however,
the law makes no distinction between charging excess fees to rich plans
or poor ones. Norman Stein, a law professor who specializes in pension
issues, explained, "the statute says you can't violate your duty and charge
excessive fees, not that you can charge excessive fees if a pension plan is
overfunded."

Alan Lebowitz, a senior Labor Department pension official, observed
that cases like that at New York Life "were inevitable because the statute
creates this situation where you can be" an official of both an investment
company and its pension plan. "The individual who is both a plan fiduciary and a company official is in a very difficult situation because you
clearly owe an obligation to both the plan participants and to the shareholders."

More than eight years later, New York Life paid $14.7 million to settle
the overcharging case. The company did not admit to wrongdoing (firms
almost never do). But the Mehling case illustrates one reason that many
millions of Americans are heading toward old age without enough resources to live out their last years well or even decently.

Mehling's essential revelation was simple: there is no way for any of
the 61 million Americans with money in 401(k) plans to know whether

those permitted to shave slices of money from their accounts are taking more than the market rate. Indeed, there is no way to know the name of every company taking some of your money or just what they are doing for their fees.

Senators and representatives have known about this for years. Congress has been told repeatedly about numerous weaknesses in the 401(k) system by its own investigative agency, the Government Accountability Office. Academic researchers, journalists, whistle-blowers and even some industry leaders like Mehling have exposed clear and present financial dangers. The poachers include bosses who steal from their workers by never passing on 401(k) money from paychecks to be invested. Some workers are forced to invest in their own employers but given no voice in how their shares are voted. Most of all, far too little money flows into 401(k) accounts, especially for workers not in the top tiers of pay.

Yet little or nothing has been done to correct abuses and protect workers, whose voices are heard far less often than those of big campaign donors and the lobbyists they employ. The result is practices that enrich some corporations not from market capitalism but market manipulation, ensuring the haves have more at the expense of those with less.

AN ACCIDENTAL SYSTEM

The problem began at the very birth of the 401(k). Starting as a favor to one industry, it grew into a system, one that carries a burden, as a cornerstone of American retirement, it was never designed to carry.

The 401(k) is really one huge tax loophole. Tax loopholes are not intended policy, but often are the unintended result of laws that do not match up, leaving some income untaxed. Loopholes can be pure accidents; sometimes clever tax lawyers spot an opening and leap through it. Other loopholes are the product of lobbyists shaping legislation and of gullible politicians, too eager to please donors and prospective employers.

The 401(k) was created at the behest of bank holding companies so that their better-paid workers could stash away some extra pay without paying taxes until they retired. Back then the top tax rate was 70 percent, so in retirement all but the most senior executives could anticipate paying much lower rates. But when a Pennsylvania compensation consultant named Ted Benna read the law more than three decades ago, he recognized something much larger. In classic entrepreneurial fashion, Benna set out with no capital to build a business for himself; by his reading of the law—and it is a correct one—not just banks but most any business could create 401(k) plans. Benna promoted the widespread use of such plans, which quickly caught the attention of people with capital, like the Ned Johnson family of Boston, who own Fidelity; the Stowers family of Kansas City, who own Century Investments; and other mutual funds. They got in on the deal and made billions, although Benna never made it beyond being a tiny player, barely compensated for his rich insight.

The annual taxes avoided because of 401(k) plans come to about $110 billion, according to Teresa Ghilarducci, a pension economist who teaches at The New School in New York. To put that number in perspective, had the IRS collected another $110 billion in 2009, total income tax revenue would have gone up by close to 13 percent.

For those who can afford to save, the plans are a happy accident. Named after a section of federal tax code numbered (you guessed it) 401(k), workers can set aside money from their pretax pay. Employers with such plans have the option to add money, matching some or all of what the workers save.

As enhancements on top of Social Security and traditional pensions, 401(k) plans are a good idea because they encourage additional savings. Viewed as a kind of financial dessert, like meringue, the 401(k) makes sense.

But instead of being dessert, this financial meringue has come to be served most often as the main course, one that is no more healthy financially than pie topping is dietetically.

Mutual funds and other promoters of 401(k) plans sold them in the eighties and nineties as a way to riches, with charts showing young people how they could retire as millionaires. But it hasn't worked out that way. Jack VanDerhei, research director for the Employee Benefits Research Institute, a straight-shooting nonprofit that gathers data, observed that "far too many people had false confidence in the past" that modest savings would make them flush in old age. "People's expectations need to come closer to reality so they will save more and delay retirement until it is financially feasible," VanDerhei said.

The rise of 401(k) plans illustrates how America is not prospering because its economic policies violate well-established principles. The typical 401(k) involves excess costs, added risks and inefficiencies that have become embedded in the law. Because of the concentrated interest of a narrow segment of the economy, people are certainly getting rich off the plans, but most of them aren't the supposed beneficiaries. What we've seen is the financial equivalent of mechanics throwing sand in the gears of machinery they do not own. It gets them work, but not work that adds value.

Corporate executives know full well that these plans are seriously flawed. *CFO*, a magazine for chief financial officers, told its readers in 2009, "True, 401(k)s have not proved to be the perfect substitute for pension plans. Workers tend not to use them to full advantage, and employers don't always follow best practices in designing them."

That's an understatement.

SLICING AND DICING

In all, 401(k) plans held about $2.2 trillion in 2010. After adding in the holdings of similar plans called 457s for government workers and 403(b) plans for nonprofit workers, the total comes to an estimated $4.5 trillion, according to the Investment Company Institute, a trade association.

Money in the trillions—that is, millions of millions—is almost incomprehensible. But divide the 401(k) pool by the 61 million people involved and you get an average of $33,375 in each account. Looking at just the 52 million workers who can add money to their plans (the others have moved on or retired), we find they did not put all that much into their accounts. Counting both worker savings and any match money from their employers, the average participant saved $4,061 in 2009, the latest year for which Labor Department data is available.

Some dollars have disappeared, as Jim Mehling warned us, due to excessive charges for record keeping, trusteeship, compliance, promotion and investment management. According to its own data, industry fees are at least a half of a percentage point per year higher than a competitive market would charge.

A half of a percentage point may not sound like much but small amounts siphoned from large pools produce big numbers. The half a percentage point in excess fees for all 401(k)-style plans works out to $22.5 billion a year. Consult your calculator, and you'll find that that amounts to an annual cost of $535 for the average 401(k) participant. After thirty years at 6 percent interest, the cumulative cost of such fees comes to an average of $42,300. That is more than the average balance of a bit more than $33,000. Looked at another way, it's the equivalent of two years of after-tax pay for a single worker making the median wage of about $500 a week in 2010, though workers at that pay level probably don't have much in their 401(k), if they have one at all. But even for a worker making

$50,000, a threshold for the top quarter of workers, that $42,300 siphoned off by Wall Street is more than a year's take-home pay.

Look deeper and you will find average balances are highly misleading. There are a few people with huge accounts—some in the millions of dollars, like Mitt Romney—but many others with less than $10,000. Mostly the 401(k) plans amount to a shallow pool where most people only get wet up to their ankles.

The lost decade of the twenty-first century, when investment returns for many were less than zero, did little to slow the steady draining of funds through fees, some hidden and some explicit. The weak stock market hurt, too. A dollar invested in Vanguard's low-cost mutual fund, Total Stock Market Index, at the market peak in 2000 lost one-third of its inflation-adjusted value by the end of 2011.

In 2007, a year when the stock market was on the rise, almost as much money came out of 401(k) plans in disbursements to retirees and people between jobs as went in from new contributions. The plans had a net gain of $223 billion or $3,700 per participant; only the next year the plans lost $723 billion as the crashing stock market more than wiped out $267 billion of new deposits.

Just in case you're thinking that people out of work due to the Great Recession tapped their 401(k)s and caused the huge loss in 2008, not so. Payouts from the plans in 2008 were 11 percent smaller than in 2007.

What the Great Recession did reveal was how much 401(k) plans are like watering holes in a drought. People migrating from a job they lost to the next will find their retirement savings pool diminished because of the market crash. If the market does not recover for years, as happened between 1966 and 1981, your 401(k), already closer to a 201(k), may quickly turn into a financial mud hole, unable to sustain you.

INEFFICIENCY COSTS YOU

Making self-directed retirement savings plans like the 401(k) the foundation of old-age income is as economically inefficient as making pins one at a time (remember Adam Smith's lesson?).

Specialization makes for economic efficiency. We do not all know how to wire our homes for electricity or plumb them to carry fresh water in and wastewater out without spilling a drop. Using self-directed investment through 401(k)-type plans is the economic equivalent of expecting every worker to be her own roofer and surgeon. Most people lack the necessary time, knowledge and highly specialized skills to manage investments and time in order to accumulate enough wealth to sustain them from the day they stop working until they die. The result of creating a population of financial do-it-yourselfers is proving to be shocking and painful, leaving people worse off than need be.

Look at it this way: if investing was something just anybody can do, the average job on Wall Street would pay average wages. But stockbrokers, investment advisers and others who become expert at subtle concepts like the time value of money, asset allocation and risk and opportunity costs make more than most people because those skills add value by reducing inefficiency and increasing returns.

The Labor Department publishes data going back to 1989 comparing investment returns of traditional pensions and 401(k) plans through 2008. The professional managers of traditional pensions performed better than individuals in their 401(k) plans in fifteen of twenty years. In every year when the stock market was down, the pension plans lost less than the 401(k) plans, numbers that reflect the steady hand of professional money managers as opposed to the less informed and sometimes panicked hands of individual amateur investors.

In 2008, when the stock market fell sharply, pension plans lost almost 20 percent of their value, but 401(k) plans lost 24.9 percent. That means that for every dollar pension plans lost, the 401(k) plans lost $1.25. Recovering from those losses will be a lot harder for 401(k) savers than those in defined benefit pension plans.

Steve Butler, a San Francisco Bay Area financial adviser who calls himself "Mr. 401k," praises 401(k) plans—*if* the costs are held down through smart shopping by the employer. His studies show that many workers pay one percentage point a year more in costs than necessary because their employers chose high-cost plans.

Again, a single percentage point may not seem like much but, over time, it adds up to a lot. Consider what happens if you put $1,000 in a 401(k) annually for forty years and earn 5 percent a year instead of 4 percent. After forty years, earning 5 percent annually would yield more than $181,000, but the other account would hold less than $137,000. That one percentage point a year of extra fees robs you of a third of your 401(k) savings at retirement.

Employers also shortchange workers by paying them with debased currency. It's an old trick, dating at least to the sixteenth century, according to David Hackett Fischer, the Brandeis University historian, in his book *The Great Wave*. In that era, Fischer tells us, the merchants of Venice and Florence got laws passed "that allowed them to insist on being paid in gold florins or ducats, which held their value, but permitted them to pay wages and taxes in silver coins, which were much debased." The result? "As a consequence rich merchants grew richer and the poor sank deeper into misery and degradation."

Modern companies debase their workers' currency when they compensate them partly in shares of company stock. Companies not only can require workers to accept company stock in their 401(k) plans, they can force them to keep the stock until they reach age fifty-five. Contrast this with the stock options issued to executives. The options only have value if the price of company stock rises. But once an executive exercises the option, he is usually free to sell his shares and diversify into other investments or take cash and spend it.

Investing in the company you work for is one of the most basic rules that financial advisers warn workers against because it concentrates their risks. If the company gets into trouble, as all companies may, both your job and your investment in company stock are at risk.

Some companies funded their entire retirement plans with company stock. The results were disastrous for workers employed by scores of big companies, among them Enron, Global Crossing and the Carter Hawley Hale department-store chain, where retirement accounts suddenly evaporated. At Enron, 62 percent of the stocks and bonds in the 401(k) plan were Enron shares, which fell in value from $80 to seventy cents before losing all value. At Lehman Brothers, the failed Wall Street investment house, a tenth of the 401(k) plan was in company shares that lost all value overnight in 2008.

Despite this, many companies still match worker savings only with company shares. At better than one in four big companies in 2009, company stock accounted for a quarter or more of the value of the 401(k) plan. At one company in twenty, 80 percent or more of the 401(k) plan assets were company stock.

A 2004 study for the Federal Reserve by three academic economists noted that "participants in plans that match with company stock end up with a highly undiversified portfolio." But most workers, who are not investment specialists, don't recognize the importance of diversification, nor do they know when and how to rebalance their holdings to maintain diversification as some of their investments grow in value and others fall behind or otherwise lose value. Executives are more likely to have such specialized knowledge, which is why they are often selling stock in their own firms to buy shares of other companies' stock.

There are those who take a reverse view of this practice. Professors Jeffrey R. Brown and Scott Weisbenner of the University of Illinois and Nellie Liang of the Federal Reserve wrote favorably about 401(k) matches in company stock, noting that "risk-tolerant individuals actually prefer" company stock to cash with which they could buy a diversified set of stocks. They reported that companies that use their own stock for their 401(k) match appear to be less likely to go bankrupt than companies generally. But even if that's true, a reduced risk of bankruptcy is cold comfort to anyone who is forced to hold their employer's stock when the firm does go under, as has happened to those who worked at Enron, Carter Hawley Hale and many other firms.

So why do companies use their own shares to make 401(k) matches? They take the position that employee ownership motivates workers, which can be true. But company shares are also cheaper than cash. The companies issue stock certificates. That means more shares are outstanding, which dilutes the value of existing shares. But they get to deduct the value of those shares as a business expense without having to spend cash. Neat trick.

Giving workers company stock and requiring them to keep it until age fifty-five seems to violate the legal basis for a retirement plan, since the courts have held retirement plans must be operated "solely and exclusively" in the interests of the workers. Yet nowhere has any court issued a definitive decision on this crucial point. Nor has Congress acted to protect workers from plans that force them to hold on to their employers' shares for long periods.

Growing inequality has marked every great shift in prices in the past millennium, David Hackett Fischer wrote in *The Great Wave*, his book about price revolutions. Using historical records of prices for everything from bread to insurance contracts, Fischer showed that a growing gap between returns to capital and returns to labor is typical of price revolutions, be they shifts from stability to inflation or, as we are experiencing, from inflation to deflation.

Whatever the historical context, companies are clearly cheating workers when they pay them in the debased currency of the employer's stock or even when they put their cash contributions into managed mutual funds. There are also winners in these plans, such as employees of Apple, with its astonishing rise in share value. But the principle of diversification should reign. Keeping company stock should be optional, not forced. And employees should be able to vote any company shares held for them in a 401(k) plan.

The numbers in the latest edition of economist Burton Malkiel's famous investing book, *A Random Walk Down Wall Street*, make the case against managed mutual funds. If you put $10,000 into an S&P 500 Index fund in 1969 and reinvested dividends, your portfolio in 2010 would have been worth $463,000. The same sum in an actively managed mutual fund would amount to $258,000. So over more than four decades, the low-cost index funds produced $1.76 for each dollar earned by the actively managed funds.

The lessons: company stock concentrates risk. Index funds are cheap. Managed funds cost more, but return less. Guess which type of fund the mutual-fund industry pushes employers to use in their 401(k)-type plan?

Official government reports, research studies and companies often refer to 401(k) plans as being "popular." But it is companies, not workers, who decide whether workers get secure, insured, efficient traditional pensions or the less reliable, uninsured and very inefficient 401(k) plans.

This is not an isolated phenomenon, as there has been a watershed shift in how retirement assets are held. In 1984 just 13 percent of companies with fifty thousand or more workers offered only a 401(k) or similar retirement savings plan. Just nine years later a majority of companies offered only this kind of plan.

Since 1980 the number of people in traditional pension plans has hardly changed. There were just under 38 million Americans in large pension plans in 1980 compared to about 42 million in 2009, annual Labor Department reports show. That's about a 10 percent increase during years when the number of Americans grew by a third. Over the same period, the number of people in all types of defined contribution plans, mostly those high-cost 401(k) plans where workers must decide how to invest, quadrupled from under 20 million to 82.5 million.

Perhaps the most telling numbers concern deposits. Consider that in 2008 employers put $107 billion into pension plans. That is $4 billion less than the $111 billion put into these plans in 1980 when adjusted for inflation. It is no wonder that the vast majority of American workers are worse off today and will be worse off in retirement than those in the generation before.

HOW MUCH DO THEY COST?

There is no way to know just how much of your 401(k) potential earnings are being siphoned off. The Securities and Exchange Commission issued a report in 2005 on conflicts of interest that put people into higher cost plans or use undisclosed services that may cost more than they are worth. Four years later, the Government Accountability Office issued its own report warning that "conflicts of interest may be especially hidden," and, in cautious bureaucratic terms, explained why you should care: "Because the risk of 401(k) investments is largely borne by the individual participant, such hidden conflicts can affect participants directly by lowering investment returns."

Despite government awareness, the law continues to insulate companies from all but the most blatant and egregious abuses in 401(k) plans. The GAO did propose a solution that would be a good first step. It would require full disclosure of all fees charged to retirement savings accounts. Every vendor getting paid by the companies that act as trustees or record keepers would have to disclose who got paid what and why. That idea has kicked around Congress for years but has never become law.

Anything short of stealing workers' money is a virtually penalty-free zone. Even when bosses steal their workers' money, as I showed a number of small employers did in the 1990s, nothing was done to most of them. The biggest case was prosecuted when in 1996 Ralph J. Corace admitted that he stole $2.3 million from 476 people who were in the 401(k) savings plan of his Long Island company. At the time of the thefts he also lent $207,000 to two of his grown children. It was an elaborate theft including faked statements, and a significant element was that some of the plan vendors did not tell the plan participants or the Labor Department when the flow of funds was interrupted and other irregularities occurred. The workers recovered next to nothing. The government let Corace plead to a single count that cited just a tenth of the actual losses, ensuring his light sentence.

A better idea would be to strengthen the laws on the duty of loyalty owed to those with 401(k) savings by their employer and the vendors it hires to hold and manage the money and keep records. We've seen this before: the lawyers call this *fiduciary duty* and, again, it means that you must put the interests of the client ahead of your own. But it is worth revisiting.

No term is more frightening to corporations than fiduciary duty. The business press is full of articles on what a burden this would be; many companies claim they would end 401(k) plans rather than sponsor these plans if they had to be fiduciaries in any meaningful sense. The mutual-fund companies and the rest of Wall Street lobby vigorously and donate generously to make sure their responsibility is limited and law enforcement is light, if not lame. As someone whose spouse is a fiduciary overseeing a quarter-billion-dollar charitable endowment, I fail to see the problem in applying the standard of loyalty first to the saver or donor while putting your own interests as manager second. My wife's fiduciary status makes her scrupulous about handling other people's money; it requires that she treat her interests as subservient to those of the donors, the institution she heads and the beneficiaries of its grants. The rules and principles are clear enough, and corporations that are scrupulous in their conduct have nothing to fear from being fiduciaries.

On the other hand, if you want occasionally to play fast and loose with other people's money or if you want to grab opportunities away from clients who have no idea you are picking their pockets, then the rigors of fiduciary duty would be intimidating.

Another solution to abuses would be to broaden responsibility from plan sponsors to make explicit a requirement that failure to deposit funds on schedule is a *per se* civil offense as well as a crime. The receivers of such funds, mostly mutual funds, should face strict liability for failing to report suspicious activity both to plan participants and the Labor Department. Making failure to report an offense would make it easier to get civil remedies and, in egregious cases, to prosecute the thieves.

The larger solution, though, is not just to stop thievery through excessive fees that are hidden, but to recognize that having workers save and invest for their own retirement is folly. The right path would be to revive traditional or defined benefit pension plans in which professionals manage the money. Companies dislike this because under current law the pension plan is a company asset, while a 401(k) plan is a separate asset. Easy fix. Make pension plans a separate asset and let companies report the values separately, provided they put in enough money every year to make sure a plan has more than 100 percent of the money needed if the plan is frozen.

Corporations will resist this option because they will be obliged to put more hard cash (rather than potentially devalued company shares) into the plans. Workers may resist, too: they may get less cash in their paychecks because a larger share of total compensation is set aside for their old age. But it would help ensure that America does not become a land of people who worked all their lives only to end up dependent on handouts.

Wimpy's Tab

I'd gladly pay you Tuesday for a hamburger today.

— J. Wellington Wimp to Popeye

18. **You may resent** paying nonexistent taxes on behalf of pipeline companies that put your life at risk unnecessarily, but there's more where that outrage comes from. Consider that you also have to pay the costs of four other tax policies that add up to far more than the imaginary tax that pipeline owners pocket. The first of these benefits corporations, the second the executives who run these companies. The third further enriches the highest-paid workers in the history of the world, namely, the speculators who run hedge funds. The fourth, and perhaps most egregious of all, results from rules that let many of the already superrich live tax-free.

Congress requires that taxes be withheld from your pay, but it lets executives and hedge fund managers pay taxes when they choose to, which is often years and sometimes decades in the future. As for profitable corporations, Congress *requires* them to delay paying part of their taxes.

Earn-now-but-pay-taxes-later schemes fill thousands of pages of fine print in tax law, regulations, confidential contracts and special tax deals known as *private letter rulings*. But let's peek behind the curtain.

BALANCING THE BOOKS

For big business, it all begins with keeping two sets of books, that same accounting oddity we encountered in talking about utilities. Once again, there's a set for shareholders and another for the Internal Revenue Service. The two sets of rules in keeping these books are known as *book accounting* and *tax accounting*. Despite all the loud complaining about the costs of government regulation and paperwork, this is an area where big business wants to endure the extra expense. Why? Because it's lucrative for companies, while you pay the cost.

The whole purpose of tax accounting is to delay paying taxes. That's it—profit now, pay later. This is achieved principally through laws that let companies write off the cost of new equipment on tax returns faster than on financial statements sent to investors. As long as a company keeps growing, the difference between the fast tax write-down and the slower shareholder (or book) write-down creates an expanding pool of money.

Congress does not require collection of data on how much these corporate tax deferrals cost, but we can get an idea from one industry that accounts for about 2 percent of the economy, the corporate-owned electric utilities. A study looked at the value of tax accounting benefits to corporate-owned electric utilities. In 2006 alone, the tax breaks were worth almost $12 billion. Looking over the entire period since accelerated depreciation began in 1954, the study found the total value of these tax breaks over fifty-three years was the equivalent of writing the industry a check in 2006 for $472 billion. That comes to more than $1,500 per American. The total is equal to almost half the $1 trillion paid that year in individual income taxes.

MSB Energy Associates in Madison, Wisconsin, prepared the study for the American Public Power Association, which represents tax-exempt electric utilities operated by cities, cooperatives and special districts. That the corporate-owned electric industry has not challenged the findings of this and previous MSB studies suggests that the actual savings are probably even larger than the study said. The delayed payment of taxes isn't a short-term thing; sometimes payment is delayed three decades or more. Some big businesses—Enron, for one—described their tax departments internally as profit centers because, plain and simple, companies like Enron make money off taxes.

Here's the mechanism. Consider a company that earns a billion-dollar profit. With the corporate tax rate at 35 percent, the company's profit and loss statement to shareholders shows $1 billion of pretax profit, reported to shareholders as a $350 million tax and a $650 million after-tax profit.

But down in the fine print of the financial statements, in a supplemental note to the cash-flow statement, the company reports how much cash it paid in taxes. In reviewing thousands of these notes over the years, seldom have I seen a "cash paid for taxes" line larger than the accounting charge. Far more often that number had parentheses around it, like this—($2,000,000)—meaning the company got back $2 million more from the government than it paid out. But let's look at a real example.

Remember Entergy, the big New Orleans utility holding company? Its operating utilities provide power to Louisiana, Arkansas and parts of Alabama and East Texas (see page 78). The "book" accounting report Entergy prepared for shareholders in 2009 illustrates the chasm between reported and actual taxes. That year Entergy reported revenues of $10.7 billion, of which it kept as profit almost $1.9 billion, or 17.5 percent, compared to just under 10 percent for most very large companies. Entergy told shareholders its profit was reduced by income taxes of $633 million, but in the footnotes Entergy revealed that it actually paid only $43 million in taxes. That meant that although its *reported* tax rate was almost 34 percent of profits, its *actual* tax payments came to just 2.3 percent of profits.

Citizens for Tax Justice uses a more sophisticated measure of taxes, one that includes the value of deductions for stock options granted to executives. Robert S. McIntyre, its no-nonsense executive director, calculated that for the ten years ending in 2011 Entergy reported profits of $15.2 billion and paid no federal corporate income taxes. Instead it got refunds of more than $1.5 billion, giving it a negative tax rate of 10 percent.

Again, write-downs and depreciation account for most of the disappearance of taxes.

That difference between what Entergy reported as tax expense on its shareholder books and its tax books constitutes an interest-free loan from the government financed with your tax dollars. That loan may be paid back in a few years or in decades, but as long as a company keeps growing, its interest-free loans of deferred taxes generally do, too.

Warren Buffett is one who has benefited from such interest-free loans. As we saw earlier, his utility holding company, MidAmerican Energy Holdings, operates electric utilities from Iowa to Oregon, as well as pipelines and other monopolies whose prices, or rates, are set by government. In the three years 2007 through 2009, MidAmerican reported revenues of $32.6 billion and pretax profits of $5.9 billion, or 18 percent. It also reported to shareholders income taxes of $1.7 billion or 29 percent of profits.

When it came to actually paying taxes, Buffett's MidAmerican made another profit. The company paid taxes in 2007, but got refunds in the next two years. For the three years, cash paid for income taxes was *minus* $141 million, giving it an income tax rate of *negative* 2.4 percent.

In 2009, MidAmerican had another $796 million in deferred taxes. The average weighted length of these interest-free loans was twenty-eight years.

Buffett would also like to keep the taxes that customers of his monopolies are required to pay him. His lobbyists won repeal of an Oregon law that required MidAmerican's PacifiCorp utility to turn over to government taxes it charged as part of customer rates or give the money back to customers. That law was passed after I revealed that Enron, which owned the Portland General Electric utility, did not pay income taxes collected from ratepayers. Nearly $1 billion paid by people in and around Portland over nine years never got to the federal or state governments, as the subsequent investigation by Congress's Joint Committee on Taxation staff confirmed.

Now, let's compare how Congress treats big businesses like Buffett's utility holding company to how Congress treats you. Congress requires that your income taxes come out of your paycheck before you even get paid. It lets Buffett's company pay its taxes years into the future. How well off would you be if you had the same deal as big business? Imagine being allowed to keep all of your income tax for thirty years before turning it over to the U.S. Treasury. Let's assume you owed $1,000 of income tax in 1982, but rather than having the money withheld from your paycheck, you used it to buy a bond that paid you the after-tax equivalent of 5 percent interest, which compounded until the bond matured in 30 years.

When 2012 arrived, you cashed in your bond, paid the government the $1,000 and pocketed more than $3,300 of interest. That would be a sweet deal, obviously, but some corporations do even better. And they do it at taxpayer expense.

Let's look at this scenario from the government's point of view. In 1982, the government borrowed $1,000 to make up for the tax that was not withheld from your paycheck. Uncle Sam paid interest at the same rate that you invested, 5 percent. Because the government spent more money than it collected every one of those thirty years (except for the last two years of the Clinton administration), that means it also borrowed the interest on the interest, compounding it.

Come 2012, the government finally collects that $1,000 from you, but only after shelling out $3,300 of interest while it waited for your taxes to arrive. And because of inflation, that $1,000 from 1982 buys only $415 worth of government services in 2012.

In summary form, what is the net result of our current policies?

- *Big Business* delays paying $1,000 for thirty years, collecting $3,300 interest on the delayed tax money.

- *Government* borrows the $1,000 that big business deferred, pays $3,300 in interest and, after finally collecting the $1,000 tax in 2012, has added $3,300 to the national debt, requiring $165 of interest per year until the debt is paid off.

- *You* have no choice but to pay your $1,000 in 1982; plus you and other taxpayers owe the $3,300 of interest government paid out to big business during the thirty-year delay and now, at 5 percent, owe $165 of annual interest on that interest for the rest of your life. You pay for it with higher taxes, fewer government services and/or more borrowing.

You and our government also took the risk that the big business that made a profit in 1982 would still be around in 2012 to pay its tax. If the big business folds, then you either have to make up for that $1,000 or accept fewer government services or pay interest on that $1,000 at 5 percent forever, making your total annual interest cost $215—the $50 interest on the tax and the $165 interest on the interest.

It's obvious why Congress does not let you earn now and pay later. So why does it let big business do so? More to the point, why, since 1954, has Congress *required* big companies to profit now and pay taxes later?

The 1954 overhaul of the tax code included a provision long sought by big business—writing off new plant and equipment faster for tax purposes than for book accounting purposes. Known as *accelerated depreciation*, it was sold on the basis that it would spur economic growth and create jobs. Just two years later, future Nobel Prize winner Robert Solow showed that accelerated depreciation deductions do not increase economic growth. Other studies by leading tax economists, including Dale Jorgenson of Harvard University and Robert Hall of the Hoover Institution at Stanford University, who chairs the committee that decides if the economy is in expansion or recession, later came to similar conclusions. Most compelling of all, the coauthor of the study that was behind the

1954 accelerated depreciation law, Evsey Domar, publicly acknowledged in 1957 that Solow was right and he was wrong—accelerated depreciation does not produce faster economic growth.

Even though accelerated depreciation does not deliver on its purpose and despite the fact that it adds to complexity in the tax system and complicates the regulation of monopolies, there has never been a serious drive to repeal it. President Reagan put in place even faster accelerated depreciation and President George W. Bush in 2003 arranged for a temporary bonus depreciation. President Barack Obama went much further. While reviled by many as antibusiness, he sponsored 100 percent immediate write-offs of all new investment during most of his first term and a 50 percent write-off during the rest of it, which should have made him a darling of business. So the next time you hear an executive or tax adviser on television complaining about the arduous complexity of the tax code, remember this: business loves complexity when it turns taxes into profits and shifts the burdens of government on to you.

PRESIDENTS WHO PAY LATER

Now what about those executives who get to earn now and pay their taxes later? This is a deal Congress says you cannot participate in unless you are an executive, a movie star, an athlete or some other highly paid worker.

Congress says you can defer without paying taxes no more than $17,000 in a 401(k) plan, provided your employer offers one, in 2012. If you are age fifty or older, you get to set aside an additional $5,500 for a maximum savings of $22,500. If your employer does not have such a plan, the most you can defer is $5,000 or, for older workers, $6,000.

Now imagine that you are an executive and you will be paid $105 million this year. You do not need that much money to live in the style to which you've become accustomed. Being a longtime executive, you have lots of investment income and enjoy an expense account that covers many of your living expenses, including golf outings with clients and celebrities. Under a 1985 tax rule, you travel by company jet at up to a 97 percent discount to actual costs, meaning a luxury cross-country trip will cost you less than a middle seat in coach. Shareholders pick up two-thirds of the cost and taxpayers the rest, minus the little bit of extra income tax you pay for your free personal flights.

So you tell your board of directors, whom you picked and on some of whom you lavish consulting fees and company business, that you want to take $5 million in taxable cash and defer $100 million until you retire.

You may have the company invest your $100 million any way you want, but there is a very good chance you will ask to earn interest from the company at a higher rate than it pays for money borrowed in the bond market. Let's say you want 7 percent when the bond market is at 5 percent.

The extra $2 million in interest paid to you the first year is money the company will not have available to invest in expanding its operations or paying its current workforce. Yet asking for 7 percent when the market is 5 is not even greedy. Jack Welch, when he ran General Electric, demanded and got 14 percent for five years on some of his deferred pay, three times what GE was paying at the time on its five-year bonds.

Artificially inflated interest rates are not the costliest part of the deal, but they are the only cost that the Securities and Exchange Commission requires be disclosed to investors in the fine print of proxy statements. The biggest part of the cost remains undisclosed, but it can be calculated from the tax rules if you know how much is being deferred.

Using our textbook example—$100 million deferred out of $105 million in annual pay—the deferred millions cannot be taken as a tax-deductible expense on the company's tax return. This is one of the rare examples where tax accounting is worse for a company than book accounting. Since that $100 million is not deducted, the company for tax purposes will report profits to the IRS that are $100 million higher than profits reported to shareholders. And that, in turn, means the company owes $35 million of federal income taxes on the deferral. Let's assume a state income tax adds another $5 million, making the total increase in company taxes $40 million. So in addition to costing the company $2 million in extra interest the first year that must be disclosed to shareholders, your pay package as CEO cost the company $40 million that is not disclosed.

Ever wonder why so many seemingly reputable companies bought tax shelters in the nineties and two thousands? They were a way to compensate for the costs of executive deferrals. Most of those tax shelters were shams, some of which I exposed in the *New York Times*. Some of the companies that bought them (but by no means all) had to pay back the taxes they tried to avoid. A few people went to jail for selling these tax shelters. But the fact that some people cheated, and some of them got away with it, does not change the fundamental economics of executive pay deferral.

Now, let's assume you are forty-five years old and your deferral runs for twenty years. On your sixty-fifth birthday, you retire and cash out. At 7 percent interest, that one-year deferral of $100 million in salary is now valued at almost $387 million, of which $121 million is from those extra two percentage points of above-market interest, money that the company could have used to expand the business. The company now gets to take a deduction for the $387 million on its tax return and you pay your taxes.

(Actually, you may be able to get around the tax bill by having the company buy life insurance in a trust for your heirs. That way the company gets its deduction and, while you don't get the money, your heirs can collect it free of tax when your time runs out.)

Back to reality. Since you are not a hypothetical CEO making $105 million a year, what does all of this mean to you? A lot.

THE COSTLY ECONOMICS OF EXECUTIVE DEFERRAL

Money to pay rank-and-file workers must be cut when executives defer part of their pay, which increases company taxes.

DOLLARS IN THOUSANDS	EXECUTIVE PAY		WORKER PAY	
	Deferral	No deferral	Deferral	No deferral
Gross pay	105,000	105,000	105	105
Taxable pay	5,000	105,000	89	105
Federal and state corporate income deduction at 40%	(2,000)	(42,000)	(42)	(42)
Deferral	100,000	0	17	0
Corporate income tax on deferral	40,000	0	0	0
Net after-tax cost of compensation	143,000	63,000	63	63
Added cost of deferrals at 10,000-employee company	($4,000) per worker	0	0	0

Source: Author calculations from IRS rules. Parentheses denote subtractions or negative numbers.

If this deal takes place where you work and your company employs 10,000 people, the tax cost alone for the chief executive's deal is the equivalent of removing $4,000 for each worker from the budget for salaries and benefits. In contrast, your piddling 401(k) wage deferral imposes no extra cost on the company.

More than just CEOs get deals like this. They are common among senior executives, as well as brand-name athletes and movie stars.

Do you wonder why your company has been cutting back on your health insurance, demanding you pay part of the premium and slapping on ever-larger co-pays? Wonder why the company says it cannot afford your defined benefit pension plan anymore? Or why it has reduced or eliminated the match for your 401(k) plan? Part of the answer is in the cost of unlimited tax deferrals for your bosses.

The third tax deal that you finance works to the benefit of hedge fund managers and private-equity managers (such as Mitt Romney, from 1984 to 1999). A quick refresher: a hedge fund is an investment pool open only to people and institutions with large amounts of money. Charitable endowments use them, as do state and local government pension funds. "Private equity" is just a fancy term for unregulated pools that invest directly in companies rather than in the stock and commodities markets.

The hedge fund leverages investors' cash with loans from banks. The industry says it typically borrows $30 for each dollar put up by investors, but court records have shown examples where ratios rose to $100 to $1 and even $250 to $1. All that borrowing can mean huge profits. Using the $30 ratio, if a hedge fund buys a stock that goes up $1, the hedge fund equity just grew by $30, minus any interest charged by the banks.

Hedge fund managers typically charge a 2 percent fee, plus they take 20 percent of the increase. James Simon, the genius mathematician turned master speculator who routinely makes more than $1 billion a year, charged clients of his Renaissance Technologies hedge fund a 5 percent fee and a 44 percent commission.

In 2009, the first half of which was officially a recession period, the top twenty-five hedge fund managers earned an average of $1 billion each. David Tepper of Appaloosa Management earned $4 billion that year. So before taxes, hedge fund managers can earn fabulous incomes. But get this: Congress gives hedge fund managers not one tax break, but two.

First, Congress lets hedge fund managers defer income taxes on the 20 percent share they take (or 44 percent in Simon's case) for as long as they keep the hedge fund in business. Second, when the hedge fund managers do cash in, they only have to pay the 15 percent tax rate on capital gains. That is an especially sweet deal because the executives have to pay 35 percent, the tax rate since 2001 on top salaries. The 35 percent rate starts at about $400,000 of taxable income. To most people that is a lot of money, but David Tepper's $4 billion means that, if he were taxed at the same rate as an executive, he would have hit the top rate fifty-one minutes after the Times Square ball came down on New Year's.

Hedge fund managers do not have any capital at risk. The pool of capital belongs to investors, and they are paying the manager the 20 percent (or larger) fee. In this way, hedge fund managers are no different from the managers of a mutual fund, of a corporation that makes widgets, or of an independent sales agent who travels around selling notions to retail stores, all of whose compensation for their services depends on their success.

When Mitt Romney disclosed his tax return for 2010 it showed he made more than $21 million and paid less than 14 percent of that in federal income taxes. His campaign, responding to a question I framed, also acknowledged in writing that the Romneys paid no gift taxes on the $100 million they put into trust for their five sons. At the time the transfers were made, the maximum they could give free of tax would, to anyone consulting the tax code, appear to be $2 million or less. The Romneys got around this limitation by giving assets that the IRS says cannot be valued, like a share of the future fees known as "carried interest" that Romney was due for deals he made while heading Bain Capital Management.

The Romneys got another sweet deal in the way they arranged this gift. They put their money into what is known as a "defective" grantor trust. Defective means Mom and Dad pay the income taxes on the trust-fund earnings and the children get their money tax-free. And it's all perfectly legal.

But the best deal of all for hedge fund managers and others among the already rich is tax-free living by simply not reporting income.

The corporate executives who defer income cannot use that money because the company has it. But in a business that depends on massive bank loans, hedge fund managers can. The hedge fund manager with a few billion in his offshore deferral account just gets a loan from his banker when he wants a few tens of millions to buy a new mansion and a Modigliani to hang over the fireplace. Typical borrowing rates? Two percent or less. That is a lot less than even the discounted 15 percent tax on withdrawals from a hedge fund. And as long as the hedge fund account keeps growing faster than the interest rate, why cash in and pay any taxes?

Almost anyone who is already very rich can live this way. Consider Frank and Jamie McCourt, former owners of the Los Angeles Dodgers baseball team. The real estate developer and his wife got into a messy divorce, with shouting matches and accusations about affairs (hers) with limo drivers. The court records that resulted contain some eye-popping numbers.

For one, from 2004 to 2008, the couple spent $109 million on their lifestyle.

Another? In petitioning a judge for $1 million a month in support for Jamie McCourt in 2009 to keep her lifestyle going while the divorce proceedings dragged on, her lawyers revealed that "the parties have not paid any federal or California income taxes since they moved to California in 2004."

The court papers also show that the couple lived on a budget, albeit an impressive one. The budget prepared for 2008 anticipated spending of $43 million. That included $25 million in new loans to fancy up two of their homes and $18 million from borrowing against Dodgers ticket revenues, which came with the added benefit of creating tax-deductible interest expenses.

The McCourts are far from unusual among people who have built up billion-dollar fortunes. Many Americans are spending millions, even tens of millions, each year while paying little or no income tax. And it's all perfectly legal, thanks to the tax regulations applicable to the richest among us. It's only surprising that the outraged voices of Occupy Wall Street only began to be heard in 2011.

An IRS Statistics of Income report known as Table 1.4 showed that nearly 322,000 taxpayers reported incomes of $1 million or more in 2008. Of these, 2,054 paid no income taxes. Their average income was $3.8 million. The number of such high-income individuals who pay no taxes has been growing rapidly. There were 959 of them in 2007. Back in 1997 they numbered just 173. Many others pay a smaller share of their income in taxes than families who work as schoolteachers and cops, nurses and truck drivers.

Terrence Wall, a Wisconsin developer, filed financial disclosure forms when he ran in the 2010 Republican Senate primary. They showed that his income was in a range between $3.5 million to $14.2 million in 2008 and the first ten months of 2009. Wall paid no income taxes and hinted that he had not paid any for years. The *Milwaukee Journal Sentinel* asked the candidate whether it was fair to the middle class that they pay taxes while he lives tax-free. Wall said, "Everyone should pay less in taxes."

Wall has all the obliviousness of a modern-day Marie Antoinette. The reality is that everyone *else* must pay more in taxes when the McCourts, Wall and thousands of others pay little or nothing.

The upward pressures on your taxes, and the downward pressure on your wages and fringe benefits, are not the only problems created by tax rules that rarely make the nightly news or even the best newspapers. Your job may have been destroyed by a tax trick—and Congress may soon double down on this ploy.

Pfizer's Bitter Pill

A democracy . . . can only exist until the voters discover they can vote themselves largesse out of the public treasury.

—ca. 1980 misquotation of words of Alexander Fraser Tytler

19. Imagine, for a moment, that you are a member of Congress in fall 2004, eager to go home to campaign. Voters are not exactly thrilled with the economy, and that makes you anxious, given the long tradition of Americans voting their pocketbooks.

Their concerns are real, as the economy is far from robust. While the 2001 recession was mild and lasted only eight months, the jobs lost were not replaced for almost four years. Job growth in the country remains mired far behind the numbers needed to serve its growing population. Those who have been working found raises rare and minimal, except at the very top. The average income of Americans fell in 2001 and again in 2002. It slipped a tad more in 2003, bringing the real average income 12 percent below the previous peak year of 2000. Even though average income has grown a bit in 2004, measured in 2010 dollars it stands lower than 2000 by $4,631 or nearly 8 percent.

Republican politicians have been reminding voters that companies that have been laying people off left and right will require more tax cuts in order to resume hiring. Democrats tend to focus on frozen pension plans, reduced health-care benefits that cut into workers' already shrunken paychecks, and fat executive pay plans.

So, as a representative or senator up for election in 2004, you're faced with delivering bad economic news. Now, imagine you have an opportunity to spend $93 billion to make things better. What would you do?

Specifically, what would you do involving the very first power the people granted you, the power to tax? Let's make this simple, with three options.

The first option would be to give voters a big, one-time tax break. You could let everyone in the bottom half pay no income taxes for 2004 and everyone in the next best-off quarter of Americans cut their income taxes by two-thirds. That way, seventy-five out of every one hundred Americans would get a benefit, but it might not help you get reelected (lower-income people are the least likely to vote). Or as a variation you could just grant everyone an 11 percent across-the-board income tax cut for 2004. That way every taxpayer would get a benefit, including those most likely to vote and those most likely to be campaign donors.

These tax savings could be achieved by simply adding a line to individual tax returns with a directive to multiply the tax owed by zero for everyone with an adjusted gross income under $31,000 and by 0.33 for those making from that amount up to $66,000 in the first case; or, if the cut was across the board, by having everyone multiply their initial tax bill by 0.89.

If you believe what President Reagan said for years on his way to the White House, you would choose the broad individual tax cut to win votes. Reagan, relying on remarks he attributed to a British judge from two centuries earlier, often said this:

> A democracy cannot exist as a permanent form of government. It can only exist until the voters discover they can vote themselves largesse out of the public treasury. From that moment on the majority . . . always votes for the candidate promising the most benefits from the treasury, with the result that democracy always collapses over a loose fiscal policy, always to be followed by a dictatorship.

Now, for your second option. You could do nothing. The government has been running chronic and worsening deficits following the 2001 and 2003 Bush tax cuts, which did not result in the promised creation of jobs. As a politician you might decide that active intervention in the economy to stimulate demand is not such a good idea.

If you are a fiscal conservative worried about deficits, you will find cutting revenues bizarre. You've long since grasped the fact that, if taxes are cut and spending keeps growing, you must borrow to make up for the shortfall and that the debt thus incurred is an implicit tax on future income. So if you're a real fiscal conservative, you might be inclined to the second, do-nothing option.

The third choice would be to give a one-time tax break to multi-national corporations with untaxed profits held offshore, provided they brought the money home. So long as these profits stay offshore they remain tax-free, but if they were returned to the United States, a 35 percent tax would come due. Say the tax break you're considering would slash the rate to a tad more than 5 percent. That's an 85 percent discount, which the Bush White House told everyone would mean jobs, jobs and more jobs.

There are other voices in Washington that favored this. Senator John Ensign (a Nevada Republican not up for election in 2004) claimed that these repatriated funds would be used "to strengthen the financial stability of U.S. companies, for expansion, for new hires and for research and development." He calls it "common-sense legislation" and predicts "the creation of more than 660,000 jobs [will] result." Ensign's jobs estimate was actually the brainchild of Allen Sinai, the economist who founded Decision Economics and formerly was the chief economist at Lehman Brothers. Creating 660,000 jobs would be a huge boost to the economy, providing work for about one in twelve jobless workers. Sinai, the source of Ensign's numbers, told me his figure is based on history and how many jobs tax reductions have generated in the past. Yet the per job price would be huge. At $455,000 per job, it would take the average American, paying the average 2004 income tax rate of 13.4 percent, sixty-two years to pay $455,000 in taxes. So even if all those jobs materialized, they were not worth anything close to the cost of the corporate tax break. But, for the moment, that was left unsaid.

So, imaginary lawmaker, which option would you choose? A broad individual tax cut to curry favor with the masses as taught by Reagan and George W. Bush; the second option of no tax cut for anyone because government was already spending much more than it was collecting in revenues; or would you vote for the third option, a highly concentrated tax cut for a few giant companies that supposedly would create jobs?

This is an essay question, by the way, because you'll need to explain your reasons for your choice, along with what steps, if any, you would require be taken later to determine whether you made the best choice or even a smart choice.

Actually, no, you don't have to answer the question. Congress already did, when a majority of actual lawmakers voted for the corporate tax cut called the American Jobs Creation Act of 2004. The final House bill got yeas from 205 of 221 Republicans, but just 75 of 199 Democrats. In the Senate, 43 out of 46 Republicans and 25 out of 39 Democrats voted yea. (Not all lawmakers voted.)

Since that decision is fading into history, we can examine its ramifications. I'd tell you what Congress learned, except the politicians forgot to include any requirement to follow up with reports from the companies that got the tax break, so they assembled no data from which lessons could be drawn. But the IRS did make a study from which much is to be gleaned. Multinational companies liked the Jobs Creation Act so much that 843 of them brought home $312 billion that qualified for the deal, escaping almost $80 billion of taxes, according to a report by Melissa Redmiles of the IRS Statistics of Income division. You'll notice that the amount of actual tax savings was less than the $93 billion estimated, but not so much less that it undermined the basic premise or the promise of many new jobs.

Much of the money came from tax havens such as Bermuda and the Cayman Islands. Firms that brought home untaxed profits from high-tax countries like Canada and Britain got an extra opportunity to take advantage of the deal because of some technical features of the law.

What was the money actually used for? That was beyond the scope of the IRS report, but studying the fine print of annual 10-K reports that companies file with the Securities and Exchange Commission yields some answers.

By far the biggest beneficiary was Pfizer. As soon as President Bush laid down his signing pen the drug maker brought home $37 billion of untaxed offshore profits. It saved $11 billion in taxes, roughly one out of every $7 saved by all 843 corporations.

Many of those profits were offshore because of earlier tax tricks. When Pfizer scientists saw promise in a new drug, like a bloodstream medication (later named Viagra) that had an unanticipated effect on male staffers, the company sold the rights to the drug to itself in a foreign jurisdiction. A drug in early stages of development has only a small value, so the price to transfer intellectual property offshore from one pocket of a company to another is small.

When Pfizer brought Viagra to market in 1998, each one of the little blue pills it sold came with a royalty to be paid to the offshore subsidiary that had acquired the rights to the formula. Pfizer listed those payments as an expense on its American corporate tax return, lowering its taxes in America as it piled up tax-free profits offshore. The 2004 American Jobs Creation Act let Pfizer bring those profits and more home at an 85 percent discount with the promise that this would mean more jobs and more research, which is vital to job growth.

So how many jobs did Pfizer create, thanks to the American Jobs

Creation Act? Well, actually, zero. Not one. In fact, Pfizer closed whole factories and fired more than a third of its employees. At the end of 2004 Pfizer employed 115,000 people, but by 2009 the workforce was down to 74,000. So a tax break that was supposed to create jobs instead was followed by the destruction of 41,000 at just one company.

Pfizer was not unique. Hewlett-Packard brought $14.5 billion of untaxed overseas profits back to America and immediately fired 14,000 employees. Other companies that brought home untaxed profits fired workers, too, though all of them waited until the American Jobs Creation Act was signed into law before collectively destroying at least 100,000 jobs.

How did Allen Sinai, the reputable business economist who predicted the creation of 660,000 jobs, get it so wrong? Sinai told me his estimates were meant to cover the broader economy, not the companies that got the benefits. He also said job creation did not work out as his economic model predicted because the relationships between corporate cash flow and job growth in the 1990s were not holding in the twenty-first century. Sinai also said he was changing his model so that future analyses would be more reliable.

So how much of the tax savings did Pfizer plow into expanding research into new drugs? Adjusted for inflation to 2010 dollars, Pfizer spent 7.5 percent *less* on research in 2006 than in 2004. Pfizer slashed research even more as time passed, except for one year when it rose slightly. By 2009 Pfizer was spending almost 11 percent less on research than in 2004. Had Pfizer just maintained research spending at the 2004 level, it would have spent $3.5 billion more over the next five years than it actually did.

Research is crucial to pharmaceutical companies. Pfizer in particular needed to spend more on research because its patents on highly profitable drugs were well on their way to expiring. Since 2004 sales of its cholesterol drug Lipitor, which generates a fifth of all Pfizer revenues, fell 7 percent while sales of Viagra softened slightly.

Buried in the fine print of the Jobs Creation Act is a hard truth: companies were not obliged to spend *one dollar* on new hiring or expanding research. Instead, corporations could use their tax savings to replace the money spent on existing pay and research. If that sounds to you like an action with all the significance of moving a dollar from your left pocket to your right, your assumption is correct. The way lobbyists wrote the bill, companies could use their tax savings for virtually anything that company executives said contributed to a firm's *ability* to retain workers and create jobs. In other words, creating jobs was not a requirement of the American Jobs Creation Act, while destroying jobs was an authorized purpose.

Let's look again at the statement from Senator Ensign, a man known not for in-depth understanding of business or economics so much as for his allegiance to right-wing ideology and subservience to big business (as well as for paying off his former chief of staff and the man's wife, who was also Ensign's mistress).

In Ensign's statement, there were four permitted uses for the tax savings. The money could be used "to strengthen the financial stability of U.S. companies, for expansion, for new hires and for research and development."

A vigorous Washington press corps would do well to parse what members of Congress saw in the same way that Cold War-era reporters parsed the Kremlin's statements. What if reporters had pressed Ensign about whether all of these purposes had to be met or just the first, vague promise of strengthening the financial stability of companies? What if they had asked why the bill did not require the creation of jobs to qualify and include a look back to take the tax savings away unless more jobs and more research actually occurred?

What the reporters covering the bill all missed (probably because none of them read it) was that the law did not even specify the United States when it came to creating jobs. Other than a perceptive piece by Joann M. Weiner in *Tax Notes*, not a single news clip that I can find showed any reporter really understood what the bill contained, as opposed to what politicians and lobbyists said it contained. Weiner, a Harvard-trained economist, figured out that because the legislation failed to specify the United States, creating non-American jobs also was an authorized use of tax savings under the American Jobs Creation Act.

"The bill was like an accounting report that takes a number out to six decimal places and therefore seems very precise, but when you read the bill it turns out it is not precise at all," Weiner explained.

Perhaps the law should have been called the 2004 Destroy American Jobs Act.

Now, it is true that had the law not passed, these companies might have fired just as many people or even more, but we would also not have handed these companies a windfall of nearly $80 billion in the form of reduced taxes.

So since Pfizer neither created jobs nor invested in more research that might someday create more jobs, just what did Pfizer do with its

$11 billion tax savings? It used it to manipulate the stock market in a perfectly legal fashion. Pfizer bought back every ninth share of its own stock, about 880 million shares between 2004 and 2009. Soon after the 2004 tax break was approved, the Pfizer board approved spending $5 billion to buy back its own shares and in 2006 it increased that to $18 billion in a desperate attempt to prop up its collapsing share price.

Why would Pfizer do that? Why would it destroy jobs and cut the research spending on which future profits depend to buy back its own shares?

The real question is this: how else are executives going to make their own stock options valuable if they are not earning real profits in a competitive market? If stock prices do not rise, then the executives cannot get rich. If Pfizer's board and executives are more focused on finances than on science, the company cannot earn a profit from investing in new drugs. And if the market thinks Pfizer is a lousy investment—which it has been for years—then one way to game the market is to buy back shares in the hope that this will mask the failings of company executives and directors. However, this fool-'em-with-stock-buybacks strategy, financed with the $11 billion in tax savings and the $3.5 billion cut in research, was yet another Pfizer flop.

Pfizer shares peaked in March 1999 at $48.60 (equal to $67.12 in 2012 dollars). At the start of 2004, Pfizer traded at almost $39 a share, but since then the trend has been mostly downhill. Pfizer shares had lost more than two-thirds of their value by early 2009 despite buying back nearly 880 million shares or 11.5 percent of those outstanding in early 2004. By May 2012 they traded at $22.

Taxpayers, meanwhile, pay interest on the $11 billion they borrowed to finance Pfizer's tax break. At 2012 federal borrowing rates, the interest came to $1 million per day. That cost will rise when interest rates go back up again, as one day they will. Whatever the interest rate, the interest expense will continue unless or until the federal debt is paid off.

Let's look at another offshore sleight of hand. Bringing money back from overseas does not require special legislation, and it can be done without paying any taxes. The drug company Merck did exactly that in 2009 when it bought Schering-Plough, a much smaller drug company that made the allergy medicine Claritin as well as Coppertone suntan lotion and Dr. Scholl's foot-care products.

Buried deep in the hundreds of pages of legalese is the one oblique paragraph of fine print that matters. Below, "Mercury" is Merck; "Saturn" is Schering-Plough:

> Overseas Financing. At the Closing, (a) Mercury will cause one or more non-U.S. Subsidiaries of Mercury (the "Mercury Overseas Subsidiaries") to lend up to $9.4 billion, in the aggregate (such amount, as determined by Mercury in its discretion, the "Repayment Amount"), to Saturn Holdings BV and Saturn Intl CV and (b) Saturn will cause Saturn Holdings BV and Saturn Intl CV to pay the Repayment Amount to Saturn and Saturn Sub in satisfaction of such portion of the Intercompany Notes as equals the amount of such payment (for these purposes, translating currencies at the spot rate in effect on the date of such payment); it being understood that, for administrative convenience, the Mercury Overseas Subsidiaries may advance the Repayment Amount directly to the Exchange Agent, in which case Saturn, Saturn Sub, Saturn Holdings BV and Saturn Intl CV will issue appropriate letters of direction confirming such payments.

In plain English, by using Caribbean tax havens (BV stands for British Virgin Islands), Merck brought $9.4 billion of profits parked offshore back to the United States, while escaping $3.3 billion of corporate income tax. From Merck's perspective, it transferred untaxed profits in its Caribbean accounts to its American accounts without ever having to pay taxes. In doing so Merck cost you money even if you do not use any of its drugs or other products because it shifted this burden on to you. Your cost? About $10 for each member of your family.

Jesse Drucker, the dogged tax reporter who dug this out for Bloomberg Business News, also reported on a corporate tax conference that showed how executives are taught to think about shifting tax burdens—every dollar of tax the executive's company escapes paying, the richer it will make the executive.

John P. Kennedy, a partner at Deloitte Tax LLP, told a November 2010 conference in Philadelphia that escaping taxes could do more to raise stock prices than increasing sales or cutting costs. Kennedy gave a textbook example of how lowering a company's actual tax rate by two percentage points could boost the stock by two dollars. Then Kennedy addressed the chief financial officers about their personal interest in finding ways to help their companies pay taxes at rates below the 35 percent rate seemingly required by Congress.

"You may think two bucks isn't much, but when you're the CFO and she has 100,000 options, that's pretty interesting," Kennedy said.

Tax Notes writer Martin Sullivan, a former Treasury Department economist, calculated that in 2008 American drug companies reported that about 80 percent of their profits were earned in tax-favored offshore jurisdictions, up from about a third of their profits in 1997. This rapid growth in foreign profits cannot be explained by increasing foreign sales, which during that time grew only from 38 percent to 52 percent of revenues.

Sullivan has shown that, at least on accounting records, the most profitable places in the world to do business are the Cayman Islands, Bermuda, Ireland and other tax havens. Moreover, in recent years U.S. multinationals' profit shifting to tax havens has become increasingly aggressive, allowing corporations to enjoy the benefits of making profits in America without sharing much in the burden of maintaining the society that makes those profits possible.

Suppose, for a moment, that American multinational corporations can persuade Congress to enact another tax holiday. With more than $1 trillion in untaxed profits overseas in 2012, they would save more than $350 billion in taxes. That's a burden that would be shifted on to you in the form of reduced services or higher taxes, the equivalent of making every family of four in America pay $4,500.

If a second so-called jobs creation act were to repeat the language of the 2004 American Jobs Creation Act, it would likely destroy several hundred thousand more American jobs while adding to the interest bill that eats up more and more tax dollars. Have you heard of this push for another "jobs creation" tax break? It would be impressive if you have. Legislation about taxes gets little coverage except for the big bills, and even then the significant details, like a "jobs creation" act with no requirement actually to create jobs, often go unmentioned or get a brief and vague mention. As long as Washington journalists are kept busy chasing ginned-up issues of no importance, and a host of corporate-backed organizations make so much trouble for reporters who provide serious coverage that their editors and producers focus on less stressful issues, Washington will remain a piggybank for the political-donor class and a prop for mismanaged corporations like Pfizer.

This brings us back to that quote that candidate Ronald Reagan loved so much, the made-up one that warned that the rabble would vote themselves the largesse of the treasury and ruin the country. The lessons here are three:

1. Reagan got it partly right. There are votes to capture the largesse of the treasury. The votes, however, come not from the citizenry, but from lawmakers whose real constituency is the political-donor class that is energetically mining the government treasury for its benefit. One way to do this is to abuse the English language by, say, drafting legislation whose title describes the opposite of what the bill says, as with the job destruction features of the 2004 American Jobs Creation Act.
2. Had Reagan been right, he would never have won election since he promised the voters less, not more, than his opponent, President Jimmy Carter.
3. Unless the voters take the time to understand giveaways (such as the Jobs Creation Act) that effectively take from the many to give to the already-rich few, which will require that the news media provide sustained, serious and skeptical coverage, then the loose fiscal policy Reagan warned about will continue to be right on the money.

Hollywood Robbery

Greed is good.

—**Gordon Gekko,** *Wall Street*

20. **You can learn** from reading tiny type on a soup can what ingredients you are about to eat. From the fine print of a loan agreement you can learn how much interest you will owe. But movie theater tickets come with no such disclosures, even though these days you are paying more than the price of a ticket to see many movies.

Perhaps you saw *Public Enemies*, the 2009 movie about the Depression-era bandit John Dillinger, whose bank heists and jailbreaks left ten men dead in nine months. *Public Enemies* starred Johnny Depp as the counter-vaulting bandit who loved submachine guns.

Part of the story involved Dillinger robbing a Racine, Wisconsin, bank, then hiding out in a northern Wisconsin lodge. History tells us that he and his gang stole about $5 million in today's money and, in doing so, ruined several small Midwest banks. History also tells us that, much more recently, General Electric, whose Universal Studios made the movie, legally robbed Wisconsin taxpayers of almost as much as Dillinger did.

This is how it worked. Many towns and forests could have been used as stand-in locations, but the producers chose to film scenes in Oshkosh and Racine. The reason was not unique scenery, but taxpayer greenery. A state law there gave the film producers tax credits totaling $4.6 million. The amount the producers spent filming in Wisconsin? They claimed $5 million.

The Wisconsin tax credit reimburses twenty-five cents on each dollar spent in Wisconsin shooting a film or commercial or making a video game. Then the state reimburses most of the wages paid to those working in a film. And on top of that are other, smaller tax benefits. In theory these credits reduce the state corporate income taxes owed on any profits from a film. But if there is no corporate income tax due, the state just cuts the filmmakers a check. That's the real benefit—cash.

When you break it all down, Universal Studios produced the Wisconsin portion of the movie at a net cost of eight cents on the dollar. To appreciate what a massive subsidy this is, consider this: most businesses would be thrilled to earn a *profit* of eight cents on the dollar. On average the nearly 5.8 million corporations that filed federal tax returns in 2007 kept as profit less than six cents on each dollar they took in from customers.

Given the opportunity to recover from Wisconsin taxpayers ninety-two cents on each dollar they spent, it should not be surprising that filmmakers found it lucrative to make brief stops in the dairy state. In 2007, the year before this giveaway began, almost no filmmaking or television production occurred in the state, but in 2008 parts of eight films, sixteen television shows and a pair of commercials for national broadcast were shot in Wisconsin. Two video games also got subsidies.

Welfare for Hollywood is bipartisan. The two biggest champions of this Wisconsin giveaway program were Lieutenant Governor Barbara Lawton, a Democrat, and state senator Ted Kanavas, a Republican. The third ranking official at the Wisconsin Commerce Department, Zach Brandon, told the *Milwaukee Journal Sentinel* that it was not as if the tax credits were a drain on the state economy. "It's a wash," he said.

Brandon needs a refresher in grammar-school arithmetic. In fact, the giveaway to General Electric was the equivalent of giving away the state's share of roughly a billion dollars of business activity in the state. That is about how much revenue corporations must collect from their customers to earn enough profits to pay as much corporate income tax as the state gave away for *Public Enemies.*

In fact, the $4.6 million that General Electric's Universal Studios received from Wisconsin taxpayers was more money than all of the corporate income taxes paid by 83 percent of the nearly 45,691 companies that filed Wisconsin tax returns in 2006, the latest year for which data is available.

Nearly thirty thousand of these companies paid no tax because they did not earn a profit. In reality, many of these firms actually did earn a profit, just not under Wisconsin law. Thanks to the generosity of Wisconsin politicians, many of these thirty thousand companies claimed that fees their local operations paid to their corporate parents ate up the profits earned in Wisconsin.

For example, chains like Target, Walmart and Hilton charge their Wisconsin operations a royalty to use their logos on signs marking their buildings. These royalty payments funnel money out of Wisconsin to states such as Delaware, Nevada, Texas and Wyoming, where corporations pay little or no tax on their profits. SC Johnson, the home products company, and two other Wisconsin businesses owned by the Johnson family paid no Wisconsin state income tax from 2000 to 2008, public records show.

When the Wisconsin profits are so big that royalties alone cannot make those profits vanish, other profit-removal devices can be used. Many corporate parents act as banks, requiring their subsidiaries to symbolically turn over all of their cash every night. A minute later the cash is lent back to the local operation, along with an interest charge.

The parent company can also charge its local operation a management overhead fee. It can inflate the prices of goods it buys and resells to the local operation. This last technique is similar to what American multinational companies do when, on paper, they ship goods through the Cayman Islands before they reach your shopping mall. This and other accounting techniques let the companies report little profit or even losses in the United States, while on paper earning their profits in tax havens like the Caymans.

The subsidy for *Public Enemies*, which earned $214 million worldwide at the box office, also shows how big businesses have arranged the laws to favor them at the expense of the family-owned businesses that dominate in numbers but are pipsqueaks in profits. Keep in mind that 80 percent of American companies have less than $5 million in assets and two-thirds have less than $500,000 in assets. After taxes these 4.7 million small businesses keep not quite three cents on each dollar they ring up at the cash register, my analysis of IRS data reveals.

Official state data show that 8,010 small Wisconsin companies eked out a profit of less than $25,000 each in 2006. Their average profit came to less than $7,000 each, on which they paid an average tax of $545. Together these small businesses paid Wisconsin nearly $4.4 million in corporate income taxes, almost exactly the amount of money that flowed out of state coffers to the makers of *Public Enemies*.

In effect, Wisconsin politicians forced the owners of these 8,000 small, family-owned and taxpaying businesses to turn over a month's profits so the money could be given to one of the biggest companies in the world, General Electric, and its partners to make a film glamorizing violent theft. This transfer illustrates how small businesses, as well as individuals, are forced via the fine print to give some of their substance to giant companies.

The question Wisconsin taxpayers should be asking is how much better off those 8,000 small businesses would be if they had been able to hold on to that $4.6 million instead of being forced to subsidize General Electric's Universal Studios. What permanent jobs or higher wages or stronger business finances would have resulted had those tax dollars stayed in Wisconsin, instead of being sent off to Hollywood and to GE headquarters in Connecticut, the highest per capita income state in the country?

State officials say the purpose of the tax credits is to create a twenty-first-century economy by helping establish a film industry in Wisconsin, a state with an economy dependent on cows, forests and a declining industrial sector that prospered in the twentieth century making Rambler automobiles and Schlitz beer. The advocates of the Hollywood giveaway argue that throwing tax money at Hollywood will build up a modern Wisconsin workforce; their interviews and speeches are filled with talk of movie-support jobs, everything from hairdressers and makeup artists to construction workers who can build sets. That's not exactly cutting-edge twenty-first-century work, even if the politicians may dream of computer graphics and other high-tech businesses serving Hollywood. The reality is that these digital jobs can be done anywhere the Internet exists, and Mumbai has a better shot at this work than Madison.

Moreover, giving money to Hollywood to create jobs, even temporary jobs, in Wisconsin makes little sense if the work goes to people from Beverly Hills, Malibu and the rest of Southern California. That is just what happened with *Public Enemies*. About $2.7 million of the $4.6 million giveaway was for work performed by people flown into Wisconsin to work on the film.

A tenth of the money went to benefit just one employee on the film, Michael Mann, best known as the producer of the stylish 1980s television series *Miami Vice* and such unusual films as *Hancock*, a comedy about two Greek gods living in modern-day Los Angeles. Wisconsin taxpayers shelled out $450,000 of the $1.8 million that GE said was paid to Mann, the writer, director and producer of *Public Enemies*, for his work during filming in Wisconsin.

The Wisconsin Commerce Department issued a report in May 2009 on the efficiency of the tax credits program. It was one of those dry tomes meant not to be read, but to collect dust on a shelf lest the voters find out how the rich are using politicians to pick the people's pockets. The study found that some local jobs were created by the Hollywood tax credit. Among these were temporary construction jobs making sets. But the study also compared the cost of these jobs to other jobs the state created through more traditional uses of tax money. The temporary film-industry jobs cost taxpayers, on average, twenty times as much as the other jobs the state created.

LOOTING THE LOCATIONS

If Wisconsin were the only state giving money away to wealthy movie-makers, the concern would be parochial. Unfortunately, forty of the fifty states have such Hollywood welfare programs. These states are now locked in competition to determine who can give the most money away, and they are also competing with giveaways by Canada and Eastern Europe. Tax welfare for Hollywood explains why careful viewers can discern Toronto towers posing as Manhattan skyscrapers.

GE's Universal Studios was not alone, either, in using pens to pry open state tax vaults and run away with tons of money. Rupert Murdoch's News Corporation, Sumner Redstone's Viacom, Dreamworks (owned by billionaires Steven Spielberg, Jeffrey Katzenberg and David Geffen), Disney and other film studios are all legally robbing taxpayers at a pace far beyond the wildest dreams of John Dillinger and his bank-robbing gang.

Louisiana gave millions to Hollywood in 2007 and then gave even more in 2008. Louisiana, New York and Rhode Island are among the states using taxpayer dollars to build soundstages to benefit Hollywood. One is proposed in Delaware, too, to be financed with tax dollars and money from a carpenters' union pension fund.

Pennsylvania taxpayers gave away $72 million in 2007–2008 to Hollywood. Among their gifts was $12 million to Murdoch's Fox Studios for *The Happening*, a film about mass suicides; $8.5 million to Dreamworks for *The Lovely Bones*, about a murdered girl who comes back to occupy another girl's body and have sex with the other girl's boyfriend; and $5.7 million for *Zack and Miri Make a Porno*, a comedy about a pair of down-on-their-luck platonic friends who seek riches by making an XXX-rated movie and fall in love along the way. The costs of subsidizing these commercial creations were borne by Pennsylvania schoolchildren and readers as budgets for public education and libraries were cut.

The most generous state in giving welfare to Hollywood is Michigan, whose fortunes have declined for more than a third of a century along with those of the domestic auto industry. Makers of thirty-two films spent $65.4 million in the Wolverine State for salaries, goods and services in 2008, according to Michigan State University researchers. The tax credits cost $48 million. That means that the state gave Hollywood filmmakers seventy-three cents of taxpayer money for each dollar Hollywood spent in Michigan, assuming the filmmakers were scrupulous in not overstating their expenses, which would increase their welfare check.

Based on the 4.95 percent tax rate Michigan applies to corporate profits, that $48 million giveaway to Hollywood represents the state's corporate taxes on $16 billion worth of revenue to business.

A report by the Michigan senate staff concluded that "the tax revenue generated from the additional activity would be unlikely to offset completely, or in some cases, even offset significantly, the cost of the proposed credits and deductions, even over the long run." That's bureaucratese for *This giveaway cannot earn back what it cost and is rapidly draining tax dollars out of Michigan.*

The Michigan senate staff report made a crucial point about why these tax giveaways to motion picture projects are a sheer waste of taxpayer money. Filming on location is inherently fickle, temporary and movable. Films shot partly in Michigan do not represent fixed investments. A movie shot on location is not like a factory, in which the owners have invested in unique manufacturing equipment and customized buildings, which they have an incentive to keep productive until they wear out decades in the future or demand for their products ebbs. Location shoots are not even like filming in a studio on soundstages that are costly to build and maintain.

The Hollywood studios just use Michigan as a location, shooting its gritty industrial cities and aging factories, its lush forests and Great Lakes shorelines. They fly in the actors, rent hotel rooms, run the cameras for a few hours and leave. All it takes to switch filming—and the jobs that go with it—from Michigan to Louisiana is a slightly larger tax credit from the Pelican State. With a quick polish of the script by a screenwriter, an Upper Peninsula hunting scene can be shot in the bayou. The loons become pelicans.

To boost their welfare checks, studios tell the companies they rent cameras from to briefly occupy a vacant space in the state where location shooting will take place. That way they can count the cost of the camera rental as an in-state expense. It's what happened when the makers of

Public Enemies rented cameras from the temporary Wisconsin storefront of a Chicago-based movie camera rental business.

The state officials whose jobs depend on maintaining these giveaways, and the moviemakers whose profits are enhanced by them, all say this is about creating jobs. That some politicians arrange to get photographed with movie stars, or give their constituents a chance to glimpse a movie set from behind police barricades, is just one of those vote-gathering perks politicians love, as long as no one notices that they are achieving this result by taxing the many to give to the few.

Meanwhile, Wisconsin is so broke it fired some of its state corporate tax auditors, even though they bring in far more money than their salaries cost. But of course it is always easier to give money away than to collect it. And what glamour is there in auditing corporations to make sure they pay their required taxes compared to politicians getting to crow to voters that they brought Johnny Depp to town?

Louisiana and Pennsylvania are among the states that have relied on a firm called Economic Research Associates to justify these Hollywood welfare programs. News reports routinely described these reports as audits or studies, implying that they are neutral searches for fact and truth. The missing descriptive words for these reports are "bought and paid for" and "superficial."

When a paying client asks, Economic Research Associates turns out "studies" that sell the absurd as fact. One such paper claimed that a nearly dead mall in Irondequoit, New York, part of whose market area is Lake Ontario, could grow sales fourteen fold from $30 million to $450 million annually. Never mind that the mall was in a county where population has been flat for decades and retail sales falling. Never mind that in the previous ten years total annual wages, adjusted for inflation, have fallen by $660 million. Never mind that the study was paid for by a developer seeking more than $250 million of taxpayer gifts, welfare he asked for while making campaign contributions to local politicians who were in a position to arrange these gifts. Never mind little details like facts and sense.

I got this study when I asked officials in surrounding Monroe County to show me their due diligence on the proposed subsidy for the dying mall. It turned out they had not one sheet of paper representing any independent inquiry to determine facts before spending money. All the officials could produce was the fantasy report by the developer hoping to pocket millions of taxpayer dollars. Reports by Economic Research Associates and other firms who get paid by those with their hands out for subtle giveaways of your tax dollars, or credits to escape taxes, should be greeted with public laughter as fairy tales for the greedy.

So just how many jobs were created in Michigan with its $48 million of tax welfare to Hollywood? The moviemakers employed nearly 2,800 people, the Michigan State University researchers reported. Some politicians trumpeted this single fact as proof that the tax credit works. But the fine print revealed that the typical "job" lasted just twenty-three days. Turn that into years of labor, and the 2,800 jobs become the equivalent of 254 full-time jobs, though such temporary employment hardly compares with steady work. Divide the $48 million giveaway by those 254 jobs and the cost to Michigan taxpayers for each came to $189,000.

For context, consider that in 2007, when most families had two breadwinners, the average American household earned $48,000 in wages. The average Michigan household did not fare as well, earning just $44,000, federal and state tax reports show. So those 254 Hollywood jobs cost taxpayers nearly five times the wages earned by the typical Michigan household.

The good news is that this welfare for Hollywood only cost the average Michigan household $12. The bad news is that state political leaders are planning on increasing their giveaways to Hollywood in the years ahead. They would never say it this way, but what they plan is to take more money from the below-average-income earners of Michigan to give to the far-above-average income people of Hollywood. This is income redistribution, not downward to relieve the poor, the disabled, the sick, but upward to help the already rich.

As with Wisconsin, the numbers show that Michigan politicians who voted for these laws flunked elementary-school arithmetic. But this story is a two-reeler and the second reel is even richer for Hollywood than the first.

TAX CREDITS FOR SALE

Michigan lawmakers were careful to make sure that Hollywood would get the full benefit of these tax breaks even if the studio did not owe any Michigan taxes. How? Technically, what Michigan gives Hollywood is a tax credit. That is a dollar-for-dollar reduction in state corporate taxes. If the film company does not make any profit in Michigan, it has no use for tax credits since it owes no taxes. On the surface, a tax credit would be worthless. But just as in Wisconsin, if the film company does not owe any taxes to Michigan, the state just writes the company a check.

Film studios can also sell their tax credits to companies that do owe Michigan taxes. Because these tax credits can be traded, when you buy a ticket to see a film that gets these deals, you are helping companies with no relationship to the movie industry escape taxes.

The producers with tax credits to sell go to brokers, who typically charge a fee of about 4 percent. The buyers of these tax credits then bid for them. The amounts the tax credits are sold for are not disclosed. But let's assume a million dollars of tax credits is sold for eighty cents on the dollar. The moviemakers collect $800,000, less the $30,000 or so in commissions to the tax credit brokers. The company that buys the Hollywood tax credits then gets to pay a million-dollar tax bill with a piece of paper that only cost $800,000. The only losers here are the taxpayers.

The trading of state tax credits is now a growing corner of business. It creates no wealth—arguably it destroys wealth, by helping the Hollywood rich collect welfare from you.

Next time you go to a movie with location shots, stick around when the action ends and watch the credits roll. Somewhere after the names of the stars, perhaps down where they list the chauffeurs and the caterers, you may see a list of people being thanked. One of the firms cited in the screen credits will probably be Tax Credits LLC, a New Jersey firm that specializes in helping studios sell their tax credits in fifteen states.

Hollywood is far from alone in arranging these deals buried deep in the fine print. A whole industry has arisen to soak the taxpayers on behalf of the rich through tradable tax credits and subsidies that put money in the pockets of filmmakers, factory owners, hotel developers, shopping mall owners and anyone else among the very rich who has no shame about being on the dole. Not having any shame is, of course, a lot easier when hardly anyone knows you are on welfare.

21

Silly Software

Reform is bad for Intuit's business.

—Professor Joe Bankman

21.   **Joe Bankman is** a Stanford University professor of tax law with a really smart idea. He knows how to end what, for many people, is the single most aggravating aspect of being an American and, in doing so, may save taxpayers billions of dollars per year, free up billions of hours of people's time and cut the cost of government.

Bankman's brainstorm? Get rid of income tax returns for most people by having government calculate their income taxes for them.

If adopted by Congress, Bankman's modest proposal could eliminate about 100 million of the more than 140 million tax returns filed annually. Plus Bankman's idea has been tried and tested. It not only works, but people who have tried it love it, with a 98 percent positive rating in surveys. "Best government program ever!" is a common response.

Think of mandatory income tax return filing for most people in the twenty-first century as the equivalent of Congress passing a law in 1908, when the first Ford Model T was sold, that every one of those newfangled automobiles come with a buggy whip. The buggy whip makers would want such a law in effect, just as the tax preparation industry likes mandatory tax returns; in both cases, one theoretical and one real, only the self-interest of an industry argues for being mired in an unnecessarily costly past.

Bankman calls his idea ReadyReturn. If embraced by Congress and the legislatures in the forty-four states with income taxes, it could eliminate the aggravation of tax return filing for most Americans. With minor tweaks in tax law, as many as 120 million federal tax returns and almost the same number of state returns could be eliminated. If Congress streamlined the tax code, only sole proprietors and people with trusts and complex international investments would have to file tax returns.

Most modern countries have already eliminated tax return filing for the vast majority of their people. The Organization for Economic Cooperation and Development, which represents thirty-four countries with modern economies, has documented how these programs are being expanded, easing burdens on taxpayers while saving money spent processing tax returns.

Taxpayer savings result because ReadyReturns are prepared automatically using the same data that government collects from employers (as well as payers of pensions, interest and dividends). Such returns by definition do not contain the kind of mistakes by taxpayers and tax return preparers that require costly review by tax agency workers. Errors, both innocent and deliberate, cost money because of the cost of audits and other enforcement actions. ReadyReturns would also eliminate the cost of keypunching data into computers.

The use of such returns could be optional. If the government makes a mistake or the taxpayer disagrees with the record sent, the taxpayer is free to file his or her own tax return. But ending tax return filing as we know it would be immensely popular, a means of ending the tortuous annual process of filling out tax forms, begun in 1943 as an emergency measure to restrain domestic spending and raise money to finance World War II. Back then, filling out paper forms was the only practical way to collect information on how much people made. Thanks to digital technology, this annual drudgery could be swept into the dustbin of history for most Americans.

People dislike filling out tax forms so much that they routinely pay to outsource the pain. Accountants and others signed as preparers on 82 million of the more than 140 million American tax returns filed in 2010. The average fee charged by accountants and tax preparers in 2009 was about $220, while tax preparers at firms such as H&R Block and Jackson-Hewitt charged an average of about $181. The software company Intuit, which specializes in tax preparation (Quicken and TurboTax are two of its products), told its shareholders in 2011 that Americans spent $22 billion for tax preparation services. That was close to double the total IRS budget of about $12 billion that year.

Americans pay others to prepare their tax returns because they find the IRS forms confusing, they do not trust their knowledge of the tax law, and for many other reasons. They worry a mistake will mean they'll be hounded or even prosecuted by the IRS. That fear is encouraged by television ads from tax services and superficial stories by journalists, but it's greatly overblown. In 2010 the government prosecuted only 1,430 cases listing any tax crimes, even as part of prosecutions for drug dealing or official corruption. An analysis of Justice Department data by the Transactional Access Records Clearinghouse at Syracuse University shows that fewer than 600 of those cases cited a tax crime as the primary offense.

As a matter of written government policy, mere mistakes are not prosecuted nor are one-time violations, unless there is compelling evidence of a plot to hide a huge income, say millions of dollars from the sale of a business.

The simplest tax return, Form 1040EZ, is so daunting that 11 million Americans, half of those who use this one-page tax return, pay an average of $50 each to have someone else fill it out for them. That cost is more than half a day's take-home pay for a worker earning the median wage of slightly more than $26,000 per year, a significant burden that would be eliminated if the IRS used ReadyReturn for most taxpayers.

WHY NOT READYRETURN?

Most of the 58 million returns completed by taxpayers were prepared using tax software like Intuit's TurboTax, the overwhelming favorite with more than 70 percent of the market. Such a large market share gives Intuit monopoly pricing power. More significant, Intuit exerts influence with government, which has been a very good friend to Intuit shareholders.

Intuit is one of the most profitable companies in America. Overall, the fourteen thousand biggest corporations, which account for 85 percent of revenues, keep about a dime out of each dollar as profit before income taxes. Intuit kept twenty-five cents out of each dollar in 2011. For Intuit, your aggravation is money in the bank.

For more than a decade, TurboTax sales have been mushrooming. Intuit sold 24 million TurboTax subscriptions on disc and online in 2011, many of which were used to prepare multiple returns. On average Intuit collected $54 for each copy of TurboTax, a total of $1.3 billion of revenue.

Sales of TurboTax have been growing much faster than the number of taxpayers. From 1998 through 2011, the number of taxpayers grew about 13 percent, but Intuit's sales increased 390 percent. TurboTax sales grew thirty times more than the number of taxpayers, partly because the software works well and gets better each year. But there was also another factor.

TurboTax sales got a significant boost from the hidden hand of government. Policies in Washington and most state capitals steered customers toward TurboTax and the other much smaller tax software firms through a host of subtle policies. Intuit will offer free state-level filing to lower-income taxpayers, but only if states promise not to prepare returns in advance (such as California's ReadyReturn) or let people fill out their forms online at a state-run Web site. And to reinforce this, when a state tax agency gets its budget cut, Intuit sometimes offers free software help in return for renewing those promises.

Because of the economics of software, as Intuit's sales grow, its profits on each copy of TurboTax should grow much faster. And TurboTax is already an exceptionally profitable product. Had you invested a dollar in the overall stock market in 1998 and another dollar in shares of Intuit, your returns would be dramatically different. By late 2011 your investment in the total stock market would have lost a bit of value, even after collecting dividends, while the dollar you put into Intuit would have grown to almost $7. For that investment to remain so lucrative, the law must continue to require people to file tax returns, even though that is a necessity whose time passed with the arrival of the digital age.

Much of the $22 million Americans paid for income tax preparation in 2011 was wasted, a drag on the economy that enriches only tax preparers and tax companies like Intuit. Intuit has told its shareholders to expect future growth of 10 percent to 15 percent annually, even though the number of taxpayers grows at only about 1 percent per year. This suggests that the more sand Intuit throws into the gears of the economy, the more it profits, an issue similar to how the telecommunications companies profit by making sure America has an Internet that is slow and serves only densely populated, higher-income areas. Policies that create profits by working against the national economy need to be replaced yesterday.

The key to understanding how to eliminate time and money wasted in preparing taxes is to remember that taxpayers fall into two broad groups: those who itemize deductions and those who do not. About one in three taxpayers, generally the more affluent and rich, fills out lengthy tax returns in which they get to deduct charitable gifts, mortgage interest, property taxes, exceptionally large medical bills and, in some cases, a wide array of other expenses, down to dry cleaning of uniforms. The majority of taxpayers only get the standard deduction plus an exemption for themselves, their spouses and any dependents. It's the two-thirds for whom the make-work of filing tax returns could easily be eliminated.

A ReadyReturn experiment began in 2005 when the state of California sent completed tax returns to fifty thousand people. All of these people were wage-earning singles. All they had to do to file their state income tax returns was sign the forms and mail them back.

These completed tax returns were sent with no public announcement, no campaign to alert people and no advance letters that the finished forms would be arriving. Some of those who got the completed tax forms thought it was a scam and threw them away. Half of those who received the completed California tax returns did not even respond, which at first suggested they were not interested. Research later showed that most of these people had already filed their tax returns.

Among those who had not yet filed, more than half signed the returns and sent them in. It involved no cost, no aggravation and only the time required to sign and date the form, then pop it into an envelope.

How did the state know how to fill out the forms? Therein lies the reason why, for most people, completing a tax return is make-work. Federal and state law already requires employers to report how much they pay workers and how much tax is withheld from paychecks. For the two-thirds of taxpayers who do not itemize, all the government needs from taxpayers is their marital status, dependents' names, and Social Security numbers. They already have the rest of the data.

California ReadyReturn was limited at the start in 2005 to singles. That made the pilot as simple as possible to both execute and evaluate. Those chosen to get prepared returns had only wage income and listed themselves as unmarried on their previous tax return. Excluding married couples and heads of households eliminated the need for any adjustments for newborn children or those no longer dependent.

ReadyReturn also allowed people to adjust their income up or down in case they made some money that was not reported or was less than their employers told the state. How many people used this feature indicated how accurate the ReadyReturns were. Just 4 percent of ReadyReturn users made adjustments. That low number suggests strongly that the returns were highly accurate. Further, it indicated that, as time passes and the system is refined, the tiny number of ReadyReturns requiring adjustments would shrink even more.

The advent of ReadyReturn made some interested parties very nervous. Intuit, for example, wanted to kill ReadyReturn, and spent at least $3.4 million making its case in lobbying expenses and in campaign donations to more than a hundred politicians just in California. It has also worked hard against such ideas in other states, including Virginia, where it persuaded lawmakers to vote for Intuit and against the constituents by keeping mandatory tax return filing.

But the best measure of its determination to get rid of ReadyReturn came in 2006, when Intuit gave a million dollars to support a single California state legislator who pledged eternal fealty to forced tax filing, which meant to Intuit's profits. The huge donation went not to the candidate, but to a group supporting Republican state senator Tony Strickland. The indirect contribution helped obscure support for Strickland, who was running in 2010 for state controller against the incumbent, Democrat John Chiang. Strickland's campaign spokesman, Michael Levoff, wrote to *Tax Notes* magazine, "Tony has been against it from day one, and always will" be against ReadyReturn.

Strickland, who lost that race, was at the time the California leader of the Club for Growth, a Washington antitax group that says it favors significantly reducing tax burdens (though, obviously, not the burden of filing or the cost savings it would produce). The Club for Growth raises money to defeat Republicans it considers weak on fighting for lower taxes, especially on investors and business owners.

ReadyReturn is also opposed by the National Taxpayers Union, which poses as a friend of taxpayers but, in this case, has befriended the tax preparation industry. The National Taxpayers Union dismissed ReadyReturn as "fools' gold for the taxpayers." Later it voiced strong support for a proposed federal law that would protect the tax-preparation industry. The bill's title was dubbed, in classic Washington doublespeak, the Taxpayer Freedom to File Protection Act.

Opponents rely on false statements to make their case against ReadyReturn. Intuit has made nine claims, all of which Dennis Ventry, another professor of tax law, has shown to be untrue. He calls them Intuit's Nine Lies.

The silliest attack, though, comes from Grover Norquist, president of Americans for Tax Reform. He says ReadyReturn and its online twin, CalFile, violate taxpayer confidentiality. In fact, as Norquist knows, all of the wage, interest, dividend, pension and other income is already reported to the authorities and, since the users are not itemizing deductions, there is no privacy to violate, only pockets to be picked by the tax-preparation industry. Norquist's group also pressures Republican politicians and Democrats in swing districts to sign pledges to never raise taxes, a pledge that violates the oath of office taken by members of Congress to make decisions unfettered by any allegiance other than to the Constitution. In 2012, Norquist promoted a new way to replace taxes: universal gambling. He urged Texas lawmakers to expand gambling, ignoring the fact that money government gets from gambling comes from taxing money that the casinos win when players lose.

Instead of ReadyReturn, Intuit has pushed for a system where it and other tax-software companies offer free tax return preparation online for some people. In theory this system covers seven out of ten taxpayers based on income, but that figure depends on the mix of offerings by all of the software firms. Each firm need only cover a smaller portion so long as together their different rules, known as "free file," are available to 70 percent of taxpayers. Not surprisingly, Intuit's offering covers a much smaller share than 70 percent of taxpayers.

Anyone who uses Intuit's free service is bombarded with ads to buy its products, many of which literally offer no value to people filing the simplest tax return, Form 1040EZ. If you thought you might save more than the cost of software by buying it, would you? Many people do. And once people buy TurboTax they are more likely to buy it again and again, as well as the company's related software, including Quicken electronic banking, and Intuit's accounting for small businesses, QuickBooks.

Professor Bankman's idea makes a great deal of sense, both for you and for efficient government. As voters, we should remind Congress that, when it passed the 1998 Taxpayer Protection Act, one of its promises was to make the tax system simpler and to make it easier to pay your income taxes. A national ReadyReturn would accomplish exactly that.

22

Pilfering Your Paycheck

> Our current governor [Pat Quinn] . . . is allowing Navistar
> to fire up to 25 percent of their workforce and still get
> millions from the state. . . . People should be outraged.
>
> **—Illinois state representative Jack Franks**

22.   **Take a look** at your pay stub. In all but six states, workers will see a deduction for state income taxes. You probably expect that money to finance public schools, the state university and college system, law enforcement and the other services that businesses and individuals rely on. Mostly it does, but in a growing number of states, your state income taxes will also be increasing the profits of your employer.

You read that right. Many employers in nineteen states can now keep state income taxes withheld from paychecks. General Electric, Goldman Sachs and Procter & Gamble have these deals, along with a host of foreign firms from the German computer maker Siemens to the Swedish appliance maker Electrolux and a host of Canadian, European and Japanese banks. In all more than 2,700 companies get to pocket the state income taxes withheld from some of their workers' paychecks.

In Illinois, for example, six big companies made deals with the state to pocket half or all of the state income taxes paid by their workers over ten years. Ford got a deal in 2007 by threatening to close an automobile assembly plant. In 2009, when the economy was in the worst shape in eight decades, Chrysler and Mitsubishi used threats of assembly plant closings to get similar deals.

In 2011, three more companies threatened to move out of Illinois. The state paid them off by letting them keep all the taxes withheld from their workers' paychecks for ten years. The German tire maker Continental will pocket $22 million of its workers' taxes, about a tenth of what it invested to modernize a tire plant in poverty-stricken southern Illinois, retaining 2,500 jobs and creating 444 more. Navistar, maker of big diesel trucks for industry and the military, threatened to go to Alabama or maybe Iowa. In return for staying put, Navistar will pocket almost $65 million.

The big winner, though, was Motorola Mobility, the cell phone maker. Just for promising not to move out of state and take three thousand jobs with it, Motorola gets to siphon $136 million from the paychecks of its well-paid high-tech workers. As if to make this transaction all the more interesting, Motorola Mobility agreed to be acquired by Google soon after the state made the big tax deal. The Motorola board then paid its CEO, Sanjay Jha, to go away. He received $66 million. Thus, Illinois taxpayers underwrote his golden parachute, which amounted to roughly half the value of the worker taxes flowing to Google.

Google hardly needs a subsidy from Illinois taxpayers. It dominates the worldwide search engine and advertising business. Its founders, Larry Page and Sergey Brin, are each worth more than $15 billion. Monopoly profits are the key to such fortunes and oversize toys: at a Capitol Hill hearing in September 2011, Senator Herb Kohl of Wisconsin asked if Google was effectively a monopoly and Eric Schmidt, Google's CEO, acknowledged, "We're in that area."

If you work for one of the above companies in Illinois, you probably have not heard that your employer is keeping the state taxes taken out of your check. The diversion is stealthy by design. No law requires the companies to notify the workers that state income taxes are being diverted. The state treats you as having paid your taxes even though it never got the money.

The few news reports about these deals, most of them scanty and vague, often characterize this pilfering of worker taxes as a public benefit that creates or saves jobs. The reality is that companies getting such benefits can actually negotiate to destroy jobs, as Navistar did. It can fire up to 900 of its 3,100 headquarters workers and still keep the taxes its remaining workers pay.

What economic argument justifies letting companies take taxes withheld from paychecks, much less companies that plan mass layoffs? In return for pocketing the taxes the companies agreed not to destroy even more jobs. Think of it as antipink slip blackmail. And like most blackmail arrangements, you never hear about them even when they happen in your neighborhood.

Warren Ribley, the director of the Illinois Department of Commerce and Economic Opportunity, told me "it's a fair question" as to whether taxpayers should be subsidizing businesses. But he said that was the duty of elected leaders, and that the public should debate the issue; assessing the pros and cons was not part of his job description.

"In the meantime," Ribley said, "I am out there competing every single day with states and countries across the entire globe. I have got to have the tools and I have to use the tools provided by the General Assembly," as the Illinois legislature is formally known.

State representative Jack Franks, a Democrat from the northern end of Illinois, said the deals "are fundamentally unfair" to taxpayers and other companies. He pushed to get copies of the contracts, which Ribley's office eventually turned over. Once Franks read the contracts he became incensed. He realized that some of the six companies made deals allowing them to fire workers en masse and yet pocket tax dollars. "Our current governor," he said, referring to fellow Democrat Pat Quinn, "had the genius idea of giving to Motorola and Navistar and others . . . yet he is allowing Navistar to fire up to twenty-five percent of their workforce and still get millions from the state" by pocketing taxes withheld from their workers' paychecks. "People should be outraged," he said.

Why would states do this? The answer is that this is the only remaining way to funnel taxpayer money to big companies without writing them checks. The biggest companies already pay little or no state income tax, thanks to friendly legislators ever grateful for campaign contributions. In Connecticut, home to about forty companies with a billion dollars or more of annual revenue (among them General Electric), only one large company paid more than a million dollars in state corporate income tax in 2003, the latest year for which the state has released such data. In Wisconsin, multibillion-dollar giants like the family-owned company SC Johnson, maker of Raid bug spray and Ziploc bags, have not paid Wisconsin income taxes in years. We know that because of an unusual Wisconsin law that, for a $4 fee, permits any state resident to get a report that discloses how much tax a corporation paid the state.

This is, of course, perfectly legal. Legislatures pass laws that let national and multinational companies pay, through a host of techniques, little or no state income tax. One of the most common is the same technique used by multinational companies to convert profits earned in America into tax-deductible expenses.

Here is how it works. A company sets up a subsidiary in a tax-free jurisdiction, nothing more than a corporate shell in, say, the Cayman Islands for a multinational or in Delaware for a domestic company. This shell then owns the parent company's patents, copyrights, brand names, logos and other intellectual property. The shell company charges royalties for the use of the intellectual property it owns. Those royalties are tax-deductible expenses at one end and untaxed profits at the other.

Another shell company acts as an internal bank. Each day all the revenue taken in at stores or factories is paid to the shell company, which then lends back whatever cash is needed at a stiff interest rate. The factory or store, burdened with debt, earns little or no profit for tax purposes, while the profits accumulate in a different jurisdiction, where they may be lightly taxed or not taxed at all.

Then there are excise and property taxes. State economic development agencies, together with local governments, routinely wipe out these levies. In Delaware, companies can get a refund on half their utility taxes. Other states give companies "green" tax credits for using renewable energy or building in areas once abandoned because of toxic spills. In many states, companies can get refunds on any sales or excise taxes they paid.

Donald Trump began his career in the 1970s with a deal to rebuild the rundown Commodore Hotel over Grand Central Station in New York, remaking it into a Grand Hyatt. He got a twenty-year property tax abatement and said his only mistake was not asking for forty. That seemed preposterous to some at the time. Now it seems prescient.

Deals to wipe out all property taxes for half a century are now common—not for your home, of course, but for property owned by big companies. Verizon, the biggest company in the immensely profitable telecommunications oligopoly, made such a deal in Lockport, New York. The deal was worth $611 million, a tax giveback in return for about 200 jobs. That's $3 million per job. Invest that amount at 5 percent and you get $150,000 annually. The Verizon jobs were going to pay at most $85,000, with many under $50,000. Yahoo made a similar deal in the same town for 125 jobs, but its subsidy was only $2.1 million per job. Still, those jobs were also worth less than the interest on the subsidy.

Then Verizon walked away from the $611 million subsidy. Why? It got a better deal elsewhere.

So many states have tax credits and giveaways that chronicling them supports a publication called *Tax Incentives Alert* that reports every bit of the fine print, together with articles critical of any reductions in these gifts, showing an especially vigorous entitlement philosophy. It provides real and useful news for those who make money off taxes, not those who pay taxes. The monthly publication costs $517 a year for both print and electronic versions, but you can save $40 by taking one or the other.

Even the myriad abatements, credits and outright gifts detailed in *Tax Incentives Alert* are not always enough to wipe out taxable profits at prosperous firms. Luckily for these companies, the politicians they help keep in office have another technique to help corporations escape taxation: laying off state tax auditors. In many states, notably South Carolina and Wisconsin, governors slashed the number of corporate tax auditors, claiming the state could no longer afford them. It is a preposterous argument. These auditors routinely bring in many times their salaries, which would seem to argue for keeping them working.

Firing auditors makes as much sense as a hospital firing doctors; in a real sense, doctors are the source of a hospital's patients and, like auditors, both amount to a sales force. But when politicians fire auditors, plenty of people cheer because their hatred of taxes or government overwhelms logic and reason. How many politicians have you heard saying we need more tax auditors? Would that change if we called them what they are—financial detectives?

At the federal level, the highest paid IRS corporate auditors, with years of experience and advanced degrees, make less than $75 an hour in pay and benefits. According to IRS data analyzed by the Transactional Records Access Clearinghouse at Syracuse University, each hour spent auditing the biggest companies produced an average of more than $9,300 of taxes owed. So firing one of these auditors saves taxpayers less than $150,000 annually while costing taxpayers more than $19 million annually in forgone tax revenue.

Once state politicians have enacted laws reducing or even wiping out income, sales, excise, utility, fuel and other miscellaneous taxes, the demands for more of the same continue. Remember the corporation is, by nature, amoral, immortal and entirely money motivated; that means the corporation is so constituted as to do anything and everything lawful to get more money. Pocketing tax dollars is an easy source of profits.

"Profits" is the right word here because no product or service is produced in return for these payments. And the companies bear no expense that they would not face without the giveaways. Taxes siphoned from workers drop right to the bottom line. Some consultants, according to *Tax Incentives Alert*, charge companies 30 percent of the take to shepherd tax giveaways through the process, presumably on small-bore deals. But on huge multimillion-dollar deals like the ones in Illinois, the rules are not that complicated and each of the companies already has experts on staff to fill out the relatively minimal paperwork.

These laws were passed with so little attention, some of them going back two decades, that I was unaware of them until the summer of 2011. David Brunori, a prominent authority on state taxes as the executive editor of the weekly state, federal and international *Tax Notes* magazines, was also in the dark. So were several tax law and accounting professors I contacted. The story was not entirely untold, however. Once I knew about these diversions I started searching the news clips. I found little items here and there, often on the inside back pages or, if prominently played, topped by vague and celebratory headlines along the lines of "Jobs Saved Thanks to State Senator So-and-So." D-list celebrities get more coverage with more telling details.

Now the essential underlying question here is: *How probable was it in the first place that these companies would close up shop and move across state lines?* Under Illinois Public Act 97-2, the justification for such tax deals is a "credible" threat that a company will leave the state. But would these companies really go, abandoning their existing investment and disrupting their operations? And furthermore, does it make sense to institutionalize threats to leave a state as the legal basis for getting tax dollars?

Motorola has three thousand highly paid workers around Schaumburg, a quick drive from the cultural amenities of Chicago. Their skills are not easily replaced. It is unlikely many of them are eager to give up their suburban enclave with easy access to museums, theater and big-time sports teams to live out their lives in, say, rural Iowa or Alabama. Moving them, especially if the company offered to pay their entire household moving costs, would impose huge costs on the company, as well as disruptions to its business. By staying put not only are these costs and disruptions avoided, but, when the current deal ends in 2021, the company can renew the flow of tax dollars by threatening—in a "credible" way, of course—to move its operations to another state.

The fine print protects.

Of Commas and Character

Be more concerned with your character than your
reputation, because your character is what you really are,
while your reputation is merely what others think you are.

—John Wooden, former UCLA basketball coach

23. **By now your** blood may be boiling at the conduct laid bare
in these pages, but what you have read is not the half of it. Researching
this book for more than four years has opened my eyes to still more
abuses beyond the scope of this book, which is the third volume in my
series examining the American economy, following *Perfectly Legal* (the
subject was taxes) and *Free Lunch* (subsidies).

To despair and think the economy is doomed, however, would be a
mistake. We can recover from the trend of permitting big business to use
our government as a shield from the economic discipline of competition.
We need not sink further into debt as individuals or as a nation. We do
not have to fall further behind our competitors, and we do not have to
endure a government that is hostile to the well-being of the vast majority.
We can end the privatized system of wealth and income redistribution
that uses monopolies and oligopolies to take from the many to unjustly
enrich the politically connected few. We can reduce cronyism and promote success based on merit.

Yet to return to the best path to prosperity and stability, we must recognize the deep forces at work that brought about our economic woes.
The core problem is with oligopolies and monopolies and their excessive
prices, lower quality services and reduced innovation. They are the principal means, enabled by government, to redistribute income and wealth
from the many to the politically connected few.

Solving problems usually begins with acknowledging them, so let's look at our most fundamental problem, a school of economic philosophy that has become the accepted truth, or rather dogma that is now treated as truth. Let me explain.

NEOCLASSICAL ECONOMICS, CHICAGO STYLE

The dogma is neoclassical economics, which, despite what we've been told, is but one way to view the production and distribution of goods and services (and, as our present circumstances demonstrate, is a highly imperfect way of doing so). The sect that promotes the dominant antitax, "deregulation" worship of this false god is the Chicago School, which assumes good behavior by people and has unquestioned faith in markets to correct themselves without any interference by government.

On paper, everything works out in neoclassical economics. In the real world, however, leaders face a less-than-ideal environment, and they must manage and compete against firms run by charlatans, incompetents and crooks, some of them aided by dishonest accounting schemes.

To the Chicago School, whose adherents seem to sit at every lever of power in Washington, regulation is regarded as a drag on the economy. The damage done by the poseurs and thieves, we are told, are anomalies that should not shape policy. One of the Chicago School's most influential figures, chief judge Frank Easterbrook of the Seventh Circuit Court of Appeals in Chicago, does not even believe in fraud laws for securities markets. (Tell that to all of the people whose savings were wiped out by the parade of accounting scandals at MCI and Enron and by the derivatives sold on Wall Street, which brought the whole economy down in 2008. The damage from those and other like events may linger for a decade or more.)

The dominant law and economics text on corporate law has for years been one by Easterbrook and Daniel Fischel, who was for a time dean of the University of Chicago's law school. They assert that "a rule against fraud is not an essential or even necessarily an important ingredient of securities markets." Their book was written after Professor Fischel worked as a consultant to three of the people at the top of America's most notorious corporate control frauds, corporations, including Enron; Charles Keating's corrupt Lincoln savings and loan empire; and Centrust, the crooked Miami banking firm. Fischel also maintains that junk bond financier Michael Milken should not have gone to prison for securities fraud. That these and other cases tested their theories—and found that they failed catastrophically in the real world—has not changed the opinions of Judge Easterbrook or Fischel. Their destructive ideas should be swept into the dustbin of history.

To assume that bad behavior does not exist or is anomalous is sheer folly. But that assumption underlies neoclassical economics and the push for "deregulation," or so-called deregulation, since the changes tend toward new rules that wipe out protections for the powerless.

Judge Easterbrook and others who share his view are, ultimately, correct that markets can be self-correcting. But how much damage will it take for self-correction to work? Should the entire economy collapse? Or would smart regulation based on principles that date to the Code of Hammurabi serve us better than the wishful thinking of the likes of Easterbrook and Fischel? Rules have long existed to rein in bad behavior through penalties and other remedies for misconduct. We also need them to promote good conduct, fair play and reasonable pricing while providing penalties and other remedies for misconduct. We don't need more of the massive securities and accounting frauds that occur when rules are dismantled.

We also need to get two words at the center of our discussion of the corruption in banking and mortgages: control fraud. That is when the CEO is a crook who uses his control of the company to run a fraud to enrich himself. We saw that William Black's diligent public service helped bring more than a thousand felony convictions of high-level insiders in the savings and loan scandals; in comparison, hardly any bankers have been indicted in the mortgage-market meltdown. That an FBI deputy director parrots the language of the banking industry—*banks are the victims of dishonest customers*—shows how blinded our government is to the obvious criminal activity of bankers, brokers and bailed-out Wall Street traders.

That our government isn't seeing what's before its eyes illustrates a much deeper problem about crony capitalism, corruption and Chicago School theories.

We have become a society where commas (it takes three to be a billionaire) count more than character. At the core of this bias in favor of the already rich is something economists call a *Pareto improvement*. It is named for Vilfredo Pareto, a brilliant Italian economist of the nineteenth century. A Pareto improvement means that when the distribution of goods or income changes, at least one person is better off, but no one is worse off.

Taken to its logical conclusion, it would be a Pareto improvement if the American economy doubled and one person enjoyed all of the gains. In fact, something not unlike that has happened in America since

Reagan's presidency, with the gains going entirely to the top 20 percent and very heavily to the top tenth of one percent.

Contrast this with the economics of Adam Smith, who recognized that competitive markets, and the signals they send about price, are at the heart of economic improvement. Smith saw competition as the great enforcer that harnessed the human desire to improve one's lot for the good of the whole society. And both he and his successor in the next great generation, Jeremy Bentham, argued for policies that benefit the majority, not the politically connected few.

If trickle-down is such a great philosophy, how do we explain the fact that after spending more than 40 percent of all the money in the world devoted to health care, we rank thirty-seventh in the quality of our health care and we still have roughly 50 million people without health insurance? In 1981, when Ronald Reagan took the oath of office, per capita health-care costs equaled 23 percent of the average salary of the bottom 90 percent of Americans. By 2007 it had risen to 49 percent with all signs pointing to a growing share of the economy going to big, inefficient but stunningly profitable health companies.

How is it that the United States ranks forty-seventh out of 224 countries in infant mortality, doing far worse than Canada, Japan, the European Union and even Cuba? Why are we forty-seventh in life expectancy at birth, according to the CIA, behind Japan, most of Western Europe and even Jordan?

Why are we forty-sixth in the world in the share of our economy spent on public education?

Why is it that forty years ago we were the greatest creditor nation in the world and now we are the biggest debtor nation?

Why is our current account deficit, measuring how much more we import than export, so large that in 2009 we ranked dead last among 190 countries? Our $378 billion shortfall is the equivalent of taking $5,000 a year from every American family of four and sending it overseas. This shortfall was greater than the combined current account deficits of Australia, Brazil, Canada, France, India, Italy, Spain and the United Kingdom.

At the other end, the top three current account surpluses were in China ($297 billion), where our manufacturing base has moved; Germany ($168 billion), which uses a competitive market philosophy to keep its economy both robust and fair; and Japan ($142 billion).

That we rank from middling to dead last among nations by so many measures represents poor choices, especially letting big business damage and destroy competition, escape tax burdens and push down wages.

RESTORE INTEGRITY

Our challenge is to restore rules and infuse our business culture with respect for integrity. Honesty benefits not just customers, but honest businesspeople who understand the real costs they must bear and are willing to do so. But when government makes it possible for some employers to avoid paying promised wages and to ignore environmental, safety and other rules, then the bad practices of the greedy few become the norm.

The typical problem is abuse of power while pursuing profit. The world isn't black and white, but our policies should aim for the lightest possible shades of gray. We have far too many executives who destroy shareholder wealth and shortchange hardworking subordinates while enriching themselves beyond reason. We have too few effective remedies for victims of abusive pricing, as we saw in the story of Barbara Keeton, her overpriced car and the threats by Wells Fargo to take away her home. We have too many big business structures that strip resources from utilities, making them more costly, less reliable and sometimes downright dangerous. And we should never have a hands-off "make your numbers" management ethos like Warren Buffett's that prompts people far down below to ask Bob Manning or anyone else to die.

The concepts we need to reintroduce into our culture to avoid sinking into an unprincipled pit—in which all that matters is money—can be summed up simply.

We need companies (and executives) who are candid. Fair. Forthright. Honest. Loyal. Prudent. Reasonable. Transparent. Reliable. Responsible.

We need to acknowledge that rules define society. When the absence of rules allows businesses to lower their standards toward the lowest common denominator, then, in time, that is what we will get. Accounting rules that lack integrity may produce short-term gains, but the whole market will gravitate toward these bad practices—as it has done.

Under the banner of deregulation, many of the rules that protected customers against abusive practices, from price gouging to unreliable service, have been swept away. The idea that profits should bear some relationship to costs is under attack. So is access to justice, as we saw with the arbitration system. We need to reverse those trends.

In the world today, those who abuse markets get rich off their abuse and taxpayers are forced to correct the egregious errors and thefts that are enabled by unregulated securities, unregulated lending, unregulated insurance and unregulated derivatives. In all of these financial abuses and crimes it is fat fees that drive the deals, not noble stewardship of other people's assets as a banker, broker or executive.

Time-tested regulation of banks, securities firms and insurance companies can prevent disasters while fostering economic growth. Honest audits can catch control frauds early.

We need to recognize that dogmas are bad for democracies. The Federal Reserve, U.S. Treasury and the major academic centers and foundations all reinforce neoclassical economics while paying little to no attention to its critics, known collectively as the heterodox economists. But it was the heterodox economists who spotted the high-tech and housing bubbles and warned of their dangers; they warned about control frauds and derivatives gone wild and numerous other problems. The neoclassical economists failed to issue warnings and, after the fact, insist that no one could have seen these disasters coming.

Our economic dogma, our campaign finance rules and our failure to recognize the need for sound economic policies are leading us away from prosperity and into a poorer future. We need to make smarter choices based on more diverse thinking. We need policies that recognize the natural human tendencies to abuse power and to covet riches at the expense of millions of others. If we choose to, we can improve our lives, our economy and our future. We can have a robust economy in which there is plenty of work and in which everyone who wants to work can; and those who work hard and handle their money prudently will live long and prosper.

If you doubt we can climb out of our deep hole, consider the end of World War II. In August 1945 Berlin lay in ruins, the work of generations lost in the mechanized horror of a war brought on by an evil regime, one in the thrall of both genetic "purity" and corporate power. Bombs had reduced Berlin and Munich and Frankfurt and other political and industrial centers to ruins. Dresden was literally burned to a crisp. Yet within a generation the Germans were prospering. Today, just sixty-six years later, their society is by many measures doing better than ours. The average German works fewer hours for more pay, runs no risk of financial ruin because of ill health and has a guaranteed base income, while the country exports far more than it imports.

The Germans achieved this by adopting economic policies that focus on competitive markets in which the government sets, and enforces, rules to keep competition vibrant. They also gave unions a real voice at the bargaining table, including a significant minority of seats on the boards of big companies.

Visit Germany and look around. That society is by no means ideal, especially in the East, where the ravages of communism still mar the physical world as well as people's souls. But in the western parts of Germany, you will not see rusty old bridges, potholed roads, and train stations where water pours down inside the building because the roof leaks, as exist everywhere in America. The trains are clean, fast, reliable and ubiquitous, just like the trains in the Netherlands, France and Italy.

Explosions of steam tunnels (like the 2007 blast in midtown Manhattan that killed one person) and bursting water mains that wash away roads, a common event in America, are virtually unheard of in Germany. The cars on the roads are overwhelmingly shiny and sound, unlike the "beater" cars seen everyday everywhere in America, rusted hulks running on nearly bald tires and listing to one side. While 15 million Americans live in trailers and the euphemistically named "manufactured housing," in Germany hardly anyone lives in trailers.

So how did the Germans achieve this? The Germans call their economic system "ordoliberalism."

This German philosophy is a market theory of competitive economics that recognizes the need to limit power and the abuses that go with it. *Ordo* comes from a Latin word meaning "inner order" (as opposed to the idea of external control).

As explained by one of its critics, ordoliberalism has "passionately affirmed competitive free markets, it was motivated from the historical observation that concentrations of power in both public and private spheres distorted functioning exchange economies. Thus, the long-term viability of free markets required a rule-bound and limited yet powerful form of government intervention."

The need for rules that ensure real competition has become an alien concept in America. As we have seen, the de facto policy in America, under the twin guises of Reaganism and the Chicago School, has allowed concentrated and largely unaccountable power, with only the most cursory government refereeing. The result has been minimal competition, oligopolies everywhere, and removal of regulations that foster candor, integrity, and a reasonable connection between cost and price.

What It All Means

America's corporate and political elites now form a regime
of their own and they're privatizing democracy. All the
benefits—the tax cuts, policies and rewards—flow in one
direction: up.

—**Bill Moyers**

24. **Now that we've** seen that big businesses artificially inflate
prices, limit competition, cut services, sell fraudulent loans and even put
your life at risk, what, finally, in practical terms, does all of this mean to
you and me?

Perhaps you don't use a telephone or the Internet, subscribe to cable
television or power any of these electronic offerings with electricity generated by burning coal. Maybe you use neither natural gas to heat your
home nor gasoline to fuel your car, so the fictitious taxes collected by
pipeline companies do not take anything from your pocket. Maybe you
even mulch your own garbage so the trash haulers do not gouge your
wallet. If you are utterly healthy, you may not require any drugs. Maybe
you have found a way to support yourself with a job independent of any
corporation.

Even so, sad to say, company policies and government rules that enable
price gouging still cost you.

Everyone pays for a rigged economy, in myriad ways, as it extracts
money from the many and concentrates it in the hands of the few. In doing so, it squanders opportunities, wastes valuable skills, costs more in
taxes and adds risks. It also helps our economic competitors by making us
less efficient. Just as poor health damages the quality of life, a weakened
economy damages the quality of life for all, including even the few gorg-
ing on the stolen fruit of the nation's economic output.

The man on the street must deal with the availability of fewer jobs. You may be losing chances to tap your talents and abilities. You will earn less money than you would in a robust and competitive economy, where workers can bargain together for their pay without government giving companies subsidies to move jobs offshore. Every big merger hurts you as well, by destroying jobs, reducing competition and concentrating economic gains.

In a rigged economy, you may be tricked into thinking you are paying less in taxes, when in reality you just pay privately, typically at higher prices, for what your taxes used to cover (as we have seen with garbage collection and health care). Add your taxes and higher personal spending, and your actual burdens are heavier than those of people in other modern countries who make less and pay higher taxes, but use the wholesale buying power of government to hold down costs.

Under the false premise that tax cuts pay for themselves, when the actual numbers show they have not, government borrowing increases at every level. This means that more and more of your taxes get diverted from services to paying interest on our growing national debt.

The official numbers showing how the fruits of the American economy are being harvested and distributed got little coverage three decades ago. As the differences between the vast majority and those at the top have widened into a huge chasm, more of this news is now being reported. Still, few Americans realize that the best-off 3 million Americans make about the same amount of money as all 150 million at the bottom. Hardly anyone knows that in 2010, the year after the Great Recession ended, in a nation of 312 million people just 15,600 households enjoyed 37 percent of all the income gains.

The data on the damage being done to the vast majority to benefit the political-donor class is extensive. Let's start with jobs.

JOBS, JOBS, JOBS

According to the U.S. Census and the Bureau of Labor Statistics reports, the population has grown about three times faster than jobs since the year 2000. The eight years of the Bush administration resulted in fewer than 3.6 million new private-sector jobs, fewer than when Eisenhower was president and the population was much smaller. This compares with 21 million jobs—six times more—created during the Clinton administration. The twenty combined years of the Reagan and two Bush admin-

INCOME TAX REVENUES FELL SHARPLY AFTER BUSH TAX CUTS

The promise that lower tax rates would result in increased revenues did not turn out that way. Total individual income taxes fell and when adjusted for population growth (second column) the revenue drop was severe.

YEAR	INDIVIDUAL INCOME TAX (IN BILLIONS OF 2010 DOLLARS)	INCOME TAX PER CAPITA (IN 2010 DOLLARS)
2000	$1,276	$4,535
2001	$1,228	$4,310
2002	$1,044	$3,628
2003	$944	$3,252
2004	$937	$3,199
2005	$1,039	$3,514
2006	$1,133	$3,796
2007	$1,228	$4,074
2008	$1,164	$3,828
2009	$934	$3,044
2010	$899	$2,910
CHANGE	($377)	($1,625)
PERCENT	-30%	-36%

Sources: OMB, Census, inflation calculations by author.

istrations produced fewer new jobs than the eight Clinton years (19.4 million private-sector jobs under Reagan and the Bushes, 1.7 million fewer than under Clinton).

This leads to a larger political comparison. From 1940 through 2009, nearly twice as many jobs were created when a Democrat was in the White House compared to when a Republican was president. Republicans controlled the presidency for more years, thirty-six out of sixty-nine, but just 35.8 percent of the jobs were created on their watch. During the thirty-three years when Democrats were in power, 64.2 percent of the jobs were created. A telling summary? The average number of jobs added per year was twice as high during Democratic administrations as Republican.

Having more workers than jobs—our problem in 2012—tends to push down wages. At the end of 2011 there were five people seeking work for every job opening. That made for a cruel variation on the game of musical chairs, only in this version four of every five players were left without seats at the economic table. In 2010 about 6 million families had no cash income, only food stamps, Jason deParle of the *New York Times* reported, a number no one has knocked down.

The job destruction caused by our faux free trade policies have so far hit factory workers hardest. What American factory workers make in an hour can be replaced with a week of labor in China, where environmental and occupational safety laws are both minimal and ignored, and independent union organizers are beaten, jailed and sometimes shot.

No wonder every third manufacturing job in America has been eliminated since the North American Free Trade Agreement was adopted in 1994—and adopted in a way that ran counter to constitutional principles. The founding document gives Congress sole authority to regulate foreign trade, but since the Nixon era, a policy known as "fast track" has transferred this power to the White House, which in turn relies on a small group of financiers, multinational companies and their lawyers to craft rules for their benefit.

If Congress had done its duty and undertaken the hard work of creating balanced, thoughtful trade policies, would 5.5 million factory jobs have gone abroad? Would we have allowed knowledge vital to understanding and improving manufacturing processes to be removed from our country?

The reality is that Congress created a host of subtle subsidies for moving jobs, investment and profits offshore, although many members of Congress, because they seldom read the bills they pass, probably even now have little idea what they did. Even if they do, few members understand the administrative regulations that implement these laws.

When companies use accounting and tax tricks to report huge profits in the Cayman Islands, Bermuda and Ireland, even though they have no employees there, they both push down your wages and push up your tax burdens.

The wage push comes from the availability of cheap labor and the free flow of goods into the United States, which in turn adds to pressure to move more jobs offshore to take advantage of cheap labor.

The tax push comes from rules in the fine print that do not just enable moving jobs offshore, but actually subsidize doing so. This movement of jobs narrows the tax base as wages and profits move outside the United States, further weakening the economic base to which taxes are applied.

Companies getting tax deals that let them bring profits home at an 85 percent discount, as Pfizer did, or tax-free, as Merck did, aren't much concerned about American job losses. If you are an executive who gets to defer paying taxes, or a hedge fund manager who gets both deferral and a super-low 15 percent tax rate, these policies look heaven-sent.

Your tax burdens increase even more when multinational corporations use their untaxed profits offshore as collateral for loans in America. The interest paid in the United States is tax deductible. That means a tax break for the company in the United States. And the long, steady decline in the share of taxes paid by corporations means that you, as an individual taxpayer, must make up for this through taxes, fewer government services or more government borrowing, which is really just a tax, plus interest, on your future income.

FAUX FREE TRADE AND JOBS

In the second decade of this century you can expect more efforts to get corporate tax holidays like the 2004 Jobs Creation Act, which was followed not by the promised 660,000 new jobs, but the destruction of more than 100,000 jobs. Pfizer, Microsoft, Dell and many other multinationals with untaxed profits offshore want another, and much bigger, Jobs Creation Act. If they get it, then expect even more Americans to be fired, which means higher tax and government debt burdens for you, if you are lucky enough to remain employed, because the burden of supporting government will be spread among fewer workers.

The Obama administration, which is closely aligned with the global financier class, wants to expand our existing wealth-destroying faux free trade agreements. His opponent, Mitt Romney, is also a champion of these policies. The political-donor class would not have it any other way.

People without jobs, or those forced to work for less pay, have less money to spend and save. Over time, that means slower economic growth, fewer opportunities and fewer jobs. Smaller manufacturers suffer. Some of them just do not have enough scale to justify the costs of going to China or even Mexico, so they stop investing in their enterprise and watch the family business dwindle because of government policy, not their own shortcomings.

One crucial fact is often left unsaid: our trade with countries where we do not have so-called free trade agreements is growing faster than with countries with which we have such agreements.

The implication is clear: free trade agreements are less about increasing trade than about lowering costs (by replacing American workers with cheap overseas labor) so owners and financiers can harvest a larger share of the economic fruits.

So far most of the lost jobs and lowered wages have come at the expense of factory workers, but that is changing. Thanks to the Internet any job that can be done on a computer can be moved offshore. Engineers, accountants, graphic designers and millions of other workers could see their jobs sent "offshore." A case in point? The Reuters news agency, for which I now work, fired twenty American and European journalists in 2004 and replaced them with sixty journalists who were paid such low wages in India that the company cut its labor costs by more than $200,000. Reuters said it was about saving money, but that shouldn't have been the headline. In fact, the job exchange was about preserving fat pay for top executives. If it were about saving money, then firing the four highest-paid Reuters executives and replacing them with a dozen talented managers in Mumbai, paid on the same salary reduction scale as the journalists, would have saved the company $968,000 a year, more than four times as much.

Moving jobs offshore comes with unseen costs. Subtle differences between cultures can lead to confusion and misunderstanding. In the late 1980s at Dow Jones, executives fretted over how much more it cost to have the European edition of the *Wall Street Journal* copyedited in Brussels than in New York. One of those who pointed out the problem of only counting costs was Fred Brock, an American copy editor then working in Brussels. "Great care was taken to ensure that the paper reflected European perspectives and European sensibilities," Brock noted, because otherwise fewer Europeans would buy the *Journal.* In time the copydesk work was shifted to America and *Journal* sales, as Brock predicted, slumped.

The depth of the job problem in America is often glossed over by politicians referring to new record-setting job numbers. American employment reached a new peak in 2007, for example, when the number of people who earned any wages totaled 155,570,422. In 2008 this figure slipped slightly, by 136,000. Then in 2009 the bottom fell out of the job market. Every thirty-fourth person who earned wages in 2008 went all of 2009 without earning a dollar.

Fewer than 151 million people earned any wages at all in 2009. That's 4.5 million people—again, one in every thirty-four Americans—who worked in 2008 but found no work during all of 2009. Add in population growth, and it means that the hands and minds of 6 million Americans were idle for the entire year. What a waste of talent.

The job loss would have been worse but for the stimulus package passed shortly after President Obama was inaugurated in January 2009. The Congressional Budget Office and other nonpartisan experts have shown that the Obama stimulus saved or created between 2 and 4 million jobs. That prevented the Great Recession from morphing into another Great Depression. But because the stimulus was much smaller than the drop in incomes, and 40 percent of it was directed at tax cuts (which by their nature are savings and thus not stimulative), Americans still saw high unemployment.

If Obama becomes a one-term president, historians will note his failure to insist on a bigger stimulus, to spend the money fast and that bussiness tax cuts do nothing for companies that pay little or no tax. Besides, no one hires workers to get a tax cut. Businesses hire more workers when they have customers who want their goods and services, not when someone dangles a tax cut in front of them.

Besides, a stimulus is not a long-term solution, only a short-term means of compensating for a lack of economic activity. Real growth stems from economic policies that encourage investments and require workers of all kinds, from janitors to mathematicians. Policies that favor moving jobs to China and investing capital offshore auger fewer jobs and lower pay for all but the very skilled.

FLAT WAGES EXCEPT AT THE TOP

For all the talk of prosperity in America, the numbers tell another story. Prosperity resides mostly among the top 10 percent or so. A third of workers in 2010 made less than $15,000. Their average pay was just $6,000 each. The numbers are stunning, aren't they? Let's look at the details.

Many of those 50 million workers only wanted part-time employment. They included students and homemakers and retirees looking for a little extra money. But also included were millions who put in forty hours a week with no paid vacation and no fringe benefits and whose gross pay never amounted to $300 a week.

Half of those with jobs earned less than $26,364 in 2010. That's $507 a week. The median wage, in 2010 dollars, fell back to the level of 1999. The trend is worrisome; in 12 years, incomes should rise, not fall. Will the future bring less and less income?

The median wage—half earn more, half less—has been stuck at just about $500 a week since 1998. Since 1990—two decades ago—it's only gone up 10 percent, or about $48 a week after adjusting for inflation.

The average wage in 2010 was $39,959—or $768 a week. Like the median wage, the average (or mean) has also been stuck at about the same level for a decade, at around $750 a week. Back in 1998 it was $700 a week. And back in 1990 it was about $636 a week.

But let's look at these numbers together.

From 1990 to 2009 the *median* wage went up 10 percent while the *average* rose almost 19 percent. In 1990 the median wage was 72 percent of the average wage. By 2009 the median wage was down to 67 percent of the average as wages for most workers stagnated or fell, while those at the

WAGES ONLY GROW AT THE TOP (IN 2012$)

Median wages—half make more, half less—were flat from 1999 through 2010, but the average or mean grew, indicating only higher-paid workers had real wage gains, especially those making more than $1 million per year.

YEAR	MEDIAN	MEAN
1999	$27,679	$40,247
2000	$27,918	$41,091
2001	$28,195	$40,907
2002	$28,247	$40,675
2003	$28,146	$40,740
2004	$28,362	$41,528
2005	$28,145	$41,637
2006	$28,323	$42,190
2007	$28,474	$42,883
2008	$28,250	$42,248
2009	$28,079	$41,988
2010	$27,735	$42,036
CHANGE	$56	$1,991
PERCENT	0.2%	4.9%

Source: Social Security Administration, inflation calculations by author.

top rose. The spread between the median and the mean grew over those years, $9,300 to $13,000.

What that tells us is that we need to examine growth moving up the income ladder.

In 2009, three out of four workers made less than $50,000. Nine out of ten made less than $80,000. Only one in sixteen made more than $100,000. Only one of 100 made more than $200,000. So the wage growth is mostly among those making at least $100,000, the top 6 percent or so.

The real growth, in fact, is way, way, way up the ladder for salary and bonuses.

From 1990 to 2009 the number of Americans making more than $1 million in salary, in 2009 dollars, increased at seventy times the size of the overall workforce. Million-dollar-plus jobs grew from fewer than 7,000 to 78,000. That high pay lifted the average, but it also served to distort our view of the average worker's income because relatively few Americans saw their pay rise much, if at all, in real terms.

These figures come from the most detailed and accurate source of jobs and pay data in the United States, the Medicare tax database. Even if you pay close attention to the official statistics on earnings, you probably have never heard or read the numbers on these pages unless you follow my work at Reuters.com. That's because no other mainstream news organization, no professional economist who blogs and no citizen journalist has used the Medicare database to analyze what is happening to the earnings of Americans.

The Medicare tax database is valuable because it is an absolute flat tax, with no exemptions or exclusions, on every dollar of compensation paid to workers. When executives exercise stock options, when bosses pay out bonuses and when teenagers at the fast-food counter get paid, their remuneration, to the penny, goes into this database (unlike statistics from the IRS, the Census Bureau, the Bureau of Labor Statistics and other government agencies which, though they routinely issue income reports, base their numbers on surveys and statistical samples).

In 2009 total wages came to $6 trillion. Or, to be precise, $6,009,831,055,912.11.

Big as that number was, it remained virtually unchanged from 2000 and was smaller than in 2007 and 2008 when figures from those years are adjusted for inflation. Indeed, in cents compared to each dollar earned in 2007, workers in 2010 made less than ninety-five cents. Total income, median income and average income were all down in 2010 compared to

2008—and were hardly changed from 2000. Together, these figures show how much the rigged economy, and the global economic downturn that it helped cause, damaged overall growth and spread misery widely.

Among all the big government agencies that gather and analyze data on people's earnings, the Social Security Administration does something unique and valuable. It breaks pay down into narrow categories, with a top category of $50 million or more. Something very significant is taking place at that rarified level, which relates to how the price gouging described in the previous chapters is damaging our economy.

Until 1994, the top income category in the Social Security Administration database was $5 million of salary and bonuses. That year two new categories were added. The new top category was $20 million and higher. Just twenty-five Americans held jobs in that top category. Their average pay was more than $45 million in 2010 dollars.

In 1997 two more high-pay categories were added. The top one measured jobs that paid $50 million or more. There were thirteen of these extremely high-paying jobs in 1997. Those twenty-five super highly paid workers in 1994 had grown in just three years to 116, of whom thirteen made more than $50 million.

In 2007, the last peak year for the American economy, there were 151 Americans whose salary and bonuses totaled more than $50 million. Their average pay was $94 million. In the recession year of 2008 the number of very top jobs fell back slightly to 131, with average pay slipping to $91.2 million. In 2009, the worst year for workers since the Great Depression, just 72 workers were paid more than $50 million. They averaged $84.1 million. In 2010 this rose to 81 workers paid an average of $79.6 million.

We do not know who these highly paid workers were. We do know that very few of them were top executives at publicly traded companies. The highest paid CEO in 2009 was Larry Ellison of Oracle, who made $84.5 million. The second highest CEO made $34 million, not enough to make the top pay category tracked by Social Security.

We also know they were not hedge fund managers. Why? Because hedge fund managers get to call their share of profits "carried interest," which is not subject to the Medicare tax (recall that Congress lets hedge fund managers defer paying their taxes for years or decades, and when they finally do pay, the rate is just 15 percent).

The seventy-two may include some Hollywood producers, assuming they, for some reason, had their share of blockbuster movies classified as ordinary income. It may include some executives who built up huge, and

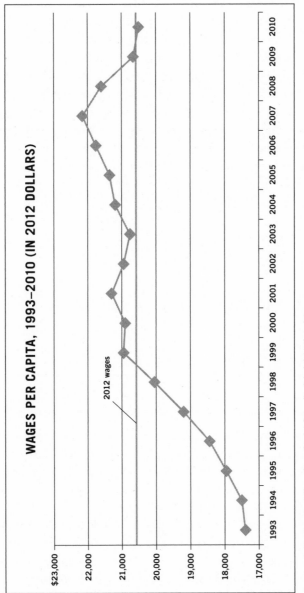

WAGES PER CAPITA, 1993–2010 (IN 2012 DOLLARS)

2012 wages

Source: Author's calculations from Social Security Administration data.

untaxed, deferral accounts that they cashed in. But most likely many of these seventy-two highly paid workers are Wall Street traders, whose bonuses are taxed as ordinary compensation. Those bonuses were made possible because taxpayers assumed the massive losses from Wall Street's bad bets.

What this data shows is that, over a long period of time, the vast majority of Americans have seen little or no improvement in their wages. Millions of people have seen their real total compensation decline as employers have raised wages just enough to keep pace with inflation, while eliminating pension plans, eliminating or reducing contributions to 401(k) savings plans, as well as requiring that workers pay a growing share of health-insurance costs out of their pockets.

So what should we do about all of this?

25

Solutions

Failure is impossible.

—Susan B. Anthony

25. **We can reverse** the pernicious public policies that are making so many worse off by taking from the many to enrich the few. If we make good choices and make our voices heard, we can get back on the path to a productive and prosperous society. What follows are solutions for specific industries, followed by an overall recommendation to get America back on the path to widespread prosperity.

COMPETITION

Nothing is more hated by big business than competition. In a competitive market with many suppliers of a good or service, the consumer shops for the best deal. That drives prices down. This pressure on prices was the great insight of Adam Smith in his 1776 book, still in print after 235 years, *An Inquiry into the Nature and Causes of the Wealth of Nations.*

Smith saw that if producers seeking profits compete against one another in a market peopled with informed consumers, the general economic improvement is akin to an invisible hand guiding the market. But the key here is competition. Simply calling a market "free" does not produce any gains; when we let one firm or a few firms capture the market, they can compete to raise prices rather than lower them.

As we saw with the telecommunications industry in Glasgow, Kentucky, and Scottsboro, Alabama, predatory pricing to keep competition at bay is all around us, but the reality has been turned on its head by big business misapplying the theory of contestable markets. The railroad industry, too, lacks competition and is today as highly concentrated as when our government first regulated corporate prices in 1887 by creating the Interstate Commerce Commission to deal with abusive railroad industry practices.

ACTION: We need to challenge the use of the term "free" markets, which has a technical meaning for economists, and replace it with support for *competitive* markets.

UTILITIES

If ever there was an industry where organized and concentrated action can bring reform it is in the regulated monopolies—utilities, railroads and pipelines. These enterprises cannot get up and leave for cheap labor in China. They have no choice but to invest and operate where they provide service. The problem is to get them to be servants of the economy, not pillagers of it.

State legislatures have repeatedly cut funding for regulatory commissions and, notably in California, have appointed industry-friendly commissioners. Meanwhile, funding for the Federal Energy Regulatory Commission grows because fees from the industry finance the commission and FERC has proven eager to enable price gouging and impose fake taxes through rigged proceedings. The process has become heavily weighted toward the utilities.

Simple and obvious reforms would improve the economy by restoring the crucial concept of just and reasonable prices, while also ensuring that assets are not sucked out of monopolies by holding companies. Reforms would have the virtue of ending the tax games that force you to pay taxes that never get to the government, as shown in earlier chapters concerning electric and pipeline industries (see pages 77 and 90), which amounts to nothing more than legalized theft.

Reform, needless to say, is conceptually easy but politically difficult. But these are problems where the interests of consumers, small business and even big business align. If these groups can work cooperatively on utility regulation, all will benefit.

Action One

Congress should require that all legal monopolies be stand-alone companies with no holding company as a parent. That was a lesson we learned back in the 1930s but conveniently forgot.

Eliminating holding-company structures would end many of the financial games that benefit Wall Street and its clients. No longer would the reliability of your electric service depend on decisions made in Bilbao or London or even Omaha. Instead, local management would mean a vested interest in local concerns. Having utility company directors whose lives and financial interests are the same as those of the local inhabitants will make them much more likely to be concerned about the reliability and quality of service today, as well as a decade or three in the future.

Many of the problems identified in this book concern legal monopolies controlled by holding companies where no market exists to discipline economic predators. When regulators reward predators, as both the FERC and the California commission have done, the economic damage is like a chronic debilitating illness that makes the host lethargic.

Holding companies are highly effective tools to shift costs and risks on to captive customers. The extensive expansion of the holding company structure in the past three decades has brought us overpriced electricity, natural gas, telecommunications, water and bulk rail freight. Electricity has become less reliable even though we live in an era when computers and extraordinarily sensitive manufacturing processes and medical procedures demand significant improvements in the reliability and quality of electric power. The pipeline industry operates in ways that put your life unnecessarily at risk, and safety problems are also built into the ways we currently regulate electric and gas utilities and railroads.

Almost eight decades ago, James C. Bonbright and Gardiner C. Means published what has become the classic text on how holding companies thwart effective price regulation, enabling abuses of railroad and utility customers. Bonbright and Means showed how holding companies could charge subsidiaries excessive fees and overcharge for services and equipment they provide the operating utilities, all the while underpaying for anything they get from the utilities. Their mundanely titled book, *The Holding Company: Its Public Significance and Its Regulation*, was an instruction manual for smart regulation to control economic predators—but it was also a field guide for executives and Wall Street on how to manipulate the system to earn unwarranted profits by foiling regulation.

Unfortunately, utility executives have read the fine print more closely than regulators.

However, by returning to the stand-alone utility model, energy suppliers and users in each market would share an interest in the other's prosperity. The utility needs a healthy local economy to sell into, at prices that sustain maintenance of existing gear and investment in new equipment; the local business and residential customers need reliable utilities that charge fair prices and plan for needs decades into the future. The holding company structure with its distant owners destroys this mutually beneficial relationship.

Action Two

Congress and each state should exempt rate-regulated monopolies from corporate income taxes.

Exempting legal monopolies from the corporate income tax will eliminate paperwork and accounting expense for the utilities, thereby improving efficiency. It will also simplify regulatory proceedings.

Remember, Congress requires companies to keep two sets of books, one for investors (and regulators) and another for the Internal Revenue Service. This reform would get utilities to use a single set of books.

As we have seen, the taxes embedded in corporate utility rates add to customer costs, but often never reach government coffers. And when fake taxes are included in rates, as with master limited partnership pipelines, tax rules are used to conceal unjust and unreasonable rates that let some investors pocket $1.75 for each dollar they are entitled to.

Eliminating the corporate income tax on utilities will end the blatant, legalized theft of billions of dollars from customers of PSEG and other electric utilities that sold their power plants (sometimes to sister companies), pocketed the taxes that had been collected from customers but not yet turned over to government, and then got a second helping of tax dollars that may also have never gotten to government.

A campaign to exempt rate-regulated monopolies from the corporate income tax will force one of two outcomes, either of which is a good deal for customers. It will either end the tax or wake people up to what has become a backdoor way to earn unjust and unreasonable profits.

While eliminating the corporate income tax for legal monopolies would save them time and effort, we must expect them to resist the idea. They will say it is unfair to others and that it will distort investment decisions. If they do fight it, the ensuing discussion will create a terrific teachable moment through which to educate the public about how our tax system takes money from the many to concentrate it in the hands of the few through dishonest policies that big business has sold to government. Imagine those politicians who rail against taxes trying to justify keeping the corporate income tax on monopolies when customers are asking for an exemption. The lesson? Taxes should finance government, not inflate corporate profits.

Reform advocates can frame the debate with a simple question to utilities: *Why do you want to be taxed?*

The idea of exempting rate-regulated monopolies from the corporate income tax was put forth in 1977 by Robert Batinovich, a wealthy businessman who was president of the California Public Utilities Commission. Batinovich still believes the efficiencies and transparency of such a reform would pay for itself many times over. It is likely that eliminating the corporate income tax will cost the government not so much as a dollar in revenue. All Congress and the state legislatures need to do is impose a gross receipts tax—a kind of sales tax—on the bills of legal monopolies exempted from the corporate income tax. No more need for two sets of books or regulatory hearings on corporate income tax costs and no more opportunities to pocket taxes embedded in electric, gas and other utility rates.

Action Three

I would go further than Batinovich. A progressive utility-consumption tax could be imposed on customers—the more kilowatts, the more water, the more telecommunications bandwidth you use, the higher your tax rate.

The tax rate for running a mansion where the air-conditioning is turned to 65 degrees in August and the outdoor swimming pool is warmed all winter could be set at two or five or ten times that for running a household where people turn off the lights in empty rooms because they cannot afford to leave them on.

A progressive add-on tax on electric utility bills would discourage consumption, which in turn would help reduce the burning of fossil fuels that is causing increased concentrations of carbon dioxide in the atmosphere. It would also encourage investment in more efficient use of fossil fuels and water.

A progressive utility-bill tax would also align the tax burden with the ancient principle that taxes should be levied according to ability to pay.

While some industries and businesses are more intensive than others in their use of electricity, natural gas and water, raising their ultimate costs would simply reflect the real economic cost of production, a virtue no honest economist could dispute. A progressive tax on utility bills would discourage waste while encouraging investment in making machinery, lights, pumps, chillers and other equipment efficient in design and use.

Action Four

Address the one-sided nature of rate-making proceedings. The utilities, pipelines and railroads have an intensely concentrated interest in the outcome, while each individual customer has a very small interest and even less knowledge about how to fight back.

An elegant solution to this problem comes from utility lawyer Patrick J. Power, who has worked for every side of the issues, including a stint as Batinovich's aide. Power is now an administrative law judge with the Oregon Public Utility Commission.

Judge Power proposes a match, with a dollar going to customer advocates for each dollar a utility spends in a rate case, on lobbying or other advocacy. He would divide the money among residential, commercial and industrial users in proportion to their shares of utility revenues.

"We all know going up against any big corporation is David versus Goliath," Judge Power says, "but [under the present system] in rate cases David pays Goliath's lawyers."

Power's reform would add credibility to the rate-making process by adequately funding adversaries with competing economic interests, thus promoting restoration of the badly damaged "just and reasonable" doctrine that is the foundation of all rate regulation of monopolies.

Another benefit of Power's plan would be that it just might discourage utility game playing. In rate cases, utilities routinely claim that crucial information is not available or too costly to get; they then deliver it at the last moment when there is little time for serious scrutiny. If every dollar a utility spends hiding evidence gets matched by a dollar to uncover the facts, maybe the utilities will find that candor and integrity are to their benefit.

It is already the law in many states that advocates can be paid for participating in rate-making and other similar proceedings. But outside of California and a few other states the sums are trivial. Power's plan would promote a level playing field. Well-funded customer advocacy would promote efficiency by exposing wasteful utility practices and encourage adequate staffing to reduce outages, fires and explosions.

Power's plan would also help advocates of very low-cost, limited services, such as Lifeline, a government policy that provides phone service for the poor, disabled and elderly for as little as a dollar a month. Society derives significant benefits from universal access to electricity, natural gas, telecommunications and other services vital to living in the modern world. Being able to dial 9-1-1 in a medical emergency can save far more money than the marginal cost of providing a connection to the telephone system. Being able to get a modicum of electricity to run a refrigerator and keep a few lights and appliances on helps elderly and disabled people with small incomes to live independently, which costs taxpayers much less than maintaining people in assisted-living and other care facilities. Yet your and everyone else's legal right to a landline telephone at any address in America is quietly being legislated away in our state capitals.

Judge Power has a related proposal that is also smart: make shareholders pay half the cost of executive salaries that are higher than those paid to the managers of utilities run by nonprofits, cooperatives and government.

Why is the head of Southern California Edison paid $3.5 million a year or more and the head of its holding company, Edison International, $4.5 million and the head of Entergy, the New Orleans utility holding company, at least $27 million? The general managers of the Los Angeles Department of Water and Power and the Sacramento Municipal Utility District each make about $350,000. These utilities have for years provided reliable service at lower cost than the corporate-owned utilities.

I would go further, making shareholders bear the entire cost of executive salaries that are higher than the average compensation of the ten highest paid municipal, cooperative and other noncorporate utilities in the same field.

Shareholders should be free to pay any salary and bonus and give any perks they want out of their profits. But since utilities, railroads and pipelines are regulated monopolies rather than competitive businesses, any premium pay should come from shareholders, not customers. In an ideal world, Congress would contribute to holding down executive pay by disallowing a tax deduction for any pay to utility executives that is greater than the average of the top ten noncorporate utilities and by requiring clear disclosure of these costs to investors.

Action Five

If Congress will not do away with the holding company for monopolies or their corporate income tax, another approach may persuade owners to move to stand-alone utilities. This reform would also create an opportunity to join the interests of consumers, locally owned businesses and opponents of the corporate income tax by making dividends paid by stand-alone utilities tax deductible to the company, while fully taxable to the recipients. That would encourage cash payments, making utilities a reliable investment for older people who need reliable income from their investments. The key is to allow tax-deductible dividends only when there is no holding company atop the utility.

Converting utilities from corporate-owned to publicly owned should be made simpler. Making public takeovers easy will also be a way to discipline utilities because, if they charge too much or provide poor service, they can lose their franchises.

Pacific Gas & Electric used wildly inflated claims of how much its property and equipment were worth when voters wanted local public ownership of the Sacramento Municipal Utility District in 2007 and when the South San Joaquin Irrigation District acted to buy a small piece in 2009. The price for assets of regulated public utilities should be set at the depreciated value on the company books plus any deferred taxes on those assets. State legislators can put this on the books and communities can put it in their franchise agreements, which should require frequent renewal, perhaps every ten years.

ARBITRATION

As an alternative to litigation in the courts, arbitration is a good idea. But as we saw with the cases of Barbara Keeton, the Casarottos' Montana Subway sandwich franchise and Ernestine Strobel's stocks, the system has become twisted to benefit big business.

Action One

A simple reform would be to require that an arbitration take place where the customer lives, not where the company chooses. Making people fly across the country to have their cases heard is an unreasonable burden on the less well-off and elderly.

Action Two

Solve the repeat player problem, in which businesses who often use the system tend to rely on those arbitrators they find friendly to their interests. This problem is tricky, but one way to shine a light on abuses would be to require a posting of how many cases an arbitrator has handled, the number and percentage decided for each side, and the average and median (half more, half less) awards not in dollars, but as a percent of the sums in dispute.

Action Three

Since arbitration is supposed to relieve congestion in the courts, let's finance it not with user fees for each arbitration, but with a fee charged to all litigants (except those who can show they are paupers). This would benefit those whose cases are heard in court by reducing demands on court time. Because arbitration fees and expenses would come from a pool, not from the warring parties, the bias in favor of repeat business litigants would shrink.

BANKING AND INSURANCE

We know how to regulate banks. We also know that lack of regulation is disastrous.

Action One

Make banks eat their own cooking, requiring them to hold on to the loans they make and buy back every loan that sours. That would be a simple, effective and self-reinforcing way to address control frauds by bank executives more interested in fast fees than interest payments.

Action Two

Increase the reserves that banks must hold to around 10 percent, with higher reserves for riskier loans. That would also help improve the integrity of lending. So would changing a host of accounting-industry rules that give lip service to the principle of providing a reasonable picture of finances but in fact hide the salient facts. For example, the Financial Standards Accounting Board should prohibit temporary swaps that on the last day of a quarter or year make liabilities appear to be assets.

Action Three

The sale of derivatives, which was at the core of the Great Recession, requires transparency, if not regulation. The pension funds, endowments, investment pools and other money held in trust for others should be barred from trading in derivatives unless there is complete disclosure of fees, costs and spreads on trades. (A spread is the difference between what the buyer and seller get—the slice taken by the trader or his proxy.)

Action Four

Credit agreements need to be in plain English. The original credit card, issued by Bank of America a little more than half a century ago, came with a half-page contract. Some Visa and other credit card contracts today run four pages of very fine print. There is no reason these cannot go back to the old length. Banking regulators can use their power to approve deals to achieve just that—simple, clear, plain English.

JOB SUBSIDIES

We need to call the so-called job subsidies what they are: wealth destruction, not job creation. Let's cease giving the likes of Alcoa a $141,000 annual discount on electricity for each job that pays less than half that much or giving Verizon $3.1 million for each job at a computer server farm. Why should we take the eternal energy from Niagara Falls and virtually give it to a few big users? Likewise, building factories for foreign companies with American tax dollars is not capitalism, but globalized corporate socialism.

Since most state constitutions already prohibit such giveaways, this problem should be easy to solve, but so far the courts have looked kindly on corporate welfare. Some inventive lawyers are arguing that the money is not a gift of taxpayer dollars, but a contract in return for creating jobs.

Action One

Here the best solution is not litigation, which we should be trying to reduce, but legislative action. Voters, especially those whose primary concern is tax burdens, should organize and press for either strengthening existing state constitutional prohibitions on gifts to corporations or new statutes that require disclosure of every aspect of the deals and require clawbacks (return of monies) when promised jobs are not created. How about requiring a bond to make sure the clawback money is there? That should be enough to dampen the competition to give away ever more.

Action Two

Don't underestimate the shame factor. Staking out CEOs and directors at public events where they can be called out for taking welfare that robs people in need of education, disability benefits and lower taxes might just make the personal price of greedy policies too high.

TAXES

No one should have to pay to have their tax return filed electronically, nor should people with modest incomes that come from their labors have to pay someone to prepare their tax returns. Thanks to professors Joseph Bankman, Dennis Ventry and others, the solution to this problem exists.

Action One

Institute a national ReadyReturn. There will be a battle—Intuit, the maker of TurboTax software, and H&R Block will fight it—but at least two-thirds of American taxpayers should not have to prepare a tax return unless they want to. If you take only the standard deduction and exemptions for yourself and any dependents, there is no reason the government should force you to spend time and effort on filing a tax return or paying someone to do it for you. The government already has the data to determine the proper amount of tax.

Privacy is not an issue, no matter how often Intuit and Grover Norquist repeat that canard, because the government has all the data for taxpayers who use only the standard deduction.

Action Two

As for the claim that if ReadyReturn were instituted millions of people might lose out on some tax break, the answer is simple: reduce unnecessary clutter in the tax code. For example, if we want to give a break to students, then all one need do is have his or her school certify enrollment, just as employers certify employment when they file annual wage reports.

Restoring the law that made small amounts of dividend and interest income free of tax would simplify tax filing for millions while encouraging more savings. Before 1980 a couple could collect $400—that's more than $1,100 in 2012 dollars—in dividends tax-free and the exemption on interest continued until 1986. Only 43 percent of taxpayers had any interest income in 2008; just 22 percent got dividends.

Exempting the first $1,000 of interest and dividends ($500 for singles) would both encourage people to save and simplify tax filing. A tax policy that encourages people to have savings that they can tap when things go wrong also reduces pressures for taxpayer-financed assistance.

Action Three

As for corporate taxes and the costly games played by most large companies, including the massive job-destroying actions of Pfizer under the American Jobs Creation Act, a simple basic reform will reduce the game playing.

As mentioned earlier, separate book and tax accounting should stop. The biggest difference between the two is accelerated depreciation, which means letting companies write off equipment faster for tax purposes. More than fifty years ago, the claim that this would increase economic growth was shown to be false, and study after study since then has verified it. Retaining the practice means you ultimately bear the cost of these loans through interest on the national debt, which robs money from your choice of lower taxes or more services. Requiring companies to pay taxes on their profits each year, with no deferrals, would plug a growing hole in your pocket.

Big business will fight this. The moguls and the business-friendly pundits will say it would be costly for business. But *you* have to pay your taxes immediately; why should big business be treated differently?

By requiring companies to pay taxes on profits as they report them, we would simplify the system, eliminate unproductive effort and reduce the need for government to borrow. That is where to focus the argument—it makes business more efficient, simplifies the tax system and treats companies the same as people by requiring taxes now, not later.

Action Four

The same solution—no more tax deferrals—should be applied to executives, movie stars, athletes and other very highly paid workers who can set aside unlimited amounts of money without paying taxes. Why should people who make more each year than you would make in ten lifetimes get to delay paying their taxes when you must pay yours on payday?

Congress should also require that existing deferrals be unwound, perhaps giving executives and others this choice: undo the deal immediately and pay your taxes in full or keep the deal on the condition that the entire contract is made public, with a plain-English explanation of the costs sent to every shareholder, every employee and every retiree on a company pension. Good deals will survive such scrutiny.

What Congress should not do is prevent executives and others from lending part or all of their paychecks to their businesses. Anyone should be free to lend money to anyone they want—provided they pay taxes on that money first.

The same antideferral principle should hold for hedge fund managers, the top twenty-five of whom collected an average of a billion dollars each in the recession year of 2009. Hedge fund managers also should have to pay taxes at the same rates as other people who get compensated for their services, not at the reduced rates for capital investments.

The only wage deferrals should be the modest sums Congress lets individuals put away for their old age in pension plans, 401(k) plans and individual retirement accounts, which are taxable when the money is withdrawn. An older self-employed worker may defer $55,000 of income annually, which is greater than the total amount most people have in their retirement accounts.

Action Five

One more reform would bring an end to rich people who live tax-free by borrowing against their assets, diminishing the amount of their fortune at death. Congress should count borrowing against untaxed assets as income. If you buy an asset—a stock, an apartment building, a painting—and sell it for a gain, you must pay taxes. By borrowing against the untaxed gain in the value of an asset, you can extract the value without paying taxes. Not fair.

Hedge fund managers with multibillion-dollar untaxed fortunes should not be allowed to borrow against untaxed assets and live on the borrowed money. Likewise people like the McCourts, the divorcing couple who owned the Los Angeles Dodgers, should not be able to borrow against assets to live on unless those assets have already been taxed. Once you have paid taxes on your assets then you can do what you want with them, but untaxed gains should not be available to dodge reporting income.

For stocks, mutual funds and bonds, this reform is easy because

Congress now requires brokerages to report the basis of these investments, a reform wrought partly after my reporting on this issue and the work of others, including Gerald Scorse, who pressed this issue with lawmakers. Like Scorse, you can affect the law if you work at it.

This reform would have the added virtue of producing data that will show just how large untaxed fortunes are in America. That is useful because it will help Americans understand the distribution of burdens and this simple fact: rich people have more wealth than they have reported income on their tax returns, while everyone else generally has more reported income than wealth.

MONEY AND POLITICS

The United States Supreme Court in 2010 reinforced its earlier decisions that giving money to politicians is a form of free speech. By way of reminder, in *Citizens United v. Federal Election Commission*, a case now generally known by the shorthand *Citizens United*, the court decided by a five to four vote that corporations could spend all the money they want to influence elections. The significance of this case—removing the relatively mild restrictions Congress and some states had placed on corporate giving in elections—can hardly be overstated.

I've said it before, but it bears repeating: *Citizens United* is to the expansion of corporate power what the big bang was to the singularity. It's the whole universe.

The high court took a narrow issue and, in a remarkably brazen act of judicial activism by judges who assert their disdain for judges doing more than narrowly interpreting the law, the majority gave political rights to corporations. It is crucial to appreciate what this means in terms of giving a megaphone to the richest among us to drown out competing points of view. Compared to most individuals or even unions, corporations have unlimited resources (what once was called "big labor," by the way, has shrunken to the degree that "little labor" might be a better name). The decision in *Citizens United* to allow corporations to spend unlimited sums to influence elections poses a grave threat not just to the economic well-being of Americans, but to the continuation of our democracy.

Corporations now have unlimited leeway to mislead, confuse and outright lie to win elections for those who will do their bidding or to stop ballot measures they oppose.

Today corporations are global, exist in perpetuity if they are well managed, and are given vast powers to do anything legal that makes money. Their size, power and scope would certainly shock and almost certainly offend the Framers.

The grant of "personhood" to corporations has had currency since 1886, although Congress never passed a law granting these rights, nor did Supreme Court justices ever vote on a decision (recall the discussion earlier of J. C. Bancroft Davis and the Southern Pacific Railroad; see page 24).

Before Davis's bit of mischief, the word "person" was understood to mean that foreign visitors and immigrants not yet naturalized enjoyed the same legal protections as citizens. This is arguably the most egregious example of how big business has abused plain English in the fine print.

Action

Congress must act. If it does not, corporations will acquire even more power. However, since money is key to elections in our era, and corporations, thanks to their special advantages, have vast resources, fighting the expansion of corporate power will be much harder. For that we can thank the Supreme Court of Chief Justice John Roberts for giving corporations vast new rights. Keep in mind that Roberts has consistently been a good friend to corporations in his rulings, even as he says he abhors judicial activism.

Just as those who opposed official racism had to live with the 1857 *Dred Scott* decision (*Dred Scott v. Sandford*) that slaves were not persons protected by the Constitution, and with the 1896 *Plessey v. Ferguson* decision that legalized forced segregation, we must live with *Citizens United*. Bad decisions eventually get overturned (*Dred Scott* by the Fourteenth Amendment in 1868 and *Plessey* by the unanimous 1954 *Brown v. Board of Education* decision ending legal segregation). But to date, the 1886 *Santa Clara* decision, a ruling by a court clerk rather than justices that affirmed that corporations were persons, still stands.

That ruling and *Citizens United* can be undone, perhaps by Congress, perhaps by a Supreme Court more respectful of the Founders' intentions. Unfortunately, it will take time and, as we've seen with the so-called self-correcting markets of the Chicago School, the damage done in the meantime may be enormous.

SUPPLY AND DEMAND

Economies are like the human body: to get the best out of life, all the parts need to function properly. Certainly, one can survive without, say, feet or the ability to see; but so afflicted, you can't run a foot race or maneuver through a maze. Quality of life, a full range of opportunities and the freedom to do as you wish are diminished with the loss of one or more functions.

Strong economies aren't so different; full function requires the presence of a robust tension between supply and demand. When there is plentiful supply from many competing enterprises, and strong demand that is distributed widely enough to serve everyone, our nation can be healthy, as income and wealth flows through the economy. But bear down too long on part of the society, cutting off its flow of money, and an initial numbness will, if the pressure isn't relieved, lead to atrophy and even death.

That is not an argument for distributing incomes and wealth equally. Your body does not require equal flows of blood to all parts. The discs in your spine that enable movement and the cornea through which you see the world require very little blood flow, while the brain requires a great deal.

Smart capitalists and the politicians their campaign contributions put into office might grasp how demand-side economics can make capital more valuable if they heeded this important observation from the middle of the nineteenth century:

> Labor is prior to and independent of capital. Capital is only the fruit of labor, and could never have existed if labor had not first existed. Labor is the superior of capital, and deserves much the higher consideration.

Those words come not from Karl Marx, but from that most famous of Republican presidents, Abraham Lincoln. Lincoln spoke those words in his first State of the Union address in December 1861. He was talking in code about slavery, but his deeper point is that capital and labor exist in symbiosis, like the algae and fungi that make lichen, like the arterial and venous blood that sustain human life. If the veins that carry away carbon dioxide and other waste are smaller than those that bring oxygen and food, the body does not remain healthy. Indeed, pools of blood form and begin to rot, which if left untreated will kill the body.

When competitive markets are turned into monopolies and oligopolies, when lousy and slow services like our second-world Internet can command premium prices, when rules almost no one knows about vitiate consumer protections, economic growth is retarded. Right now our economic sickness is so severe that those stores of idle greenbacks piling up at the biggest businesses are rotting, just like lettuce left too long on the shelf. In 2008, the latest IRS data show, nonfinancial companies held a record $3.7 trillion of cash. That is close to $12,000 for every man, woman and child in America. It is a gross excess of money that has no place to be profitably invested and so it is not circulating.

We all pay a high price for this. Our economic competitors are gaining by following different policies. We face a future where we operate at a disadvantage. Consider the super low-cost telecommunications in France and Japan; the much lower cost of health care in every other industrialized country, which also does not burden small business with the costs and paperwork; the improving quality of infrastructure in Europe and Asia; and the growing investments in education and research being made in China and Europe.

We are being robbed blind by rules that the politically favored few have buried in the fine print. Just a penny a day per person is $1.1 billion a year; an unwarranted buck a day redistributes $113 billion upward to the politically connected few who write the contracts and get government to write the rules in their favor, all the while undoing the discipline of competitive markets.

Unless we fight back, the economic elite will continue to stuff their pockets, while weakening markets and stagnant-to-falling incomes for the vast majority damage the stability of our society. No one else will do this job. That is the whole idea of a democracy—people decide for themselves what kind of government—what kind of fine print—they want. They decide by their actions: whether to speak up, whether to organize, whether or not to vote.

If you want a stronger, wealthier and fairer America, then act. Turn off *Dancing with the Stars* and go talk to others. Vote. Join an organization or organize others yourself. Study. Write brief letters to the editor. Call in to talk-radio programs with concise points. Meet with politicians and, if a little more pressure seems appropriate, badger them some at public forums by salting the room with people who have prepared tough, polished questions in advance. And don't expect overnight success.

Change is not easy. As Frederick Douglass, the runaway slave who became publisher of the antislavery *North Star* newspaper, observed in

1857, "if there is no struggle, there is no progress. Those who profess to favor freedom and yet depreciate agitation . . . want rain without thunder and lightning. . . . Power concedes nothing without a demand. It never did and it never will."

But consider how far we have come because people just like you acted. People who believed that the world can be a better place and who worked for that to happen. Slavery is gone. Women have the right to vote. We have child-labor laws despite all the factory owners who railed against them. We have minimum-wage laws and environmental laws (though both are under attack under our faux free trade policies).

Progress is not a straight line uphill. We are living in an era of setbacks, an era that the future will look back upon and see for all its follies, especially the naïve idea that markets will just run themselves efficiently and honestly and that cutting wages and taxes is the path to prosperity.

Change takes time, persistence and recognition that knowledge is power. Remember the words of Susan B. Anthony on her deathbed in 1906, after a lifetime of seeking the vote for all women and more than fourteen years before the Nineteenth Amendment was enacted: "Failure is impossible."

Make yourself informed, dedicated and powerful. Organize or join and support organizations dedicated to a better, fairer, more productive America, where the goal is to give everyone a shot at success.

Real change comes from the bottom up. Popular power can break through any glass ceiling, any artificial barrier, because voters elect our government leaders. So get out the vote. And remember that no one will do it if you do not.

Reform begins with you.

[ADDING IT ALL UP]

Below are estimated annual costs borne by the average family of four because of artificially inflated prices due to corporate and government policies. Not everyone will face every cost.

401(k) fees	$140
Bank fees	$120
Electric utility tax favors	$150
Electricity corporate-owned costs above public power	$500
Corporate electric utility stranded costs	$200
Garbage companies	$100
Pipeline "fake tax"	$40
Pipeline monopoly overcharges	$100
Railroad monopoly overcharges	$100
State and local gifts to corporations	$940
Telephone and cable TV companies (compared with France)	$1,440
TOTAL	**$2,390**

[ACKNOWLEDGMENTS]

Many more people than I will be able to name here helped in one way or another during the four years I researched this book in the United States, Europe and Asia. To those who are left out, my apologies and my appreciation for the time you took to teach and to ferret out obscure records and to interpret them, especially the clerks and other record keepers in government offices and executives and specialists at companies named here who asked not to be identified.

At Reuters, Jim Impoco, who brought me in as a columnist in July 2011, and my editor, Howard Goller. At *Tax Notes*, where I was a columnist for three years until July 2011, CEO Chris Bergin and the editors, including David Brunori, Joseph Thorndike, Jeremy Scott, John Bell, Robert Goulder and Meredith Fath.

At Syracuse University College of Law, all of my colleagues, but especially Dean Hannah Arterian and assistant deans Aviva Abramovsky, Christian Day and Terry L. Turnipseed, professors David Driesen and Rob Nassau and my research assistants since 2009, Megan E. Dodge, Jacqueline S. Lawrence, Jessalyn M. Mastrianni, Fred Pugliese, Kenneth R. Williams and Ju-Hyun Yoo, now practicing law in Seoul. Also, my Syracuse colleagues Keith Bybee, Len Burman and Eric Kingson at the Maxwell School and Joseph Comprix at Whitman School of Management, where I have a joint appointment.

On taxes, John Buckley at Georgetown Law, Professor Michael

McIntyre of Wayne State University, H. David Rosenbloom of Caplin
& Drysdale and New York University Law School, Robert S. McIntyre
at Citizens for Tax Justice and the rest of the staff at CTJ, and Ed
Meyers at the Institute on Taxation and Economic Policy.

At the University of Missouri–Kansas City, professors Bill Black,
June Carbone, L. Randall Wray, Stephanie Kelton and John F. Henry.
At the University of California–Riverside, Mason Gaffney. At the Tax
Policy Center, Gene Steuerle, Jeff Rohaly and Bill Gale, and Elizabeth
Boris at the Urban Institute.

On medical and public health matters, Drs. Stephen Bezruchka,
Michael J. DeVivo, Art Moss and Marvin Hoffman as well as Nancy
Yanes Hoffman.

In Oregon, David Bean, Ann Fisher, Mary Geddry, Bob Jenks, Nigel
Jaquiss, Dan Meek, Chuck Sheketoff and my brother Eric, whose blue-
collar insights always inform.

On utilities, Charles Acquard, Jim Baller, Dan Berman, Patrick
Crowley, Charlie Harak, Robert McCullough, Pat Power, Harry
Trebing, Howard Spinner, as well as Judge Richard D. Cudahy of the
Seventh Circuit Court of Appeals and Professor William D. Henderson
of Indiana University. On contracts, Professor Judith Resnik at Yale
Law School, Ralph Nader and many others.

On geology and coal mining, Ronald C. Surdam, the former
Wyoming state geologist; on coal mining, Geoff O'Gara, John Meklin
and Ray Ring, now or formerly of *High Country Times*; on unions, Leo
Gerard, president of the United Steelworkers; on public finance, Irene
Rubin; on railroads, Richard White of Stanford University, and Gerald
McCullough; on wealth distribution, economists Brad DeLong and
Emmanuel Saez of the University of California–Berkeley, G. William
Domhoff of UC–Santa Cruz, and Ed Wolff of New York University;
on subsidies, Greg LeRoy, Phil Mattera and Bettina Damiani of Good
Jobs First, Kenneth Thomas of the University of Missouri–St. Louis
and Bruce Fisher of Buffalo State College; and on Census Department
data, Steve Doig of the Arizona State University.

On investing, John C. Bogle, the founder of Vanguard, and my
stockbroker friends Nannette Nocon and Mike Millard.

For their advice and thoughtful criticism, Dean Baker, Kate Berry,
Fred Brock, Lynnley Browning, Pablo Eisenberg, Glenn Hubbard,
Emily Kaminski, Sherm Levey, Lauren Lipton, Susan Long, Betty
Lukas, Kevin Morrissey, Danelle Morton, Mindy Spatt, Chi Chi Wu,
and the great reporters David Burnham, formerly of the *New York*

Times, and Morton Mintz, formerly of the *Washington Post*, for reminders of abuses past.

My Portfolio publisher, Adrian Zackheim, whose idea this book was, showed remarkable patience. My editor for much of the book, Courtney Young, provided valuable help, as did my loyal literary agent, Alice Fried Martell. Hugh Howard polished the final manuscript.

And, as always, those among my eight children who helped, this time Andy, Kate, Marke, Molly, Steven and especially Amy, as well as my wonderful wife, Jennifer Leonard, CEO of the Rochester Area Community Foundation and a guiding light on integrity and compassion whose motto is: always do your best.

Reuters, which hired me after it was largely completed, has no role in this work.

[NOTES]

A Note on Sources

This book is based on hundreds of interviews and the reading of many tens of thousands of pages of official government documents as well as law reviews, corporate and academic studies and innumerable books. Words in quotation marks were actually spoken or written by those named.

Readers who wish additional documentation beyond the Notes should write to the author at davidcayjohnston@me.com. The documents, if digital, or references to print will be posted at davidcayjohnston.com in the section for this book's sourcing.

Chapter One: Jacking Up Prices

3 **Kushnick knew a research gold mine:** Bruce Kushnick, "The $300 Billion Broadband Scandal." Teletruth ebook. www.newnetworks .com/broadbandscandals.htm.

7 **Since 1913 Americans:** "Milestones in AT&T History." www.corp.att .com/history/milestones.html.

9 **The worst of these are laws:** http://blogs.reuters.com/david-cay -johnston/2012/04/12/taxed-by-the-boss/ and http://blogs.reuters.com/ david-cay-johnston/2011/07/19/paying-taxes-your-employer-keeps/ and www.youtube.com/watch?v=SF4J-y7wJc0 and www.goodjobsfirst .org/taxestotheboss.

10 **In deciding Ostrowski's suit:** Opinion in *Bordeleau v. State of New York.* www.courts.state.ny.us/CTAPPS/Decisions/2011/Nov11/190opn11.pdf.

11 **What does it cost banks:** *Perdue v. Crocker Nat'l Bank*, 38 Cal.3d 913, 702 P.2d 503 (Cal. Sup. Ct. 1985).

Chapter Two: Corporate Power Unlimited

17　**Nearly four thousand years ago:** L. W. King translation of Hammurabi's Code at www.fordham.edu/halsall/ancient/hamcode .asp.

18　**We give the Athenians:** Maureen B. Cavanaugh, "Democracy, Equality, and Taxes." *Alabama Law Review*, Winter 2003.

19　**In ancient Rome:** Cullen Murphy, *Are We Rome? The Fall of an Empire and the Fate of America*. Boston: Houghton Mifflin, 2007.

20　**The poor have become:** Miguel Helft, "Google Founders' Ultimate Perk: A NASA Runway." *New York Times*, September 13, 2007. www.nytimes.com/2007/09/13/technology/13google.html.

21　**Back on earth:** David Cay Johnston, "First Look at US Pay Data, It's Awful." October 19, 2011, http://blogs.reuters.com/david-cay-johnston/2011/10/19/first-look-at-us-pay-data-its-awful/ and "The Richest Get Richer," March 15, 2012, http://blogs.reuters.com/david-cay-johnston/2012/03/15/the-richest-get-richer/.

21　**More recently, when the economy:** Author calculations from www.ssa.gov/cgi-bin/netcomp.cgi?year=2009 and http://www.ssa.gov/cgi-bin/netcomp.cgi?year=2008.

23　**Among the world's:** OECD, "Divided We Stand: Why Inequality Keeps Rising," May 5, 2011. www.oecd.org/document/40/0,3746,en_21571361_44315115_49166760_1_1_1_1,00.html.

24　**The Southern Pacific Railroad:** Jack Beatty, *The Age of Betrayal: The Triumph of Money in America, 1865–1900*. New York: Alfred A. Knopf, 2008, p. 173.

25　**Very much later Associate Justice:** *First National Bank of Boston v. Bellotti*, 435 U.S. 765 (1978). http://caselaw.lp.findlaw.com/cgi-bin/getcase .pl?court=us&vol=435&invol=765.

Chapter Three: Buffett Buys a Railroad

31　**Buffet paid a stiff premium:** Berkshire Hathaway announcement at www.bnsf.com/media/news-releases/2009/november/2009-11-03a .html.

32　**A look at government data:** Laurits R. Christensen Associates, "A Study of Competition in the U.S. Freight Railroad Industry and Analysis of Proposals That Might Enhance Competition: Final Report." Madison, Wis., Nov. 2008 available at www.stb.dot.gov/stb/elibrary/ CompetitionStudy.html.

34　**In recent public talks:** Mulvey PowerPoint at www.naco.org/ searchcenter/pages/results.aspx?k=mulvey.

36　**This means:** Hoover's electric generation guide at www.hoovers .com/industry/electric-power-generation/1856-1.html.

37 **Wall Street even measures:** http://news.morningstar.com/articlenet/
article.aspx?id=91441, last accessed May 24, 2012.

38 **As a result of my work:** David Cay Johnston, "Enron Avoided Income
Taxes In 4 of 5 Years." *New York Times,* January. 17, 2002, www
.nytimes.com/2002/01/17/business/enron-s-collapse-the-havens-enron
-avoided-income-taxes-in-4-of-5-years.html.

40 **This assertion is belied:** John Boyd, "US Railroads Are Holding Up as
the Healthiest Segment of the North American Freight Carrying
Industry." *Journal of Commerce,* August 17, 2009.

Chapter Four: Railroaded

44 **In a quirky:** "Surface Transportation Board Announces Second
Favorable Appeals Court Ruling in 'Bottleneck' Cases." STB release no.
00-11, February 17, 2000.

44 **Big railroads also erect:** "Unfair Federal Policies" in *Consumers United
for Rail Equity,* www.railcure.org/issue/issue_unfair.asp.

47 **The evidence of a lack of competition:** "Railroad Regulation," GAO,
RCED-87-109, June 1987; available at http://archive.gao.gov/
d28t5/133518.pdf.

Chapter Five: In Twenty-ninth Place and Fading Fast

57 **Braverman later wrote:** Burt Braverman, "Cities Should Stay Out of
the Cable Business," Multichannel News, April 28, 2003.

60 **South Korea has taken:** "Pando Networks Releases Global Internet
Speed Study." September 22, 2011. www.pandonetworks.com/Pando
-Networks-Releases-Global-Internet-Speed-Study.

60 **We do consistently rank:** Product-offering brochures of Orange.com
and bills sent to Dana Kennedy in Vieux Nice, France.

61 **In terms of job creation:** Michael Spence and Sandile Hlatshwayo,
"The Evolving Structure of the American Economy and the
Employment Challenge." Council on Foreign Relations, Greenberg
Center, http://b.rw/gEq7Wo.

Chapter Six: Profits Upkeep Commissions

65 **PG&E diverted much:** California Public Utilities Commission, Pacific
Gas and Electric Company, 2011 General rate case, prepared testimony
exhibit (PG&E-2), December 21, 2009.

67 **This story is as old:** "Edison's Electric Light: 'The Times' Building
Illumination by Electricity." *New York Times,* September 5, 1882.

69 **But we're not quite done:** State of New Jersey Board of Public Utilities.
In the matter of the Energy Master Plan Phase II proceeding to

investigate the future structure of the electric power industry, docket no. EX94120585Y, attachment H: testimony of Dr. Colin J. Loxley.

71 **These and other tax benefits:** MSB Energy Associates, "Major Federal Tax Breaks that Lower Investor-owned Electric Company Costs and U.S. Treasury Revenues 2006." www.publicpower.org/files/PDFs/ MajorIOUTaxBreaks2006.pdf.

72 **Bill Bagley:** Phillip Matier and Andrew Ross, "CPUC Foundation to Raise Money from Utilities." Wednesday, January 26, 2011. *SFGate*, www.sfgate.com/cgi-bin/article.cgi?f=/c/a/2011/01/26/BAEI1HE615 .DTL.

73 **Niagara Falls generates massive:** James Heaney, "Power Failure: Region Home to Cheap Power, High Bills and Huge Corporate Subsidies." *Buffalo News*, April 29, 2007.

76 **In reality, Wyatt wrote:** Dennis Wyatt, "CPUC: California's Profits Upkeep Commission," *Manteca Bulletin*, Dec. 12, 2010. www .mantecabulletin.com/archives/19207/.

Chapter Seven: "We Lead the Industry with Integrity"

78 **Joe Seeber knows:** David Cay Johnston, "Businessman Ordered Jailed in Dispute with Utility," September 12, 2007, and "Businessman Avoids Jail in Dispute With Utility." *New York Times*, September 13, 2007.

78 **Joe Seeber owns:** www.tristem.com/.

79 **Late in 2009, the small:** *City of Beaumont v. Entergy Texas*, Jefferson County District Court 172 case E184-962, filed September 21, 2009.

89 **And the attempt:** "Code of Entegrity," www.entergy.com/about _entergy/entegrity/.

Chapter Eight: Paying Other People's Taxes

93 **The court reversed:** *BP West Coast Products LLC v. FERC et al.*, 374 F.3d 1263, 362 U.S. App. D.C. 438.

96 **This time Judge Sentelle:** *ExxonMobil v. FERC* 04-112, www.ll .georgetown.edu/federal/judicial/dc/opinions/04opinions/04-1102a.pdf.

97 **In California, SFPP sought:** David Cay Johnston, "Tax.com Helps Win One for Taxpayers." Tax.com, June 28, 2011, www.tax.com/taxcom/ taxblog.nsf/permalink/uben-8j9kyv?opendocument.

98 **Gooch says that corporate-owned:** David Cay Johnston, "Pipeline Profiteering." Reuters, October 17, 2011. http://blogs.reuters.com/david- cay-johnston/2011/10/17/pipeline-profiteering/.

98 **How many other rules:** The Shelf Project at www.utexas.edu/law/ faculty/calvinjohnson/shelf_project_inventory_subject_matter.pdf.

Chapter Nine: Investors Beware

103 **We met Sam Insull:** Hon. Richard D. Cudahy and William D. Henderson, "From Insull to Enron: Corporate (Re) Regulation after the Rise and Fall of Two Energy Icons." *Energy Law Journal* 25, no. 1 (2005): 35–110.

Chapter Ten: Playing with Fire

105 **The explosion came:** Ellis E. Cinklin, "Boys Who Died Were 'Unwitting Heroes' in Pipeline Fire." *Seattle Post-Intelligencer,* June 18, 1999.

106 **Rushing down to the Pecos River:** Carol M. Parker, "The Pipeline Industry Meets Grief Unimaginable: Congress Reacts with the Pipeline Safety Improvement Act of 2002." *Natural Resources Journal* (Winter 2004).

107 **If you live in an urban:** David Cay Johnston, "Poorly Maintained Gas Pipelines Put Increasing Numbers at Risk." *Remapping Debate,* Dec. 14, 2010. www.remappingdebate.org/article/corroding-pipelines.

109 **At pipeline safety conferences:** Jeff Nesmith and Ralph K. M. Haurwitz, "Pipeline Office Is Small Agency with Big Job and Many Critics." *Austin American-Statesman,* July 22, 2001.

114 **In the Carlsbad disaster:** National Transportation Safety Board, Pipeline Accident Report: Natural Gas Pipeline Rupture and Fire Near Carlsbad, New Mexico, August 19, 2000; TSB/PAR-03/01 PB2003 -916501 Notation 7310B adopted February 11, 2003, at p. 32.

117 **Prior to protests from parents:** Dina Capielli, "Pipelines: What Lies Beneath." *Houston Chronicle,* Nov. 12, 2006.

Chapter Eleven: Draining Pockets

119 **How high can it go?:** Tim Reiterman, "Small Towns Tell a Cautionary Tale About the Private Control of Water." *Los Angeles Times,* May 30, 2006.

120 **In Felton, California:** Felton FLOW, www.feltonflow.org/.

123 **Then, in 2005:** "Felton Backs Water Buyout." *Santa Cruz Sentinel,* July 27, 2005.

Chapter Twelve: How We Beat the Garbage Gougers and Their Stinking High Prices

134 **One community:** "Firefighters Watch as Home Burns to the Ground." WPSD Local 6 News, www.wpsdlocal6.com/news/local/Firefighters -watch-as-home-burns-to-the-ground-104052668.html.

136 **The 1911 Triangle:** "141 Men and Girls Die in Waist Factory Fire,"
New York Times, March 26, 1911.

138 **These prices should:** Waste Management 10-k reports.

Chapter Thirteen: Fee Fatigue

149 **The United States Comptroller:** OCC's Quarterly Report on Bank
Trading and Derivatives Activities, Fourth Quarter, 2011. www
.occ.gov/topics/capital-markets/financial-markets/trading/derivatives/
dq411.pdf.

149 **By waiving Rule 23A:** www.federalreserve.gov/aboutthefed/section23a
.htm.

151 **One set of those blinders:** www.fbi.gov/news/testimony/fbi
-efforts-to-combat-mortgage-and-other-financial-frauds.

152 **Many people saw:** David Cay Johnston, "A $1,000 Prize for
Disagreeing," January 18, 2004, and "In Debate Over Housing Bubble, a
Winner Also Loses." *New York Times*, April 11, 2004.

Chapter Fourteen: "Wells Fargo Will Take Your House"

156 **Margaret L. Moses:** Margaret L. Moses, "Statutory Misconstruction:
How the Supreme Court Created a Federal Arbitration Law Never
Enacted By Congress." *Florida State University Law Review* 34 (Fall
2006): 99, http://papers.ssrn.com/sol3/papers.cfm?abstract
_id=939609#%23.

159 **Paul and Pamela Casarotto:** Scott J. Burnham, "The War Against
Arbitration in Montana." *Montana Law Review* (Winter 2005): 66. Mont.
L. Rev. 139.

Chapter Fifteen: Giving to Goldman

166 **Treasury Secretary—and former:** Gretchen Morgenson, "Behind
Biggest Insurer's Crisis, a Blind Eye to a Web of Risks." *New York Times*,
September 28, 2008.

166 **In October 2008:** David Cay Johnston, "Invade the Caymans!" *Tax
Notes*, Dec. 22, 2008.

167 **As an extraordinarily profitable:** Goldman 10-K, 2004–2011.

167 **In 2009 alone:** Author calculations from Goldman 10-K and IRS data.

168 **Taxpayers are not the only ones:** Delaware Chancery Court Civil
Action No. 6949-CS, decision February 29, 2012.

171 **Phil Angelides:** David Cay Johnston, "Meltdown Redux." Reuters, Nov.
15, 2012, http://blogs.reuters.com/david-cay-johnston/2011/11/15/
meltdown-redux/.

Chapter Sixteen: Please Die Soon

172 **Bob Manning enjoyed a wonderful life:** David Cay Johnston, "Paralyzed Since Fall in 1962, Man Is Still Seeking Benefits." *New York Times,* May 5, 1995. www.nytimes.com/1997/05/05/nyregion/paralyzed-since-fall-in-1962-man-is-still-seeking-benefits.html.

173 **While luckily none of the locked-in:** "The McWane Story." PBS *Frontline,* www.pbs.org/wgbh/pages/frontline/shows/workplace/mcwane/.

175 **Massey Energy contributed:** *Caperton v. A. T. Massey Coal Co.,* 129 S. Ct. 2252 (2009).

176 **First, a little background:** 2009 California Workers' Compensation Losses and Expenses, Workers' Compensation Insurance Rating Bureau of California, June 2010. https://wcirbonline.org/wcirb/resources/data_reports/pdf/2009_loss_and_expenses.pdf.

Chapter Seventeen: Your 201(k) Plan

185 **Mehling's essential:** Staff Report Concerning Examinations of Select Pension Consultants, May 16, 2005. Available at www.sec.gov/news/studies/pensionexamstudy.pdf.

188 **In all, 401(k):** Investment Company Institute at www.ici.org/pressroom/news/ret_10_q4.

190 **Employers also shortchange workers:** David Hackett Fischer, *The Great Wave: Price Revolutions and the Rhythm of History.* Oxford University Press, 1996, p. 29.

193 **There is no way to know:** Report and Recommendations Pursuant to Section 401(c) of the Sarbanes-Oxley Act of 2002 on Arrangements with Off-Balance Sheet Implications, Special Purpose Entities, and Transparency of Filings by Issuers. Available at www.sec.gov/news/studies/soxoffbalancerpt.pdf.

194 **Despite government awareness:** Private Pensions: Conflicts of Interest Can Affect Defined Benefit and Defined Contribution Plans, May 24, 2009. Available at www.gao.gov/assets/130/122042.pdf.

Chapter Eighteen: Wimpy's Tab

197 **Congress does not require:** MSB Energy Associates, "Major Federal Tax Breaks that Lower Investor-Owned Electric Company Costs and U.S. Treasury Revenues 2006." American Public Power Association, December 2008.

200 **The 1954 overhaul:** Robert M. Solow, "The Production Function and the Theory of Capital." *Review of Economic Studies* 23, no. 2: 101–8.

202 **The extra $2 million:** Christopher Drew and David Cay Johnston, "Special Tax Breaks Enrich Savings of Many in the Ranks of

Management." *New York Times*, October 13, 1996. Available at www
.nytimes.com/1996/10/13/business/special-tax-breaks-enrich
-savings-of-many-in-the-ranks-of-management.html.

205 **When Mitt Romney disclosed:** David Cay Johnston, "Romney's
Gift from Congress." Reuters, January 31, 2012. Available at http://blogs
.reuters.com/david-cay-johnston/2012/01/31/romneys-gift-from
-congress/.

206 **Almost anyone who is already very rich:** David Cay Johnston, "Tax-
Free Living: How Some Wealthy Dodge the Top 400 Taxpayers List."
Tax Notes, March 15, 2010, p. 1411.

Chapter Nineteen: Pfizer's Bitter Pill

210 **There are other voices:** David Cay Johnston, "Largesse Out of the
Public Treasury." *Tax Notes*, July 7, 2008, p. 73.

212 **So how much of the tax:** Pfizer 10-K, 2004–2009.

213 **Let's look again at the statement:** Jesse Drucker, "Dodging
Repatriation Tax Lets U.S. Companies Bring Home Cash." *Bloomberg*,
December 29, 2010.

216 *Tax Notes* **writer:** Martin Sullivan, "Transfer Pricing Abuse Is
Job-Killing Corporate Welfare." *Tax Notes*, August 2, 2010.

Chapter Twenty: Hollywood Robbery

219 **The Wisconsin tax credit:** David Cay Johnston, "Killing the Future:
Tea Parties, Tax Credits, and Hollywood Jobs." *Tax Notes*, April 27,
2009, p. 479.

223 **The most generous state:** Steven R. Miller and Abdul Abdulkadri,
"The Economic Impact of Michigan's Motion Picture Production
Industry and the Michigan Motion Picture Production Credit." Center
for Economic Analysis, Michigan State University.

223 **The Michigan senate staff report:** Available at www.legislature
.mi.gov/documents/2007-2008/billanalysis/Senate/pdf/2007-SFA-5841-F
.pdf.

Chapter Twenty-one: Silly Software

227 **Joe Bankman is a Stanford:** Joseph Bankman, "Simple Filing for
Average Citizens: The California ReadyReturn." *Tax Notes*, June 13,
2005, p. 1431.

228 **People dislike filling out tax forms:** Intuit Investor Day 2011
presentation, http://investors.intuit.com/events.cfm.

232 **ReadyReturn is also opposed:** Dennis J. Ventry Jr., "Intuit's Nine Lies

Kill State E-Filing Programs and Keep 'Free' File Alive." *State Tax Notes*, Aug. 30, 2010, p. 555.

Chapter Twenty-two: Pilfering Your Paycheck

234 **You read that right:** David Cay Johnston, "Taxed by the Boss." Reuters, April 12, 2012; available at http://blogs.reuters.com/david-cay-johnston/2012/04/12/taxed-by-the-boss/ and "More companies pocket workers' state income taxes," available at www.youtube.com/watch?v=SF4J-y7wJc0.

234 **In Illinois, for example:** David Cay Johnston, "Paying Taxes Your Employer Keeps." Reuters, July 19, 2001, available at http://blogs.reuters.com/david-cay-johnston/2011/07/19/paying-taxes-your-employer-keeps/ and www.goodjobsfirst.org/taxestotheboss.

237 **Donald Trump began his career:** Wayne Barrett, *Trump: The Deals and the Downfall*. New York: HarperCollins, 1992.

Chapter Twenty-three: Of Commas and Character

241 **The dominant law:** Frank H. Easterbrook and Daniel R. Fischel, *The Economic Structure of Corporate Law*. Cambridge, MA: Harvard University Press, 1991, p. 283. "A rule against fraud is not an essential or even necessarily an important ingredient of securities markets."

246 **As explained:** Johannes R. B. Ritterhausen, "The Postwar West German Economic Transition: From Ordoliberalism to Keynesianism." IWP Discussion Paper no. 2007/1, January 2007.

Chapter Twenty-four: What It All Means

252 **Then in 2009:** David Cay Johnston, "Scary New Wage Data." *Tax.com*, www.tax.com/taxcom/taxblog.nsf/Permalink/UBEN-8AGMUZ.

253 **For all the talk:** David Cay Johnston, "Forget Taxes, It's Wages that Plague Americans." Reuters, August 6, 2011, http://blogs.reuters.com/david-cay-johnston/2011/08/06/forget-taxes-its-wages-that-plague-americans/.

Chapter Twenty-five: Solutions

261 **Almost eight decades:** James C. Bonbright and Gardiner C. Means, *The Holding Company: Its Public Significance and Its Regulation*. New York: McGraw-Hill, 1932.

274 **"Labor is prior to":** Lincoln's December 1861 address to Congress, available at http://www.presidency.ucsb.edu/ws/index.php?pid=29502#axzz1tvhQqnUM.

[INDEX]

Telecommunications Act (1996), 56
telemarketing companies, 4
telephone bills, 1–2, 5–6, 51
    extra charges on, 3–4
    misunderstanding of, 6–7
telephone industry, 1–8
    fiber-optic network created by, 50–51
    record keeping in, 52
Telescripps, 55, 56–57
Tennessee, 134
Tepper, David, 204, 205
terrorism, pipelines and, 113
Theofanous, Theo, 111–12, 114
Thomas, Clarence, 26
Thomas, Kenneth, 9
Tilden, Kevin, 124
Time Warner, 56, 60
Transactional Records Access
    Clearinghouse, 229, 238
Transportation Department, U.S., 12,
    108, 109, 112, 114
Trapp, George J., 184–85
Treasury, U.S., 245
Triangle Shirtwaist Company, 136, 173
trickle-down economics, 20, 243
Trieweiler, Terry N., 159, 160–61
TriStem Consulting, 78–79, 81, 82,
    83–84, 86–87, 88
Trump, Donald, 237
trusts, duty of, 18
truth-in-billing policy, 6
Tsiorvas, Stephen, 105, 106
TurboTax, 228, 229–33, 269
Turk, Ron, 130
Tyco, 20
Tytler, Alexander Fraser, 208

UBS, 150
unemployment, 22, 208, 250, 252–53
Union Pacific Railroad Company, 39, 42,
    43, 44, 45, 46, 48
unions, 147, 245
United Steelworkers Union, 166
Universal Studios, 218, 219, 222
Upper Big Branch mine explosion, 174
utilities, 67, 72, 260–66
    average equity of, 80
    executive salaries in, 265
    holding companies and, 67–68,
        260–62, 265
    overbilling by, 82–83

progressive consumption tax for,
    263–64
public takeovers and, 266
ratemaking proceedings and,
    264–65
see also specific utilities
Utilities Mutual, 177–81
utility-consumption tax, 263–64
Utility Rate Network, The (TURN), 7
Utility Workers Union of America,
    116, 125

Vanderbilt University, 147
VanDerhei, Jack, 187
Vanguard, 189
Venice, 190–91
Ventry, Dennis, 232, 269
Verizon, 8, 51, 53, 237, 268
Verizon Wireless, 4
Vermillion, S.Dak., 116
Viacom, 222
Viagra, 211, 212
Virginia, 232
Visa, 143, 268
Vonage, 53

wages, 21–23, 250, 252, 253–58
    median vs. average, 253–55
    per capita, 257
    stagnation of, 54
Wall Street Journal, 152, 252
Wall, Terrence, 206–7
Walmart, 23, 134, 162–63, 173
Waste Management, 128–29, 132, 138,
    140, 141
water companies, 118–27
water systems, 118–27
    privatization of, 119–24, 126
Wealth of Nations, see Inquiry into the
    Nature and Causes of the Wealth of
    Nations
Weimer, Carl, 109, 115
Weiner, Joann M., 213
Weisbenner, Scott, 192
Weisshaar, Ben and Rita, 64–65
Welch, Jack, 202
Wells Fargo Bank, 11, 154, 164, 244
Whatcom Falls Creek, 105
Williams Companies, 102
Wired for Greed (Seeber), 87–88
wire maintenance fee, 5